THE STATE WE'RE IN

Wyse Series in Social Anthropology

Editors:
James Laidlaw, William Wyse Professor of Social Anthropology, University of Cambridge, and Fellow of King's College, Cambridge
Maryon McDonald, Fellow and Director of Studies, Robinson College, University of Cambridge
Joel Robbins, Sigrid Rausing Professor of Social Anthropology, University of Cambridge, and Fellow of Trinity College, Cambridge

Social Anthropology is a vibrant discipline of relevance to many areas – economics, politics, business, humanities, health and public policy. This series, published in association with the Cambridge Department of Social Anthropology but open to all scholars, focuses on key interventions in Social Anthropology, based on innovative theory and research of relevance to contemporary social issues and debates.

Volume 1
Sociality: New Directions
Edited by Nicholas J. Long and Henrietta L. Moore

Volume 2
The Social Life of Achievement
Edited by Nicholas J. Long and Henrietta L. Moore

Volume 3
The State We're In: Reflecting on Democracy's Troubles
Edited by Joanna Cook, Nicholas J. Long and Henrietta L. Moore

THE STATE WE'RE IN

Reflecting on Democracy's Troubles

Edited by

Joanna Cook, Nicholas J. Long and Henrietta L. Moore

berghahn

NEW YORK · OXFORD

www.berghahnbooks.com

First published in 2016 by
Berghahn Books
www.berghahnbooks.com

Library of Congress Cataloging-in-Publication Data
A C.I.P. cataloging record is available from the Library of Congress

British Library Cataloguing in Publication Data
A catalogue record for this book is available from the British Library

ISBN 978-1-78533-224-1 hardback
ISBN 978-1-78920-510-7 paperback
ISBN 978-1-78533-225-8 ebook

Contents

Figures

Acknowledgements

This book has grown out of a series of scholarly conversations on the character and future of contemporary democracy. Although only nine of us are represented in the present volume, we are very grateful for the support, interest and ideas of our interlocutors in those discussions, including Azra Hromadzic, Jim Glassman, Tom Grisaffi, Insa Koch, Hirokazu Miyazaki, June Nash, Ruth Prince, Natalia Roudakova, Stefanie Strulik and Andre Willis. We offer our very warmest thanks to the Wenner-Gren Foundation for Anthropological Research and the Centre for Research in the Arts, Social Sciences and Humanities at the University of Cambridge, who generously helped us bring the authors of the present volume together to refine their arguments in the light of each other's work. Marie Lemaire, Matthew McGuire, Patrick O'Hare, Laurie Obbink, Jonas Tinius, Louis Wenham and Alex Worsnip all provided invaluable assistance. Particular thanks to the two anonymous reviewers for their helpful comments and suggestions, to Agnes Upshall for attentive copyediting, to Larry Sweazy for compiling the index, and to Caroline Kuhtz, Charlotte Mosedale, Molly Mosher, Ben Parker and Dhara Patel at Berghahn.

Introduction
When Democracy 'Goes Wrong'

Joanna Cook

Nicholas J. Long

Henrietta L. Moore

In March 2014, *The Economist* – a news weekly that enjoys a global circulation of over 1.4 million copies – ran a front cover that asked in stark scarlet, 'What's gone wrong with democracy?' The framing of the question was revealing in itself. The issue's eponymous essay was not a text that sought to debate whether democracy really had gone wrong; the answer to that seemed to be self-evident. Instead the writers sought to provide a retrospective diagnosis of democracy's difficulties. As they pointed out, it seemed remarkable to be undertaking such a task so early in the twenty-first century given that democracy had been touted by many as 'the most successful idea' of the twentieth.[1]

So are we facing a global crisis of democracy? Many would argue so.[2] The citizens of post-colonial and post-socialist states who had once pinned their hopes on 'democracy' increasingly appear to have lost faith in its emancipatory promise (Diamond 2008b). Longstanding democracies in North America and Western Europe are beleaguered by a sense of 'democratic malaise' among their citizens (Hay 2007; Kupchan 2012), and the 'post-democratic' encroachment of corporate interests into representative politics (Crouch 2004). Even among those who have campaigned most vociferously in the name of democracy – the networks behind the anti-globalisation and Occupy movements – there is now intense debate as to whether the moniker and practices of 'democracy' need to be left behind.

The present collection is an attempt to make sense of this moment. We asked scholars with a deep knowledge of settings in which democracy seemed to be losing momentum to contribute chapters exploring how and why this situation had come about, their brief being less to evaluate whether democracy actually had 'gone wrong' in any of these settings (although such judgements were by no means precluded), and rather to investigate who thought and felt it had: on what basis did those people reach such a judgement, what were the circumstances that precipitated it, and how did they act in response? We were interested to see what, if anything, these different settings had in common and what factors divided them. Did it make any intellectual sense to talk of this phenomenon as a single 'global crisis of democracy', in the ways that the popular media and some academic commentary seemed to invite? If, as we suspected, it did not, then what could account for the fact that there had been such a wellspring of democratic distemper in the early years of the twenty-first century, and what was allowing a narrative of 'democracy having gone wrong' to coalesce and prove so compelling to so many people around the world?

At a more theoretical level, we were interested in using this material to develop a better understanding of how and why people become dissatisfied with the circumstances in which they live. Did discontent regarding democracy reflect 'fault-lines' (Agüero 1998) and structural tensions intrinsic to 'democracy' as both a principle and a practice? Or was it – as scholars such as Crouch (2004) and Kupchan (2012) suggest – a response to recent but problematic developments in the forms of statecraft that go by the name of 'democracy'? Both explanations seemed plausible. Yet although they could reveal the conditions of possibility under which feelings of democratic malaise might become likely, neither line of argument seemed to provide a convincing answer as to what led individuals or populations to cross a threshold dividing tacit acquiescence to a suboptimal situation and outright dissatisfaction with it. Nor could they explain why some subjects were prompted to abandon their democratic commitments altogether, while others felt compelled to 'reclaim' or 'reinvigorate' democracy. These are puzzles that clearly require an investigation into political subjectivities, and a consideration of how such subjectivities both affect and are affected by the broader systems in which they are embedded.

For readers concerned with understanding why the practices and principles of democracy are in flux, sometimes even proving intolerable and unsustainable, the contributions to this volume – which offer an overview of how citizens in a wide range of countries experience and express dissatisfaction with democracy – point towards two important conclusions. The first is that there is no – and can be no – easy master narrative to encompass and explain all these diverse experiences. Secondly, and following from this, the volume demonstrates that if accounts of political dissatisfaction are to have either intellectual credibility or practical value, they have to be grounded in the specificities of citizens' subjective experiences, with particular attention paid to the factors that structure their visions of how best to relate to themselves and others, as well as to ideas, objects and institutions. This involves thinking about citizens' own criteria for evaluating democracy on a much more intimate scale than is usual in political analysis, even as those criteria are themselves partially generated by the activities of capital and the state. The chapters in this book thus build on and move beyond the insights of the now-familiar structural and political-economy approaches to democracy and its discontents to shed a fresh light on the difficulties facing democracy in contemporary times.

For readers interested in the character of political subjectivity, the volume offers provocative case studies that illuminate the changing and sometimes mercurial way in which the democratic is not only thought about, but also felt and experienced. The volume thus builds upon recent work in social and cultural studies that emphasises the role of the affective and the experiential as a driving feature of political life (e.g. Ahmed 2004; 2010; Berlant 2011; Crociani-Windland and Hogget 2012; Long 2013; Navaro-Yashin 2012). Our contribution to this literature comes in developing accounts of political subjectivity that not only recognise the importance of affective engagements with democracy – as ideal, institution, procedure and experience – but also seek to account for their character and force.

Democracy, Sociality and Subjectivity

What might people be talking about when they claim that democracy has 'gone wrong' or is something that they have 'lost faith in'? One way to approach this puzzle would be to ask: 'What is democracy?' This question, simple enough on the surface, has bitterly divided political thinkers, some of whom consider democracy's essence to be the hosting of elections that are free, fair and – perhaps – proportional (Powell 2000), or the state distribution of wealth, leisure and opportunities (Lenin 1965 [1919]); others of whom see it as a condition of egalitarian decision making, in which there should be no state present at all (Graeber 2007: 329–374). For the purposes of this volume, it is not our intent to advocate any one normative definition of 'democracy'. Instead we note, following Paley (2002: 473–479), that many different political forms can lay claim to being 'democracies'. Nevertheless, one particular heuristic has become globally hegemonic: the 'liberal democratic' system of statecraft, in which regular elections are held, such elections are free and fair, an established opposition exists to hold the government to account, there is a free press, an independent judiciary, and the state upholds the rule of law and displays a commitment to human rights. Certainly, in all of the cases discussed in this volume, this is at least part of what our informants have in mind when they refer to the failures and disappointments of 'democracy'.

A related, but less frequently posed question concerns what kind of analytic object democracy should be considered to be. Most writers using the term either consider it to be a technique of governance and/or a principle by which the body politic is constituted and political life ordered (as Agamben (2012) notes, many commentators conflate the two, even though they are analytically distinct). In this volume, though, we favour a more expansive definition that includes but also exceeds these familiar connotations. In the spirit of classic thinkers such as de Tocqueville (2003 [1835]), and Dewey (1988 [1939]) as well as more recent scholars of democracy, including Banerjee (2008) and Michelutti (2007), we prefer to think of democracy as a total way of life: a form of human sociality. This expansive definition is the one that affords the most accurate purchase on the multiple ways in which our informants might understand and experience 'democracy', and thus stands to give the most insight into contemporary varieties of democratic malaise.

By sociality, we mean the dynamic and interactive relational matrix into which an entity is created, through which it comes to have an effect in the world and through which, if it is sapient, it comes to know the world and find meaning and purpose within it (Long and Moore 2013: 2). Social scientists now recognise that all entities, human and non-human, exist in co-productive and dynamic matrices of relations; sociality is a property foundational to all of them. However, the character of that sociality is not always the same. What distinguishes human sociality in particular is its capacity to take many forms and its remarkable plasticity: human relations can be and have been organised in ways that range from egalitarian communes to intensely hierarchical court societies.

Each form of sociality distributes authority, access to resources and access to opportunities in particular ways: in other words, it constitutes a body politic. But that is not the limit of its 'political' effects. It also has a distinctive bearing on subjects' relations to themselves and to others, inflecting all aspects of social life. Classic liberal democracy, for example, is a form of sociality in which members can and do disagree publicly (Long 2006), where they periodically enjoy the thrill (or the burden) of evaluating what kind of person they would most like to be in authority over them (Simandjuntak 2009), and where individual citizens discipline themselves (and each other) to obey the law and fulfil their obligations towards the state (Cruikshank 1999). All these relations are part of and come to shape the same dynamic system – which is why we find it helpful to talk of democracy as a 'total way of life' rather than simply a political principle or administrative technique. But the totality of a way of life does not equate to its durability: like all forms of sociality, democracy is continually emergent, generated through the relations that comprise it, and as such inherently fragile and open to the possibility of change.

Importantly, though, this change is not just a result of external pressures: it frequently arises from within. This is why, as Long and Moore (2013) have argued, the variability and changeability of human sociality can only be satisfactorily explained if one subscribes to a strong notion of the human subject who is born into and made within a dynamic and malleable matrix of relations, but avowed of sufficient critical and imaginative faculties to imagine how that matrix might be otherwise and – if material circumstances allow – to choose whether to transform it. These faculties include the human capacity for virtuality (Moore 2012), the will or effort required to persist in or transform a particular mode of being (Povinelli 2012), and what Moore (2011: 16) has termed 'the ethical imagination': the forms and means through which individuals not only imagine relationships to themselves and to others but also, and crucially, adjudicate them.

One of the most important aspects of the ethical imagination is its multidimensional character. That is to say, it may involve the processes of rational deliberation and *askesis* that scholars inspired by Foucault have emphasised as a primary means by which human beings might attempt to open up (or shut down) alternative ways of being (Long and Moore 2013: 10–11). But it might also stem from forms of unknowing, the unconscious, fantasy, affect, and the use and experience of the body (Moore 2011: 16). Typically, all of these elements are present to varying degrees (see e.g. Long 2012). It should also be emphasised that, because the ethically imaginative subject has been created through a long history of social relations within a specific dynamic matrix, the way in which that subject imagines their relationships to themselves and others will be shaped by that history. This includes the social imaginaries and ideologies to which they have been exposed, but also the emotional tonalities of the events they have previously experienced. The ethical imagination is not unconstrained. It is nevertheless an important site of cultural invention, calling new forms of social arrangement to mind and motivating the subject to move towards them to the extent that their circumstances allow (Moore 2011: 16–18).

People's perspectives towards and imaginative engagements with the kinds of people they would like to be or become, as well as with objects, ideas, institutions and procedures, are shaped by communal and individual efforts to create ongoing and sustainable infrastructures (both practical and affective) for daily living. And as Lauren Berlant (2011: 23–24) suggests, all attachments – including attachments to existing or aspirational forms of sociality – are 'optimistic' in that they provide a means and a reason for continuing to live and for wanting to be in the world. Three important points follow from this. The first is that self-other relations are foundational for the political at the formative levels and structures of the subject (see Moore 2011 and this volume). This is one of the many reasons why kinship ideas, idioms and experiences are so key for understanding forms of political identification and dissatisfaction, including subjective investments in democracy (see Borneman, Long, this volume; Herzfeld 1997). Secondly, human attachments to, and identifications with, their worlds are ambivalent because human behaviour is not just a matter of rational calculation and well worked-out ideas, but also about the role of affect, suggestion and sensation. Democracy, like any other form of human sociality, is partly set up in fantasy and constituted by and through strong ties of identification and ambivalence which may work in concert or in counterpoint with each other. This is key to understanding the tensions and ambiguities inherent in the nature of people's dissatisfactions with democracy explored in the case studies in this volume. Third, dissatisfaction and desire for political change are not necessarily liberatory, as evidenced in this volume by turns to theocracy, populism and authoritarian rule, but the fact of change – whether desired or actualised, structural or symbolic – is itself part of the human possibilities that make up the political, part of the strategies individuals use in imaging and living out their relations to themselves and to others (Moore 2011: 29).

Democratic Discontent: Re-setting the Agenda

It follows from the principles outlined above that any evaluation of 'democracy', any attempt to compare it with alternatives (theocracy, say, or autocracy, or even a radically refashioned vision of what 'democracy' might be) is ultimately an assessment of the way a particular matrix of relations is organised. It is a reflection upon 'democracy' as a form of sociality, and as such is driven by the ethical imagination of the subject in question. In some cases, this is made very explicit – as when the Israeli politician Rehavam Ze'evi spoke of his aspirations to 'live in a democracy, in which all of its citizens are able to vote and be voted on; without two types of citizens, no masters and no slaves' (in Bat-Adam n.d.). Here 'democracy' was minimally associated with the principle of universal suffrage but, as Ze'evi acknowledged, this has implications for the entire way in which social relations are constituted. Indeed, as Wolin (1983: 3) notes, democracy has historically 'been the means by which the many have sought access to political power in the hope that it could be used to redress their economic and social lot', thereby exposing the illegitimacy of drawing sharp ontological distinctions between 'the political' and 'the social' (as found, for example, in the thought of Hannah Arendt), and highlighting that what is at stake in democracy (or any other form of 'political' organisation) is world-making in its broadest sense (Barthes 1972: 143). This has significant implications for investigating democratic malaise because it reminds us that for all that democracy is typically envisaged as a way of distributing power or rule (reflecting its etymological roots in the Greek *krátos*), dissatisfaction with it could have roots in *any* aspect of the entire form of sociality to which that distribution gives rise. Even the 'classic' features of liberal democracy (elections, the rule of law, the guarantee of political and social rights, etc.) are by necessity embedded within entire ways of life – *any* elements of which might be sources of pleasure or frustration, and *any* elements of which might be the triggers for a profound sense of democratic malaise. Identifying what those problematic elements are – and when and why they serve as lightning rods for specific citizens' discontent – is the empirical task at the heart of this volume.

This allows us to develop a novel approach to the problem in hand. To date, most authors who have tried to account for feelings of dissatisfaction with democracy have focused their attention on the relations between citizens and either their leaders or their state's political institutions. These are of course often very important issues, featuring prominently in citizens' own accounts of why they feel as they do. But they are not the only relations that may be salient: democracy also leads to subjects having distinctive relationships with themselves, other citizens, and with the sense of a national or global world order in which they are embedded. Such relations may all have normative associations drawn from cultural imaginaries regarding how they ought to be conducted; they are also necessarily set up in unconscious fantasy (since one can never fully know oneself or another person, let alone distant global others to whom one nevertheless feels connected), and so have a complex emotional tonality that influences the way in which the subject responds to them (Moore 2007: 6–7). Since the ethical imagination is multidimensional, attention to *both* explicit ethical reflection and less readily articulated tonalities and feelings is vital for understanding why self-avowedly democratic forms of life might provoke its disapproval. We need, in other words, to engage with subjectivity in its broadest sense. This does not mean studying individual subjectivities in isolation or ahistorically, but rather examining their relation to the broader social imaginaries of personhood and politics that circulate within any given place and time, as well as reflecting on how the specific histories of the democratic forms in which subjects are embedded may themselves come to affect the parameters by which 'democracy' is experienced and adjudicated.

The principles we have outlined here make for a deliberately broad and foundational model: one that can be used as a starting point for understanding all of the cases discussed in this volume and that therefore serves as a basis for comparison between them. In the sections that follow, we examine how our emphasis on subjectivity and the ethical imagination adds new layers to the three most widely touted explanations for citizen discontent with democratic socialities, namely that democracy contains inherent aggravating fault-lines, that it has 'failed to deliver', and/or that it has been intolerably adulterated by its entanglements with global capitalism.

The Inherent Tensions of Democracy

Because every political system is a mode of sociality, every political system is capable of attracting the critical attention of the subjects who inhabit it, and of being thought of otherwise. This is an inevitable corollary to the model of political subjectivity that we have outlined, and democracy is not exceptional in this regard. There are, nevertheless, certain structural features, broadly shared among the modes of sociality that call themselves democracies, that make it especially likely that the inhabitants of a democracy will have their ethical imaginations engaged in such a way as to reflect critically on the 'democratic ideal'. The points on which we focus here stand apart from the 'fault-lines' that emerge during the process of democratisation, which are often closely linked both to the legacies of the political systems that preceded democratisation and the manner of the latter's implementation (Agüero 1998; O'Donnell 1993: 1359–1360). We ask instead how the relational forms that a democracy necessitates place particular pressures and demands upon the subject, and whether institutional workings of a democratic polity contain inherent tensions, contradictions and 'fault-lines' that can – in certain circumstances – turn into potent sources of democratic malaise.

Most so-called democracies organise themselves – or at least legitimise themselves – with reference to the principle of popular sovereignty. Democracy is government in the name of the *demos*; of the people, by the people and for the people. The 'empowerment' that such a principle supposedly provides is often advocated as one of democracy's greatest strengths (see e.g. Fung 2006). Yet, because democracy locates sovereignty within individual citizens, it also by necessity makes the way in which that sovereignty is realised – and thus the subject's relationship to others and to 'the political' – stand out as an explicit object of reflection and anxiety (see Hansen 2012). This is further compounded by democracy's promise that the subject has the capacity to change the political, should she wish. 'What am I for the political?' and 'What is the political for me?' are thus questions that continually recur for the inhabitant of a democratic system, unlike those living in more feudal or patrimonial systems, where, although such reflection is of course possible, the particular forms of political subjectivity involved deflect sustained reflection away from the constructed notion of the political.

As Brown (2012: 45–46) argues, popular sovereignty is an 'unfinished principle', offering no specific criteria as to how that rule should be made legitimately manifest: the concept of democracy in and of itself 'specifies neither *what* powers must be shared among us for the people's rule to be practised, *how* this rule is to be organised, nor by *which* institutions or supplemental conditions it is enabled or secured'. Thus, although democratic governance – which in the present day is almost always that of a state – typically seeks to claim its legitimacy through recourse to the principle of popular rule, its actual manifestation will always reflect the historically and geographically particular manner in which that principle has been 'finished'. This observation can help to explain the multiplicity of political forms that lay claim to being 'democracies', and the controversy that surrounds their entitlement to such a designation (Collier and Levitsky 1997). It also sheds important light on perceptions that democracy has 'gone wrong'. As David Nugent argues in his contribution to this volume, such claims may not in fact reflect a malfunction of the 'democratic' political system, but rather the inevitable slippage between the ideal of popular rule as citizens understand it and its instantiation in the practice of statecraft and the experience of social life.

Nugent illustrates his argument with reference to the classic 'liberal representative democracy' – a political form frequently touted as 'the best possible form of government' in both advanced and transitioning democracies (Diamond 1999: 2–7) – which he suggests is predisposed to generate a sense that democracy is in crisis or going wrong. He terms this phenomenon 'the democracy effect'. There are two dimensions to his analysis. Firstly, he identifies tensions embedded deep within the notion of liberal representative democracy: the very practice of electing a representative – while touted as being exemplary of popular rule – actually disempowers the citizen, who is forced to relinquish her sovereignty to a representative drawn from a limited pool of possibilities.[3] Benedict Anderson (1996: 14) described this as a 'domestication'. And yet, as Remmer (1995) notes, without some degree of citizen 'domestication', the state becomes so vulnerable to political buffeting that it is unlikely to survive. This generates a paradox at the heart of democratic nation states: popular sovereignty is both the bedrock of a democracy and yet also something that must be curtailed.

Secondly, Nugent notes that despite such contradictions, subjects are often affectively bound to and invested in the ideal of popular rule – a claim he illustrates with reference to the APRA movement in early twentieth-century Peru. The combination of attachment to an ideal, with its inherent inability to be fully realised within a state, generates a sense of inadequacy surrounding the political. This is his 'democracy effect'. Subjective attachment to the idea of popular rule also makes it especially likely that this sense will be articulated through tropes which sustain the fantasy that popular sovereignty can and should be supported within the apparatus of a state society. Consequently, critique is based on an illusion of 'properly functioning democracy' elsewhere in space and time, fanning the flames of local dissatisfactions.

Henrietta Moore's chapter identifies further tensions which, while arguably intrinsic to all democracies, are becoming especially visible in the context of the self-consciously 'plural' nation states that are so widespread today. Such polities are saturated by social imaginaries drawing strong taxonomic distinctions on the basis of ethnicity, race, religion and culture, and as a result, issues of representation and inclusion are particularly likely to stand out as matters of concern for the ethical imagination. This is especially true given that democratic states predominantly operate as 'pluralist democracies', in which citizens vote according to specific interests, and the spectre of marginalisation looms large for minorities. This can involve more than just economic marginalisation; the relegation of one's deeply held moral principles is also at stake. As Feldman (2012: 671–673) notes, the intrinsic ethical relativism of pluralist democracy marks a radical departure from the earlier model of 'republican democracy', in which the gratification of voters' desires was subordinated to the maintenance of virtue and an explicit pursuit of 'the common good', a shift that alarmed European émigré intellectuals such as Arendt, Strauss and Voegelin, who saw in it the potential for 'anti-democratic masses' to 'gain a power position in the state by legal means' as had previously happened in Nazi Germany (Voegelin 1941: 163–164). Even today, the rise of far-right parties scares liberals with the prospect that democracy might usher in resurgent totalitarianism, while controversial policies – from gay rights to welfare cuts to the United Kingdom's ban on fox-hunting – can chill voters with the realisation that democracy offers no guarantee of upholding their core moral principles, and that their voices will only carry so far in the public sphere.

Such developments may result in claims that 'democracy' – as a system designed to respect the voices of all its citizens – is broken and in need of 'Occupation' or a revitalising 'spring', as Moore documents among French anti-gay-marriage activists. They may also result in forms of passionate violence that, as she shows through the case study of Kenya, can themselves lead to a democracy being judged (by both its citizens and international observers) as 'failing' or 'in decline'. Moore shows that these seemingly diverse responses to contemporary democracy share at their core a common set of preoccupations – those of voice, belonging, authority and legitimacy. And yet to understand the form that a subject's response to feelings of dissatisfaction takes, such concerns must be studied alongside other matters that influence the ethical imagination. For the French activists, the feelings of 'betrayal' are heightened by their identification with the ideals of the French Republic, while Kenyan voters exerted great efforts to prevent violence in the wake of the

2013 election not because they had come to view democracy more positively, but because of their investment in being held in esteem by an imagined wider world. Her material thus demonstrates that the ways in which deep-rooted and shared anxieties about voice, belonging and authority are expressed should be understood in the context of the full range of imaginaries and identifications animating the ethical imagination.

In different ways, each of Moore's cases illustrates the difficulty of finding a way to secure the 'agonism of adversaries' that Mouffe (2000: 15–16) considers to be characteristic of a well-functioning democracy, while avoiding the alternative pitfalls of a consensus managerial state or the explosion of antagonisms that cannot be managed within the democratic process. Indeed, many new experimental political forms grapple precisely with how to achieve the forms of political agonism that appear so difficult to realise within the framework of the electoral state (see e.g. Frenzel 2011; Maeckelbergh, this volume). In terms of identifying factors that might precipitate democratic malaise, we can now add to the inherent tension that comes from the way a democracy domesticates its citizens democracy's simultaneous mandate and incapacity to allow all voices to be fully heard.

The structure of the electoral democratic process can also be a wellspring of democratic discontent. Firstly, as studies in both the United Kingdom (Koch 2016) and Bolivia (Grisaffi 2013) have shown, electoral campaigning often involves a highly personalised and affectively charged set of interactions, in which the voter comes to believe that the politician takes interest in the small-scale concerns that animate their lifeworlds, will care for them when in office, and may even allow them to influence policy via some form of 'direct politics'. Yet once elected, the politician faces so many demands from so many constituents (as well as lobby groups and corporate interests) that it is impossible to fulfil them all. This frequently results in voters feeling betrayed and disappointed. (Note once again the role that identification and desire play in this material.) Secondly, as Runciman (2013) has argued, the very quality that has led to democracy being such a durable political form – the adaptability and capacity to experiment afforded by regular elections – can lead to a sense that democratic governments lack clear direction and are simply 'muddling through' incipient crises, further stoking anxieties that democracy is not fit for purpose.

Indeed, outright satisfaction with democracy will always be unlikely given that the many goods it promises to realise for its citizens will of necessity be delivered at an uneven pace (Holston and Caldeira 1998); democracy is inherently disjunctive and can never be fully realised. While critique arising from this incompleteness might generate forward momentum and political innovation (Holston 2008: 310-311), it may also result in a profound sense of apathy, a crippling democratic malaise, or a turn to an altogether different form of government. To understand what makes the difference, then – and as both Nugent and Moore's contributions to this volume emphasise – we need to move beyond a generalising account of the fault-lines that run through democracy and combine this with a historically, ethnographically and individually specific analysis of the affects and desires that underpin the ethical imagination's engagements with democratic sociality and political life.

Turning Points: The Affective Basis of Democratic Dissatisfaction

To explore this further, we begin with those cases in which citizens who had once seemed quite enthusiastic about the democratic ideal come to feel intensely dissatisfied with it: instances where what the subject thinks or feels is a desirable way to live has been rendered impossible or seriously compromised, resulting either in efforts to reformulate 'democracy' or a turn towards other modes of political organisation. This latter phenomenon, sometimes labelled 'democratic recession' or 'democratic rollback'[4] has been most widely investigated in the new, emerging or 'transitional' democracies associated with the late twentieth century's 'third wave' of democratisation – although, as we will discuss shortly, similar rhetoric is becoming increasingly widespread in societies where democratic statecraft has an older vintage. The key question that such material raises is why a turn away from democracy is taking place among populations where the idea once enjoyed a widespread currency. In this regard we are addressing a fundamentally different issue to that which arises in settings where populations have *always* been hostile to democracy – viewing it as immoral, dangerous or incompatible with local models of deliberative consensus – but have nevertheless had a democratic system of governance imposed (see e.g. Ferme 1998; Hickel 2015; West 2008). Rather, following Ahmad (2009), we place the emphasis of our enquiry on the processes through which 'incompatibilities with democracy' or feelings of dissatisfaction are socially produced within democratic forms of life.

Drawing extensively on the findings of longitudinal 'barometer surveys' that measure shifts in public opinion regarding democracy and its alternatives in particular nations and world regions,[5] authors in the 'democratic recession' school have forcefully argued that citizens turn against democratic ideals when faced with high levels of corruption, poor economic performance, and low levels of security – in other words, when they receive 'poor governance' (Diamond 2008a, 2008b; Fernandez and Kenzi 2006; Kurlantzick 2013; Önnudóttir and Harðarson 2011). This, the literature suggests, may be because the low quality of democratic governance leads citizens to look back on their previous experiences of authoritarian governance with nostalgic fondness (Chang et al. 2007: 74–75). Alternatively, the tremendous socio-economic success of relatively undemocratic, authoritarian regimes such as Singapore, Malaysia and China might enhance support for managerial strongman politicians who position themselves as national or regional 'CEOs' (ibid.: 78).

While this focus on governance in its broadest sense has been an important corrective to the assumption in many policy circles that free-market economic growth in and of itself was the ticket to democratic consolidation, there are questions that surround it as a generalisable thesis. Firstly, one might ask whether issues of governance are really the most fundamental factors that turn citizens against democratic forms of statecraft (and the principles that underpin it), or simply the most readily reportable. Secondly, if problematic governance really is the issue at hand, a question remains as to why this should have become the key locus of subjective investment:

> Although people in countries with weak democratic governments naturally lament their governments' failings, they are also often aware, either through past experi-ence in their own country or from knowledge of other countries, that authoritarian governments often do not perform well either. ... The various ways democratic governments treat their citizens better than authoritarian governments do—such as repressing them less, allowing them to express themselves and take part in political life—also count for something. (Carothers 2009: 12)

Thus, if Diamond and his colleagues are correct, then *why* socio-economic per-formance and 'good governance' should have trumped the apparent pleasures of new freedoms stands out as an urgent question for analysis. Perhaps more urgent still is the question of how comprehensive a portrait is gained when one's analysis hinges on the assumption of a rational-choice political actor, picking and choosing political systems according to their costs and benefits (and seem-ingly equipped with accurate information in this regard). This is a premise that runs deep in both the democratic recession literature and Carothers' rejoinder to it. As such, while studies of democratic recession have told us a great deal about the form in which democratic malaise is publicly expressed – a vital issue if we are to understand its structural effects – an anthropological engagement with citizens' subjectivity has the potential to further illuminate the motiva-tional dynamics that underpin it.

Nicholas Long's contribution to this volume does exactly that, using the insights afforded by person-centred ethnography to shed a fresh light on the growing levels of public distaste for democracy in Indonesia. Underneath a surface discourse of dissatisfaction with governance, he finds a host of much more personal issues that convince his informants that democracy is dangerous or bad. Each case can be understood by examining the subject's ethical imagina-tion within the context of both personal and national history. For example, he shows how state policy, primary education and the favoured family forms that existed under Suharto's authoritarian New Order regime systematically pathol-ogised the expression of individual desires among youth, giving rise to conflicted subjectivities that were at once attracted to democracy because of the capacity it afforded them to articulate their aspirations, yet also, contrary to Carothers's expectations, disgusted by these 'freer' and more 'selfish' versions of themselves. Some older Indonesians, by contrast, who had become used to imposing their views on others in their roles as heads of households, were drawn to democracy because it offered an opportunity to do exactly that in settings beyond the family home. When faced with the forms of agonism, disagreement and manipulation that characterise democratic politics, however, their identifications and sense of self became so threatened that they turned against democracy as a mode of sociality entirely.

In these cases it is psychodynamically motivated, affectively charged and only partially conscious desires regarding who one wants to be, and how one wants to share the world with others, that can account for both subjects' initial enthusiasms for democracy and their sharp turns away from it. While this demonstrates the importance of conducting an expansive enquiry into the dissatisfactions of democracy, Long also argues that even critiques that are *prima facie* focused on governance may be (partially) motivated by deeper psychodynamic concerns. Some of his informants lamented the failing economy and high levels of corruption even as they admitted that they knew that there had been improvements in these areas. Such 'enlightened false consciousness' (Sloterdijk 1988) hardly fits the democratic recession school's model of a rational-choice actor, but makes sense when the language of bad governance is understood as an 'idiom of distress' (Nichter 1981), or a fantasy that conceals deeper anxieties regarding the failure to live as one wants to in a world where the horizons of the good life have been shaped by the legacies of authoritarianism and the growth of consumerism.

John Borneman's chapter offers a complementary perspective to Long's by asking not just why citizens might turn away from democracy and its institutionalised opposition but also what circumstances encourage authoritarianism to flourish: a question he explores through a comparison of the former GDR and contemporary Syria. As with all the contributions in this volume, Borneman insists on the importance of studying political subjectivity in a richly historicised manner, noting that the inherited cultural context in which a form of sociality or political system is emplaced exerts a 'historical weight and influence' that can influence emergent outcomes. He identifies two factors that are of particular importance. The first is kinship, by which he refers less to the specificities of individual households and families (cf. Long, this volume) and more to the ways in which principles of descent, affiliation and alliance serve as a model of libidinal desires that come to endow meaning and grant cultural legitimacy to all social and political forms. The second factor is whether a society has any history of institutionalised opposition or turn-taking, itself something made considerably more likely by a commitment to the bilateral reckoning of kinship. East Germany, in which an initial democratic period quickly gave way to an authoritarian gerontocracy, did have such a heritage, which Borneman suggests may explain the democratic reflex that eventually led to the GDR's segue into a liberal democracy.

For Syria, Borneman notes that while the strong presence of the United States and various EU member states in Syria may have led to forms of identification prompting Syrians to aspire to a 'democratic' constitutional order, the uprisings themselves were not in fact lobbying for democracy as is often (but erroneously) assumed. Both the 'people' in whose name the protests took place and the 'freedom' and 'liberty' that they demanded were concepts couched in a psychologically compelling maternal register (*umma* and *al-hurriyah*, respectively), emphasising freedom from authoritarian repression, but in favour of a binding and connecting of the people in the name of 'community' that also precluded opposition. Taken together, both Borneman and Long's chapters show the significance of an attention to affect, identification and psychodynamics – to subjectivity – in the study of political ideals and satisfactions, while also revealing the importance of grounding such affects in the historical and biographical contexts that give them their 'structured precision' (Hemmings 2005: 562).

The importance of understanding turning points through a focus on subjective identification is developed further in Jan-Jonathan Bock's chapter on emergent political subjectivities in a disaster-struck region of Italy. Bock notes that many people in the central Italian town of L'Aquila had not been especially reflective about democracy prior to the disasters, describing its role in their lives as that of an 'abstract concept'. Suspicion towards politicians and frustration with 'wasteful' local administrations may have been the norm, but there was often an implicit trust in the state as having a basic duty of care towards its citizens. Yet as events unfolded following a devastating earthquake, this faith in the state began to founder, leading voters to reconfigure the government's disaster management not as a caring interventionist response but a cynical management strategy. To the extent that Italian political life had previously been infused *either* with an ethics of clientelistic reciprocity *or* an ethics of trusting the experts, the Aquilani's understandings of the relations they had with leaders were now shattered. Bock understands this as a 'decision-event' – a moment where the matrix of relations in which one is embedded comes into sharp relief, and which elicits a need for subjects to reflect on whether to continue with the status quo or seek to transform it.

The Aquilani responded in a range of ways: some resigned themselves to mediatised democracy or succumbed to authoritarian nostalgia, while others embraced a more vigorous re-engagement with participation in democratic politics. Strikingly, though, what comes forward in Bock's material is the extent to which the motivation for such democratic re-engagement is not only a sense of betrayal by and disillusionment with the state as it currently exists, but also a sense of needing to do justice to the memory of deceased relatives, so that their deaths were not in vain. Once again, we can see how a motivation to rethink politics might stem not only from an intellectual deconstruction of the shortcomings of the present situation, but also intense personal affects (grief, bereavement, fury) that charge political life with personal meaning.

The Pain of Post-democracy

As we have argued, feelings that democracy has 'gone wrong' or should be abandoned can partly be accounted for if one attends to the ways in which ethical imaginations, driven by their own distinctive experiences and idealisations of self/other relations underpinning libidinal and affective investments in the political, engage with the contradictions and relations inherent to the project of democratic statecraft. Building on this, we now engage more closely with a growing body of scholarship on post-democracy that identifies systemic changes in democratic practice – on a widespread if not global scale

– that might in and of themselves dispose citizens to a sense of democratic malaise.

Such scholarship is most frequently concerned with the ways in which state-craft in so-called democracies has drifted away from the vibrant ideological clashing of adversaries – Mouffe's (2000) 'agonistic politics' – and towards a consensual managerialism and non-democratic paternalism that is authoritarian in all but name. Writing of the United Kingdom, Ramsay (2012: 223) traces this to the ascendancy of neoliberalism as a political-economic model that has been able to capture the political imaginations of both the Left and Right. The 'mutual ruin of the old political movements', Ramsay argues, 'has denuded mainstream politics of significantly different versions of society, and reduced competition between the [political] parties to point scoring over tax and spend, and the best technical mix of public and private service provision'. Such 'technicalisation of politics' (Ong 2006: 178) has led to a sense of apathy and disengagement among many citizens, who no longer feel that their voice makes a difference (Crouch 2004; Hay 2007), a disposition compounded by the increasingly limited efficacy of national policy making in a globalised world (Kupchan 2012).

For analysts such as Crouch (2004), Rancière (2006), and Wolin (2008), this situation demonstrates how principles that many imagine should be core to a democracy – such as popular participation and representation – have been eviscerated. The popular mandate no longer sets the policy agenda. This is a problem that extends beyond the mere fact of policy makers exercising decree powers (which, as noted earlier, may be an inevitable corollary of the state system) to incorporate the question of whose interests political decisions are calibrated to advance. Crouch (2004) suggests it is often the interests of global corporations, whose economic resources afford them a much greater capac-ity to influence political decision making than voters or civil society groups; a situation compounded by the fact that economic growth – and hence the flour-ishing of these businesses – is among the top priorities of many governments. As Stark (1998: 76) notes, such difficulties may be even more acute in the Global South, where the need to maintain an attractive climate for investment depends in turn upon developing policies that will be endorsed by major finan-cial institutions and fund managers. Keane (2009), meanwhile, observes that politicians frequently construe the public interest according to how that public is represented by media outlets, identifying a further way in which the citizen-representative relationship is transformed by the activity of corporate interests.

Scholars within this tradition frequently make use of the term 'post-democracy', and such analyses are positioned very interestingly with regard to the question of democratic malaise, because as much as they seek to explain it, they also inhabit it and seek to instigate it in others so that change might take place and the hegemony of neoliberalism be shaken. To an extent, then, their own writings can be analysed within the framework of Nugent's 'democ-racy effect': a perspective which helps explain why many authors have found the term 'post-democracy' a helpful indictment of contemporary affairs, as opposed to available synonyms such as 'oligarchy', 'kleptocracy', or 'technocratic managerialism'.[6] Highlighting the possibility that 'democracy' – to which many readers are affectively bound and which they may consider themselves to be comfortably inhabiting – has been superseded gives the notion of 'the post-democratic' considerable rhetorical force (Ward 2009: 73). It provokes outrage over the state we're in, while sustaining the illusion that there was once or could one day be a truly 'democratic' state of affairs (Crouch 2004: 7–9). However, while this opens the post-democracy literature to critique on the grounds that state governance can never be perfectly democratic, the malaise at the heart of these contemporary critiques cannot be fully accounted for by Nugent's 'democracy effect'. The anger and disappointment at their core stems not (just) from the fact that popular sovereignty is imperfectly realised: a bitter but inevitable truth. Rather, malaise stems from the substantive decline in the extent to which popular sovereignty has been realised in many contexts since at least the 1970s.

Many of the contributions to this volume do corroborate the claim that there has been a fundamental change in the operations of democratic statecraft over the past fifty years. Moreover, by presenting accounts of political life in the wake of the 2008 financial crisis, they also provide an important update to the models of 'post-democracy' that were developed during a time of economic growth. This is perhaps most evident in the complementary analyses of the crises afflicting democracy in contemporary Europe provided in the chapters by Giorgos Katsambekis and Yannis Stavrakakis.

In his analysis of Greek statecraft, Katsambekis illustrates how the role of the popular mandate has not only been systematically displaced but ideologically denigrated through an anti-populist discourse, which sees the people as lacking 'qualification to rule' (Rancière 2011: 3) and thus inferior in their judgements to technocratic experts.[7] Such rhetoric has not only been used by Greek governments to disparage those who opposed austerity measures, whom they dubbed 'populist' and 'unpatriotic'; it was also used by European heads of state to force the Greek Prime Minister George Papandreou to cancel his planned referendum on the EU-IMF bail-out deal. This not only subverts the principle of representation but also, and perhaps even more crucially, sabotages the principle of opposition, which as Borneman (this volume) argues, is fundamental to the very concept of democracy. Unsurprisingly this situation has left some contemporary Greeks feeling torn between their attachments to democracy and their attachments to nationalism, others feeling outraged that democracy has been trammelled by the technocratic juggernaut of EU authoritarianism, and others still wondering what the role of democracy can or should be in their immediate future.

While accounts of post-democracy are helpful for describing the structural eviscerations of representative democracy that have given rise to this state of affairs, there are several crucial dimensions of the situation they struggle to explain. Most notably, the insistence and zeal with which austerity policies are being applied in Greece (and elsewhere) stand sharply at odds with post-democratic theory's image of detached, rational managerialism; the 'expertocracy' that is stifling democracy and calling its future into question quite evidently has a complex affective dynamics of its own. In his chapter, Yannis Stravrakakis demonstrates why, drawing on psychoanalysis and affect theory to show how Europe's current post-democratic tendencies are anchored in the distinctive subjectivities engendered by relations of consumer debt. Although democratisation is often read as a trajectory of electoralisation or the implementation of social and political rights, Stavrakakis observes that it could equally be understood as a genealogy of consumerism, where consumption has been progressively democratised through the increasing availability of credit. The consequences for subjectivity are profound since debt relations, and the sense of guilt they inspire, are highly individualising and moralising, such that problems are blamed on the personal failings of individual consumers (including oneself) rather than on the broader structures in which they are embedded. Stavrakakis explores how the elite consensus on austerity feeds on notions of personal and subjective failure and drives a sadistic desire to inflict punishment. Since the infliction of punishment itself performatively reiterates the illusion of blameworthiness, a vicious cycle is established that upholds the austerity agenda regardless of its merits and drawbacks as a policy and sustains the disregard of the popular mandate.

The current economic crisis in Europe has thus not only witnessed important transformations in the character of 'democratic' statecraft, it has also witnessed the emergence of new aspirations as local forms of the ethical imagination shift towards alternative forms of self/other relations, forms of sociality that might be preferable to existing political and social matrices. Although attachments to 'democracy' as a powerful signifier, charged with associations of 'the good' (Mason 1982: 32) have prompted some to seek its reinvigoration (see e.g. Bock, this volume), an increasing number of people seem willing to embrace entirely alternative conceptions of how political life might be organised. The public embrace of authoritarianism is part of this shift, but so, too, is an apparent surge in affection for 'benevolent' leaders without a popular mandate such as Queen Elizabeth II and Pope Francis – a trend that leads Freedland (2013) to conclude that democracy is 'looking fragile'. Alternatives to democracy have entered debate in popular culture. In the United Kingdom, the actor and comedian Russell Brand famously declared on the BBC news show *Newsnight* that he refused to vote, and subsequently published a monograph urging his readers to pursue a 'revolution' (Brand 2014). He emphasised that his unwillingness to even participate in an election stemmed from a refusal 'to be complicit in a system that persistently disempowered the underclass' and that he was instead 'looking elsewhere for alternatives that might be of service to humanity; alternative means, alternative political systems'.[8] Challenged as to what such an alternative might be, Brand admitted he had 'not invented it yet', but the interview became well enough known via social media for many to begin to argue it was indeed time for a new form of government; the romantic appeal of an undefined 'revolution' capturing the ethical imagination in a way that the tawdriness of pursuing change through the ballot box could not.

Marianne Maeckelbergh's chapter considers the painstaking efforts taken to create and implement a new political system by members of social movements such as 15M, Occupy, and the alter-globalisation movement. For many years, these groups have advocated a form of political practice known as 'horizontality', in which participants communally participate in decision making in ways that seek to avoid any form of hierarchy or domination. The principles of representation, and indeed the nation state structure, are rejected by this innovation. Liberal democracy's founding assumption of equality among all citizens is discarded in favour of a recognition of the ways in which difference and disadvantage can impact upon participation. The authoritarian correlates of the ideal of democratic consensus are surmounted by allowing multiple conflicting outcomes to be decided upon should parties be unable to agree. Clearly, this represents a thoroughly different way of ordering sociality to that which is hegemonically understood as 'democracy'.

Horizontality's proximity to the ideals of popular sovereignty, democratic agonism and 'Athenian' styles of politics has often led to it being championed as the reinvigoration of democracy, true democracy or 'direct democracy' (Graeber 2013; Rasza and Kurnik 2012). Yet Maeckelbergh notes that a growing number in the movement she has worked with reject this characterisation of their practice. For these figures, the ideal of 'democracy' has been so tainted by its associations with the state and, latterly, corporate capitalism, that horizontality should be pursued as the successor to democracy rather than its purification.

Her ethnography thus reveals a tension at the heart of the movement over how 'democratic' its participants should conceive, imagine and experience themselves and others to be. This is in part a tactical question engaging the reflexive and rational dimensions of participants' ethical imaginations, since positioning themselves against democracy affords scope to educate the public against democracy's shortcomings, yet deprives them of the positive moral valence that the term so readily invokes. But it is also an identificatory and affective issue, as the term 'democracy' increasingly elicits disgust or disdain, and yet foregoing the understanding of oneself as a democrat is not always easy. Indeed, it is precisely because of the term's affective hold on contemporary subjects that the terminological question stands out as a matter of tactical concern. What this reveals is that democracy is not just a label for certain forms of sociality, as a nominalist approach to democracy's multiple meanings might highlight. It is also, as a term – and as a psychological object – co-productive of those very forms of sociality. How readily the rhetoric of democracy can be dispensed with is consequently – as Maeckelbergh shows – dependent on the specific history of democracy in each country and – by extension – in the life of each community and individual within that country, and therefore a matter for detailed and particularist enquiry.

Conclusion: A Global Crisis of Democracy?

Taken together, the chapters in this volume reveal that we should exercise extreme caution before advancing the claim that we are facing a 'global crisis of democracy'. The cases do share certain factors in common. All are fundamentally concerned with the exercise of the ethical imagination, with human subjects reflecting upon the dynamic matrix of relations in which they are embedded and deciding that it in some way needs to change its character and/ or its form. And all involve people either expressing dissatisfaction with or thinking beyond forms of liberal democratic statecraft that not only contain inherent contradictions, but have, under the most recent phase of globalisation, come to acquire distinct new authoritarian characteristics and have often become subject to the exigencies of extraterritorial actors. These trends in and of themselves could be seen as evidence of democracy being in worldwide crisis. Yet the chapters in this volume highlight the importance of paying attention to the specifics: the different time-depth of democratic social imaginaries, the historically contingent collective identities that are seen as being at the heart of 'democracy', and the differing ways in which factors such as kinship, consumerism and unforeseeable natural and economic disasters influence what stands out as a matter of concern for citizens as they reflect upon the political. Even when people are apparently responding to the same sets of problems or difficulties, what those challenges actually *mean* is fully embedded within a specific web of social and historical relations.

Nevertheless, a huge number of the people whose voices are captured in this volume persist in the belief that they inhabit a democratic predicament that is fundamentally shared not only by their countrymen, but by their counterparts around the world – demonstrating once again that the ethical imagination and self/other relations are foundational both for the political and for subjectivity. The flows of representations that Appadurai (1996) and others have argued to characterise the present age, transnational mass media flows being foremost among them, ensure that citizens are regularly exposed to images – often fleeting, fragmentary and incomplete – of other people's dissatisfaction with democracy, and find within these a sense of similarity. But such viewings are never straightforward, and despite the apparent sense of linkage to 'distant but familiar others' (Boellstorff 2005: 211), the potential for miscommunication and misunderstanding remains high. Images are not the sources of objective knowledge that they first appear to be; they are 'fantasised point[s] of interconnection ... that make the position of the individual and the nation intellectually and emotionally plausible within an imagined global space' (Moore 2011: 60).

This finds vivid illustration in a fieldwork episode from Indonesia. It was August 2011, and Nicholas Long had recently arrived in the Riau Islands Province to investigate local attitudes to democracy. Yet when he broached the subject, it was not Indonesian politics that was foremost in his informants' minds. The riots that had swept England that month – in which several people were killed and hundreds of businesses and homes were looted and set on fire

– attracted widespread coverage in the Indonesian media and was often met with horror and incomprehension. For many who had long been committed to the ideals of democracy and human rights, Western countries had been their source of inspiration, a model to be emulated. But as their news bulletins showed footage of riots and violent demonstrations in the 'developed' world that they had hoped their country would one day parallel, they began to wonder whether the problems Indonesia was having were not just caused by Indonesians' inexperience with democracy, or inability to implement it effectively. Perhaps they were inherent to democracy itself.

'I was so shocked to see the riots in the UK!' said Arifin, a Malay businessman friend of Long's as, they discussed the day's news in a Tanjung Pinang coffee shop. 'Even though you have been a democracy for hundreds of years! And your country is much richer than ours. How can it be that you are still having the same problems that we are?' Reflecting on the unrest that followed in the wake of the Greek debt crisis, another man at the table remarked that even though democracy had been invented in Ancient Greece, it had done nothing to secure the nation's socio-economic prosperity. He had heard that even Greek people were saying that they had had enough of it. Perhaps, he suggested, it was time that Indonesians looked for a more 'Indonesian' solution as to how to govern their country: something closer to Sukarno's authoritarian 'Guided Democracy', an Islamic state, or a feudal system of military rule.

This case shows how the fantasised interconnections of a shared global predicament can generate a sense of democracy's inevitable failure, and inflect the concept of democratisation with an affect of despondency. But they do so by eliding important differences between the various situations in hand. These Indonesian businessmen looked at the riots in London and Athens and saw anger at democracy's failures to provide socio-economic prosperity: an issue of particular concern to them. This was, of course, an ingredient of the rioting. But what they did not see was the anger at police brutality that triggered the rioting in both Britain and Greece, nor the bitter history of institutionalised racism and class inequality in Britain, nor the sense of deep democratic betrayal that came from the Liberal Democrats' *volte face* on tuition fees and the government's failure to adequately regulate the banking sector. They did not see the Greek public's anger at the ideological sadism of austerity measures, nor at the extent to which their country's policies were being determined by overseas powers. As such, and in a cruel twist of fate, anger at the way that democracy had been eviscerated and replaced with a rapacious, authoritarian state in Europe came to be taken as compelling evidence in favour of implementing a new brand of authoritarianism in Indonesia. The same process happens in reverse; while few Euro-Americans pay much attention to Indonesian democracy, the so-called 'Arab Winter' that saw political Islamists rise to power in elections across the Middle East has become interpreted by Euro-American cosmopolitans as a rejection or short-circuiting of the turn to democratisation that was the Arab Spring, and as sure-fire evidence that 'democracy is going through a difficult time' – to quote the article from *The Economist* with which this essay opened. This has become the dominant narrative of Middle Eastern and North African politics, despite the fact that – as Borneman (this volume) shows – the protests at the heart of the 'Arab Spring' were always more concerned with rejecting existing authoritarianism than embracing Western-style democracy.

The disparate cases of democratic malaise that we discuss in this book thus cannot be understood in isolation because the nature of the ethical imagination, and the way selves imaginatively engage with others across distances of time and space, means that they are increasingly becoming evidence for and productive of each other. When a question such as 'What's Gone Wrong With Democracy?' is plastered across the cover of a respected news weekly, it creates the very crisis it announces, stoking it further with the juxtaposition of fundamentally incommensurable case studies that overwhelm the reader with their sheer volume and their shared grimness. Such a situation will likely intensify any disillusionment that citizens have regarding democracy. Given the potency of imaginative identifications and their potential consequences for political change around the world, the excitement of discovering similarities between contemporary engagements with democracy's troubles must be balanced with a sobering appreciation of their differences. It is precisely in that spirit that our present contribution is made.

Notes

1   http://www.economist.com/news/essays/21596796-democracy-was-most-successful -political-idea-20th-century-why-has-it-run-trouble-and-what-can-be-do (accessed 15 July 2014).
2   See for instance Diamond (2014), who warns we are on 'the brink' of one, Pavel (2010), who considers it 'obvious' that we are in one, and various other scholars, journalists and public intellectuals who have sought to call attention to its presence and its character (e.g. Kaldor in Šimečka et al. 2009; Thakur 2011; Žižek 2013).
3   When one considers that the field of candidates is typically drawn from a pre-existing elite political class, this situation only appears graver. It is compounded by voting mechanisms that may lead to parties or personalities with relatively low proportions of vote-share or seat-share nevertheless being declared the victor in an election.
4   While the scope of this term extends beyond an interest in citizens' attitudes to democracy (encompassing among other things the elite capture of democratic institutions and failures of the rule of law), the turn of public opinion away from democracy and towards more authoritarian alternatives is a central problematic in the literature.
5   See for example the work of Chang et al. (2007) on East and Southeast Asia, Fernandez and Kenzi (2006) on Africa, Lagos (2008) on Latin America, and Steves et al. (2011) on Europe.
6   'Post-democracy' has also been used by Hocking and Lewis (2007) and Rorty (2004), to describe the new forms of statecraft that have emerged to confront international terrorism and signal their deviation from the workings of a classic liberal democracy.
7   Concerns about poor vote quality have long dogged discussions of democracy (see Friedman 1998 for an overview). For an alternate perspective, see Oppenheimer and Edwards's (2012) argument that, however poor an individual voter's decision making

might be, popular sovereignty has systemic effects that lead to better quality governance and citizenship than less representative systems.
8   See https://www.youtube.com/watch?v=3YR4CseY9pk (accessed 25 July 2014).

References

Agamben, G. 2012. Introductory Note on the Concept of Democracy. In *Democracy
    in What State?* (eds) G. Agamben, A. Badiou, D. Bensaïd, W. Brown, J-L. Nancy,
    J. Rancière, K. Ross and S. Žižek, 1–5. New York: Columbia University Press.
Agüero, F. 1998. Conflicting Assessments of Democratization: Exploring the Fault Lines.
    In *Fault Lines of Democracy in Post-Transition Latin America* (eds) F. Agüero and
    J. Stark, 1–20. Coral Gables: North-South Center Press.
Ahmad, I. 2009. *Islamism and Democracy in India: The Transformation of Jamaat-e-
    Islami*. Princeton: Princeton University Press.
Ahmed, S. 2004. *The Cultural Politics of Emotion.* Edinburgh: Edinburgh University Press.
———. 2010. *The Promise of Happiness*. Durham: Duke University Press.
Anderson, B.R. 1996. Elections and Participation in Three Southeast Asian Countries.
    In *The Politics of Elections in Southeast Asia* (ed.) R.H. Taylor, 12–33. Cambridge:
    Cambridge University Press.
Appadurai, A. 1996. *Modernity at Large: Cultural Dimensions of Globalization.*
    Minneapolis: University of Minnesota Press.
Banerjee, M. 2008. Democracy, Sacred and Everyday: An Ethnographic Case from India.
    In *Democracy: Anthropological Approaches* (ed.) J. Paley. Santa Fe: SAR Press.
Barthes, R. 1972. *Mythologies* (trans. A. Lavers). New York: Noonday Press.
Bat-Adam, S. n.d. Ghandi's Political Path. <http://www.gandi.org.il/Site/en/pages/
    inPage.asp?catID=3&subID=27> (accessed 20 July 2015).
Berlant, L. 2011. *Cruel Optimism*. Durham: Duke University Press.
Boellstorff, T. 2005. *The Gay Archipelago: Sexuality and Nation in Indonesia*. Princeton:
    Princeton University Press.
Brand, R. 2014. *Revolution*. London: Century.
Brown, W. 2012. 'We Are All Democrats Now...'. In *Democracy in What State?* (eds)
    G. Agamben, A. Badiou, D. Bensaïd, W. Brown, J-L. Nancy, J. Rancière, K. Ross and
    S. Žižek. New York: Columbia University Press.
Carothers, T. 2009. *Stepping Back from Democratic Pessimism.* Washington, DC:
    Carnegie Endowment for International Peace.
Chang, Y.T., Y.H. Chu and C.M. Park. 2007. Authoritarian Nostalgia in Asia. *Journal of
    Democracy* 18, no. 3: 66–80.
Collier, D., and S. Levitsky. 1997. Democracy with Adjectives: Conceptual Innovation in
    Comparative Research. *World Politics* 49, no. 3: 430–451.
Crociani-Windland, L., and P. Hogget. 2012. Politics and Affect. *Subjectivity* 5, no. 2:
    161–179.
Crouch, C. 2004. *Post-Democracy*. Cambridge: Polity Press.
Cruikshank, B. 1999. *The Will to Empower: Democratic Citizens and Other Subjects.*
    Ithaca: Cornell University Press.
de Tocqueville, A. [1835] 2003. *Democracy in America: And Two Essays on America.*
    London: Penguin.
Dewey, J. [1939] 1988. Creative Democracy – The Task before Us. In *John Dewey: The
    Later Works, 1925–1953. Volume 14* (ed.) J.A. Boydston, 224–230. Carbondale:
    Southern Illinois University Press.

Diamond, L. 1999. *Developing Democracy: Toward Consolidation.* Baltimore: The Johns Hopkins University Press.

———. 2008a. The Democratic Rollback: The Resurgence of the Predatory State. *Foreign Affairs* 87, no. 2: 36–48.

———. 2008b. *The Spirit of Democracy: The Struggle to Build Free Societies Throughout the World.* New York: Times Books.

———. 2014. Is There an Emerging Crisis of Democracy? <http://cddrl.fsi.stanford.edu/events/is_there_an_emerging_crisis_of_democracy> (accessed 10 September 2014).

Feldman, S.M. 2012. Democracy and Dissent: Strauss, Arendt, and Voegelin in America. *Denver University Law Review* 89, no. 3: 671–697.

Ferme, M. 1998. The Violence of Numbers: Consensus, Competition and the Negotiation of Disputes in Sierra Leone. *Cahiers d'Etudes Africaines* 150–152, no. xxxviii-2-4: 555–580.

Fernandez, K.E., and M. Kenzi. 2006. *Crime and Support for Democracy: Revisiting Modernization Theory.* Cape Town, Legon-Accra and East Lansing: Afrobarometer.

Freedland, J. 2013. After a Night at the Theatre with the Queen, I Worry About Our Democracy. <http://www.theguardian.com/commentisfree/2013/mar/22/theatre-queen-worry-democracy-politicians> (accessed 7 September 2014).

Frenzel, F. 2011. *'Exit the System': Crafting the Place of Protest Camps between Antagonism and Exception.* Working Paper. Bristol: University of the West of England.

Friedman, J. 1998. Public Ignorance and Democratic Theory. *Critical Review* 12, no. 4: 397–411.

Fung, A. 2006. *Empowered Participation: Reinventing Urban Democracy.* Princeton: Princeton University Press.

Graeber, D. 2007. *Possibilities: Essays on Hierarchy, Rebellion, and Desire.* Oakland: AK Press.

———. 2013. *The Democracy Project: A History. A Crisis. A Movement.* London: Allen Lane.

Grisaffi, T. 2013. 'All of Us Are Presidents': Radical Democracy and Citizenship in the Chapare Province, Bolivia. *Critique of Anthropology* 33, no. 1: 47–65.

Hansen, T.B. 2012. *Melancholia of Freedom: Social Life in an Indian Township in South Africa.* Princeton: Princeton University Press.

Hay, C. 2007. *Why We Hate Politics.* Cambridge: Polity Press.

Hemmings, C. 2005. Invoking Affect: Cultural Theory and the Ontological Turn. *Cultural Studies* 19, no. 5: 548–567.

Herzfeld, M. 1997. *Cultural Intimacy: Social Poetics in the Nation-State.* London and New York: Routledge.

Hickel, J. 2015. *Democracy as Death: The Moral Order of Anti-Liberal Politics in South Africa.* Berkeley: University of California Press.

Hocking, J., and C. Lewis (eds) 2007. *Counter-Terrorism and the Post-Democratic State.* Cheltenham: Edward Elgar.

Holston, J. 2008. *Insurgent Citizenship: Disjunctions of Democracy and Modernity in Brazil.* Princeton: Princeton University Press.

Holston, J., and T.P.R. Caldeira. 1998. Democracy, Law, and Violence: Disjunctions of Brazilian Citizenship. In *Fault Lines of Democracy in Post-Transition Latin America* (eds) F. Agüero and J. Stark, 263–296. Coral Gables: North-South Center Press.

Keane, J. 2009. Media Decadence and Democracy. <http://johnkeane.info/media/pdfs/keane_28_aug_2009_senate_lecture_canberra.pdf> (accessed 22 February 2013).

Koch, I. 2016. Bread and Butter Politics: Democratic Disenchantment and Everyday Politics on an English Council Estate. *American Ethnologist* 43, no. 2.

Kupchan, C.A. 2012. The Democratic Malaise: Globalization and the Threat to the West. *Foreign Affairs* 91, no. 1: 62–67.

Kurlantzick, J. 2013. *Democracy in Retreat: The Revolt of the Middle Class and the Worldwide Decline of Representative Government*. New Haven: Yale University Press.

Lagos, M. 2008. Latin America's Diversity of Views. *Journal of Democracy* 19, no. 1: 111–125.

Lenin, V.I. [1919] 1965. First Congress of the Communist International, March 2–6, 1919. In *V.I. Lenin: Collected Works, Volume 28* (ed.) V.I. Lenin, 455–477. Moscow: Progress Publishers.

Long, N.J. 2006. Debating Democracy: School Debaters Struggle against Social Norms to Promote Change. *Inside Indonesia* 88: 33–34.

———. 2012. Utopian Sociality. Online. *Cambridge Anthropology* 30, no. 1: 80–94.

———. 2013. *Being Malay in Indonesia: Histories, Hopes and Citizenship in the Riau Archipelago*. Singapore: NUS Press.

Long, N.J., and H.L. Moore. 2013. Introduction: Sociality's New Directions. In *Sociality: New Directions* (eds) N.J. Long and H.L. Moore, 1–24. Oxford and New York: Berghahn.

Mason, R.M. 1982. *Participatory and Workplace Democracy: A Theoretical Development in Critique of Liberalism*. Carbondale: Southern Illinois University Press.

Michelutti, L. 2007. The Vernacularization of Democracy: Political Participation and Popular Politics in North India. *Journal of the Royal Anthropological Institute* 13, no. 3: 639–656.

Moore, H.L. 2007. *The Subject of Anthropology: Gender, Symbolism and Psychoanalysis*. Cambridge: Polity Press.

———. 2011. *Still Life: Hopes, Desires and Satisfactions*. Cambridge: Polity Press.

———. 2012. Avatars and Robots: The Imaginary Present and the Socialities of the Inorganic. *Cambridge Anthropology* 30, no. 1: 48–63.

Mouffe, C. 2000. *Deliberative Democracy or Agonistic Pluralism?* Vienna: Institute for Advanced Studies.

Navaro-Yashin, Y. 2012. *The Make-Believe Space: Affective Geography in a Postwar Polity*. Durham: Duke University Press.

Nichter, M. 1981. Idioms of Distress: Alternatives in the Expression of Psychosocial Distress: A Case Study from South India. *Culture, Medicine and Psychiatry* 5, no. 4: 379–408.

O'Donnell, G. 1993. On the State, Democratization and Some Conceptual Problems: A Latin American View with Glances at Some Postcommunist Countries. *World Development* 21, no. 8: 1355–1369.

Ong, A. 2006. *Neoliberalism as Exception: Mutations in Citizenship and Sovereignty*. Durham: Duke University Press.

Önnudóttir, E.H., and Ó.Þ. Harðarson. 2011. Policy Performance and Satisfaction with Democracy. *Stjórnmál og Stjórnsýsla* 7, no. 2: 417–436.

Oppenheimer, D., and M. Edwards. 2012. *Democracy Despite Itself: Why a System That Shouldn't Work at All Works So Well*. Cambridge, MA: MIT Press.

Paley, J. 2002. Toward an Anthropology of Democracy. *Annual Review of Anthropology* 31: 469–496.

Pavel, D. 2010. Civic, Noncivic, Anticivic Sau: 'The Theory of Civil Society Revisited'. *Sfera Politicii*, no. 144: 3–20.

Povinelli, E.A. 2012. The Will to Be Otherwise / The Effort of Endurance. *The South Atlantic Quarterly* 111, no. 3: 453–475.

Powell, G.B. 2000. *Elections as Instruments of Democracy: Majoritarian and Proportional Visions*. New Haven: Yale University Press.

Ramsay, P. 2012. *The Insecurity State: Vulnerable Autonomy and the Right to Security in the Criminal Law*. Oxford: Oxford University Press.

Rancière, J. 2006. *Hatred of Democracy* (trans. S. Corcoran). New York: Verso.

———. 2011. The Thinking of Dissensus: Politics and Aesthetics. In *Reading Rancière* (eds) P. Bowman and R. Stamp. London and New York: Continuum.

Rasza, M., and A. Kurnik. 2012. The Occupy Movement in Žižek's Hometown: Direct Democracy and a Politics of Becoming. *American Ethnologist* 39, no. 2: 238–258.

Remmer, K.L. 1995. New Theoretical Perspectives on Democratization. *Comparative Politics* 28, no. 1: 103–122.

Rorty, R. 2004. Post-Democracy. *London Review of Books* 26, no. 7: 10–11.

Runciman, D. 2013. *The Confidence Trap: A History of Democracy in Crisis from World War I to the Present*. Princeton: Princeton University Press.

Simandjuntak, D. 2009. Milk Coffee at 10am: Encountering the State through Pilkada in North Sumatra. In *State of Authority: The State in Society in Indonesia* (eds) G. van Klinken and J. Barker, 73–94. Ithaca: Southeast Asia Program Publications, Cornell University.

Šimečka, M.M., M. Kaldor, K. Schwarzenberg, B. Schmögnerová and W. Martens. 2009. Open Society in Crisis. <http://ceeforum.eu/en/2009/11/otvorena-spolocnost-uprostred-krizy/> (accessed 10 September 2014).

Sloterdijk, P. 1988. *Critique of Cynical Reason*. London and New York: Verso.

Stark, J. 1998. Globalization and Democracy in Latin America. In *Fault Lines of Democracy in Post-Transition Latin America* (eds) F. Agüero and J. Stark, 67–96. Coral Gables, FL: North-South Center Press.

Steves, F., E. Berglöf, J. Zettelmeyer, B. Bidani, M.F. Diagne, S. Zaidi, F. Ricka, P. Sanfey, D. Ringold, A. Teytelboym and E. Fodor. 2011. *Life in Transition: After the Crisis*. Brussels: European Bank for Reconstruction and Development.

Thakur, R. 2011. Global Crisis of Democracy. *The Japan Times*, 28 October 2011.

Voegelin, E. 1941. Some Problems of German Hegemony. *The Journal of Politics* 3, no. 2: 154–168.

Ward, G. 2009. *The Politics of Discipleship: Becoming Postmaterial Citizens*. Grand Rapids: Baker Academic.

West, H. 2008. 'Govern Yourselves!': Democracy and Carnage in Northern Mozambique. In *Democracy: Anthropological Approaches* (ed.) J. Paley, 97–121. Santa Fe: SAR Press.

Wolin, S.S. 1983. Hannah Arendt: Democracy and the Political. *Salmagundi* 60: 3–19.

———. 2008. *Democracy Incorporated: Managed Democracy and the Specter of Inverted Totalitarianism*. Princeton: Princeton University Press.

Žižek, S. 2013. The West's Crisis Is One of Democracy as Much as Finance. <http://www.theguardian.com/commentisfree/2013/jan/16/west-crisis-democracy-finance-spirit-dictators> (accessed 10 September 2014).

Joanna Cook is a reader in medical anthropology at University College London.

Nicholas J. Long is Assistant Professor of anthropology at the London School of Economics and Political Science.

Henrietta L. Moore is the founder and director of the Institute for Global Prosperity, and Chair in philosophy, culture and design at University College London.

1

After (?) Democracy
Time, Space and Affect in Peruvian Political Imaginaries

David Nugent

The opening decades of the twenty-first century have been witness to what many regard as a sea change in the principles of political legitimacy. A fundamental breakdown of trust between politicians and electorates is said to have given rise to a widespread sense of 'malaise' and disaffection among the citizens of democratic polities (Kupchan 2012). For some scholars (cf. Diamond 2008), these developments represent a 'recession' of democratic ideals and practices. For many other scholars (cf. Fraser 2014), however, contemporary developments are more serious than the term 'recession' implies. Only the notion of 'democratic crisis', they argue, can capture the scope and scale of the sweeping transformations taking place in political life.

In the pages that follow I argue that the crisis of democracy interpretation, while important, does not provide a wholly adequate explanation for why so many people of late appear to have rejected the democratic ideal. Drawing on ethnographic materials from the northern Peruvian Andes during the middle decades of the twentieth century, I explore this point by focusing on the temporality of democracy that is implicit in the crisis view, and the normative claims associated with that temporality. My argument has several components. First, I show that the crisis interpretation, while accurate in many respects, is also partial and incomplete. The notion that democracy is in crisis is anything but a recent development. To the contrary: extreme scepticism about the merits of the democratic ideal, and about the future of democracy, has been widespread and continuous, virtually since this form of political order became institutionalised in select countries of the North Atlantic in the late eighteenth century. Indeed, as I shall argue, in democratic social orders crisis is inevitable rather than exceptional.

The second component of my argument builds on this first one to show that perceptions of crisis – even when they are as widespread as they are today – are embedded in a more complex field of responses to democracy. Multiple understandings of the democratic ideal, I suggest, generally coexist within the same social field, and vie with one another for public support and recognition. Among the most interesting aspects of these different views of democracy is that they often contradict one another. With respect to the notion that we have entered into a period of crisis, however, what is relevant about these different forms of democracy is that each has its own distinctive temporality. What may appear to be a post-democratic moment for some, for example, is often regarded as a democratic or even a pre-democratic moment by others.

I argue that there is much to be gained by recognising the full range of democracies and democratic temporalities that characterise any given social context. I argue that it is equally important to pay close attention to the antinomies between these coexisting democracies. Doing so allows us to understand democracy as a contested field of legitimating claims and understandings (Roseberry 1994) rather than a set of institutions, conditions or social accomplishments. As I will show presently, the very same institutions, conditions and accomplishments may be interpreted in very different terms – as democratic, non-democratic, pre-democratic or post-democratic – by different constituencies, each of which may have its own understanding of the democratic ideal. As a result, these constituencies may renounce some versions of democracy even as they embrace others. Rejection of any particular form of expression of democracy does not mean rejection of democracy.

From this perspective, it would be important to subject to careful scrutiny all claims about the temporality of democracy – to ask, for example, who argues that we are in the midst of a sea change in political legitimacy. It would be equally important to ask what kind of work is performed, what kinds of legitimating claims are being made, by means of such an assertion. It would also be important to explore the possibility that other forms and other temporalities of democracy exist alongside the form that is said to be in crisis – to ask what views are rendered opaque or invisible by asserting that we are passing out of democracy and into something post-democratic. To fail to ask these questions is to neglect the full range of moral and political imaginaries that are expressed through the democratic ideal. It is also to assert a particular, and quite interested understanding of democracy and its history as normative (cf. Nugent 2008) – a point to which I will return. Finally, it is to silence the many alternative voices that view the temporality and spatiality of democratic social processes in ways that cannot be captured by the thesis of epochal change.

Democracy as Ideal and as Practice

Later in the chapter I present a brief discussion of the multiple temporalities of democracy that coexisted in northern Peru during the middle decades of the twentieth century. Before doing so, however, I offer some preliminary thoughts about democracy as a conceptual category – thoughts that have been provoked by the unusually interesting way in which the editors of this volume have framed our project in theoretical terms. In describing the book's orientations and aims, the editors emphasise that the point of our discussions is not simply to explore why people become dissatisfied with this or that set of political circumstances or forms of statecraft. Instead of solely focusing on democracy as a set of institutions or social conditions, the editors explain, they would also like us to engage with the problem of democracy as an ideal. They would like us to analyse people's changing relationships to democracy as an ideal – to explore why they are led, in some times and places, to reject the entire notion of democracy. I will use this distinction between ideal and practice as my point of departure for the discussion that follows. I will begin with democracy as political and cultural ideal.

It is in the very nature of ideals, of course, to be unrealisable in practice. Democracy is no exception. But democracy is no ordinary ideal. The first task we face in seeking to understand people's changing relationships to democracy as an ideal is to understand the specific kind of ideal that democracy is. What makes democracy distinctive as an ideal, I argue, is that it is not only an ideal. In addition, it has also acted as a core principle of political legitimacy across much of the globe for at least a century.

Because democracy-as-ideal has been so extensively used as a means of legitimation, and in such widely different circumstances, the term has been used to refer to a startlingly broad range of social conditions and political practices (see below). This fact alone adds greatly to the complexities involved in thinking through the significance of the crisis that democracy is currently undergoing in some parts of the world. But the challenges of doing so do not end here. Because of its double life as an ideal and as a means of legitimation, democracy has also been employed to defend a great range of context-specific (and often opposed) claims concerning how political life should be, could be, might be, must be, used to be and is sure to be lived. Democracy has been used in an equally broad range of settings, however, to defend a very different set of assertions – concerning how life should never be, could never be, should not currently be and never will be lived.

In some contexts, democracy is described as an aspiration – as a passionate, heartfelt desire for an imagined state that is absent rather than present, one that would help liberate people from conditions of servitude or oppression. But in other contexts democracy is characterised as the culmination of such a process of struggle and emancipation – not as a wish but as a fact, as a political state, which has been won through great sacrifice, and is present rather than absent.

In still other contexts, however, democracy signals neither aspiration nor a state of emancipation but a set of institutions and political processes, often (but not always) those associated with elections and representation. A related but distinct use of democracy is to refer to a category of nation state, as in the common reference to the 'established democracies' – a term that invokes a global hierarchy of polities, some of which are more securely democratic (and legitimate) than others. Finally, democracy is commonly used to refer to what a particular regime, time period, etc., fails to be when it fails to live up to people's material and moral-ethical expectations – when it fails to provide them with what they believe they are entitled to.

In these latter circumstances, democracy is viewed not as something that lies ahead of people, something they should reach toward, something they should work hard to achieve. Rather, democracy is seen as something that people should distance themselves from, something they should put behind them. It is seen as something that should be a part of their past, that may unfortunately be a part of their present, but that should definitely not be a part of their future.

What is revealed about democracy by even this cursory examination of some of the diverse ways in which it is mobilised and imagined? Democracy may be used to refer at once to an emotion and an institution, to conditions desired and those rejected, to a category of polity and a state of being. Indeed, because democracy is used in such a promiscuous manner, a striking range of what are often mutually incompatible institutions, conditions, practices and accomplishments have come to be associated with this term. Small wonder, then, that it is so difficult (but also so productive) to analyse people's changing relationships to democracy, both as ideal and as practice. For it is not at all clear what the referent of the term is.

The fact that this one term is used to refer such a wide range of activities, aspirations, conditions, accomplishments and failures speaks to the importance of democracy as a category of cultural meaning – one that is involved in framing a great many contemporary political and moral imaginaries. Indeed, whether it is regarded as a force for good or evil, as something to be accepted or rejected, it would appear that democracy is an unusually powerful and compelling principle of order. The fact that it is so, and is also an unattainable ideal or aspiration, is important in understanding people's relationships to democracy as an ideal. For it means that people's experiences of democracy are almost inevitably accompanied by a sense of something missing, something incomplete. But this is more than something that is simply absent. Because of the power of democracy as a legitimating principle, it is also a sense of something absent that *should* be present.

As a result, democracy often finds itself in question. The unresolved tension between the 'should' and the 'is' of this form of political life means that some constituencies are forever finding democracy wanting, are continually led to re-imagine its contours, at times (as of late) to reject it outright. Indeed, it is democracy's failure to be what it is supposed to be that has led many (but not all) people in the contemporary world to wash their hands of it – to discard democracy completely.

Democracy, Capitalism and Inequality

The sense that there is something missing in contemporary manifestations of democracy is a function of more, however, than the disjuncture between should and is. Equally important is the particular form of political practice that has come to be regarded as democracy in much of the world, and the relationship between this normative form of democracy (Nugent 2008) and capitalism. In that contemporary discussions of crisis focus on one or more aspects of this specific expression of the democratic ideal it is worth examining this form of practice in more detail. Doing so will make it possible to 'provincialise' (cf. Chakrabarty 2000) this particular expression of democracy – to distinguish between it and Democracy with a capital D. Doing so will also help clarify what is at stake when crisis theorists invoke the demise of this form of political practice as signalling the end of democracy itself.

As noted by a number of scholars (cf. Wood 1994), the birth of capitalism in the North Atlantic in the eighteenth century coincides with the institutionalisation of a particular form of political practice – what has come to be known in the scholarly literature as liberal representative democracy. This form of democratic practice is not of one piece. Rather, it is made up of separate components, which together constitute an odd hybrid of unrelated rights and rituals that we have come to think of as a single undifferentiated whole. These rights and rituals have little to do with the original meaning of democracy – in the sense of rule by the people, or the *demos*. Each of the different components that make up the hybrid that is liberal representative democracy stands in a different relationship to the principles of popular rule. It is to this topic that I now turn.

One of the components that make up liberal representative democracy is the liberal component – a term that refers to the rights and protections enshrined in the constitutions of many countries around the world. These rights originally took shape in Western Europe, in the early modern period. They did so as the ascending commercial classes associated with the rise of market capitalism successfully challenged the position of centralising states and powerful agrarian elites, and in the process opened up a new political space. The commercial classes did so by consolidating a group of entitlements (that we call 'individual rights and protections'), a set of social institutions (civil society; cf. Keane 1998), and also a public sphere (cf. Habermas 1989), that was autonomous of, and that set real limits to state power.

It was these entitlements, etc. that came to form part of the core of modern democratic citizenship, that helped establish the institutions of political democracy, and that remain central to what democracy means to many people today. These liberal entitlements included, for example, the 'freedoms of' speech, religion, movement (of people, commodities, ideas, messages), etc. They included as well the 'freedoms from' (arbitrary search and seizure, etc.), and protections of person and property. They also established the autonomous (white, bourgeois male) *individual* as the sovereign holder of jural rights. Overall, these entitlements set legal and practical limits on the ability of government officials to interfere with everyday social life.

Part of the origin myth of Euro-American democracy is that it is the most recent manifestation of a millennia-long democratic tradition that originated with the Greeks in ancient Athens. It is interesting to compare democracy in these two settings; as such, a comparison brings out just how distinctive

Euro-American democracy is. Actually, the liberal rights that make up this component of Euro-American democracy have little if anything to do with popular understandings of Athenian democracy. What we are taught about democracy in ancient Athens is that it was based on *citizen control*, on insuring that the citizenry exercised a direct and powerful voice in all community affairs. That is, Athenian democracy sought to guarantee extensive 'input from below' – from the mass of the population, who were to determine the conditions of their own existence. Liberal rights, however, address a quite different problem. They are focused on the state rather than the citizenry, and seek to limit 'input from above'. In other words, liberal rights seek to map out a terrain where state power may *not* be exercised. They are intended as, and developed historically as, brakes on the centralisation of power (Wood 1994). They have little to do with democracy understood as 'rule by the people'.

A second component of the hybrid mix of unrelated practices that has come together to form liberal representative democracy concerns the processes associated with representation. The representative component of liberal representative democracy refers to the highly ritualised process by which individuals (or groups) cede or relinquish direct decision-making power to other individuals, who go on to make key decisions in the political arena. Unlike the liberal component, this one is directly concerned with the problem of democracy – with the ability of the citizenry to exercise a voice in political affairs. As is widely recognised, the representative component of liberal representative democracy significantly disempowers those who are compelled to relinquish their voice. In relation to the problematic of rule by the people, it is worth noting that processes of representation were viewed with outright disdain in ancient Athens, as was voting more generally (cf. Wood 1988).

As many scholars have shown, 'representation' favours the maintenance of inequalities in power and wealth. This is because it is generally members of the privileged classes who succeed in dominating positions of representation. In this regard it is revealing that, historically, elite groups have viewed more direct, participatory forms of democracy with outright horror (cf. Linebaugh and Rediker 2000). Elite groups have been strong advocates of representative democracy, however, as it offers an effective means of maintaining their positions of privilege in the face of democratising demands 'from below'.

Understanding the hybrid nature of liberal representative democracy thus requires that we distinguish between its liberal and its representative components. Doing so provides us with a vantage point from which we may better understand the challenges involved in interpreting people's acceptance or rejection of democracy. For these two components of liberal representative democracy may combine in distinctive ways to confront people with qualitatively different institutional environments. Because all tend to travel under the name of democracy, however, people use the same term to refer to quite different phenomena.

Regardless of the conclusions that people reach about the particular practices that (are said to) represent democracy – whether democracy should be embraced or abandoned, rejected or reformed – two facts seem salient. First, the practices to which the groups in these various circumstances respond are not the same – even though they are treated as if they were. Second, the groups in question do not draw upon a shared vocabulary or set of meanings when they make their assessments of the practices that represent democracy.

Thus far, I have suggested that it is important to disaggregate liberal representative democracy into its two major component parts. There is a third set of institutional arrangements, however, that is crucial to the operation of liberal representative democracy.[1] Most scholars regard these arrangements as interfering with or limiting the ability of the general population to control the conditions of their own lives – and thus as being profoundly anti-democratic. In its most common form, this component combines with the other two components to help create a unique constellation of forces – one that represents a distinctive set of conditions that structure the disjuncture between should and is. This final component of liberal representative democracy is usefully thought of in terms of a 'delineation of spheres'.

Liberal representative democracy is based on the delineation of separate spheres, only some of which are regarded as open to processes of democratic decision making. The most important sphere that is so regarded, of course, is the *political* sphere. The integrity of liberal representative democracy depends crucially on maintaining a clear separation between a formal realm of politics (which involves the operation of the government apparatus, the passing of laws, the holding of elections, voting rights, etc.), and economic, social and cultural spheres.

In liberal representative democracy it is particularly the *economy* that must remain outside the realm of democratic decision making. In many contemporary societies, voting rights are more or less generalised among the population writ large.[2] Were the mass of the citizenry able to use elections to change the organisation of material life or the distribution of wealth in any appreciable way, they would threaten to undermine the entire structure of class, property and exchange upon which capitalism is based.[3] If voting is to be generalised without endangering the economic structure, then the franchise in liberal representative democracies must be organised in such a way that voting affects spheres other than the economy.

The widely noted 'autonomy' of the economic sphere (Polanyi 1944) both reinforces, and is reinforced by, liberal representative democracy's institutionalised separation of the political and the economic. The spread of 'neoliberal' ideologies, practices and policies in recent decades, especially since the debt crisis of 1980, and the establishment of bodies like the World Trade Organisation (in 1995), have reinforced the autonomy of the economy *vis-à-vis* the sphere of formal politics, expanding greatly the range of activities that are subject to a market logic. These same processes have also undermined the wellbeing of groups that had long been sheltered from the vicissitudes of the market. It is ironic that the spread of these non-democratic forces – which are explicitly intended to undermine public decision making – has been accompanied by the widespread embrace and expansion of elections, and electoral processes (cf. Robinson 1996). As this indicates, liberal representative democracy is fully compatible with the most undemocratic of processes imaginable. Furthermore, as noted earlier, it always has been. Indeed, the liberal, representative variant of democratic practice relies crucially on the maintenance of such processes, and was designed with the goal of reproducing them.

In many circles, liberal representative democracy has become synonymous with democracy itself. Because of the role of liberal, representative democracy in perpetuating stratified social orders that violate the principles of popular sovereignty – principles of equality, egalitarianism, participation and inclusion – however, liberal representative democracy has a tendency to generate its own opposition. Furthermore, it tends to do so in the name of the very principles that this form of political practice is said to represent.

The Democracy Effect

For the reasons outlined above, as it is actually practised in any given set of circumstances, democracy tends to be in tension with its own ideals. Focusing on the unresolved tension between the 'should' and the 'is' of democracy, I argue, offers an unusually fruitful vantage point from which to theorise democracy and post-democracy. It does so for several reasons. First, a focus on the tension between should and is highlights the fact that democracy is in a constant state of becoming. Second, it locates the source of that becoming in processes of the most mundane and ordinary kind – processes that anthropologists are accustomed to investigating. This suggests that if we are to understand people's changing relationships to the ideal of democracy we would do well to direct our attention towards what we might think of as the everyday construction of democratic life. By this term I reference a seemingly unremarkable process that occurs countless times and in innumerable iterations, on a continual, ongoing basis, all around the globe. This is the culturally charged, affectively loaded process by which people assess, pass judgement on and evaluate the legitimacy of the conditions in which they live.

The fact that democracy occupies a central place in so many of these endless, ordinary assessments – regardless of whether democracy is viewed as positive or negative, whether it is regarded as something we should accept or reject – is indicative of the enormous power that the concept continues to exercise.[4] Focusing on democracy as (contested) ideal, and dwelling upon the disjunction between ideal and everyday practice, allows us to grasp the instability, mutability and movement that is inherent in practice and in the ideal. It does so by focusing our attention on the fact that democracy is constantly and inevitably being reinvented in the process of its everyday construction. It is useful to think of this process in the following terms: people who are located in a given set of circumstances seize upon the specific disconnect between practice and ideal represented by the constellation of institutional practices with which they are

confronted to produce vernacularised versions of democracy and non-democracy (Nugent 2008) – versions of the ideal reflected in forms of practice that they
can regard as their own. In some instances (see e.g. Long, this volume), people
go so far as to reject democracy completely. In others (cf. Juris 2012), however,
they seek to revise or reform democracy. In still other contexts (Paley 2008),
they cling fiercely to actually existing forms of democracy, or take great risks in
an effort to make democracy a reality. And in still other cases (see below) people
simultaneously reject some forms of democracy even as they embrace others.

There are other reasons why there is much to be gained by focusing on the
problem of democracy as political ideal. As the foregoing suggests, prominent
among them is the fact that there is no such thing as *the* democratic ideal.
Democracy does not have, nor has it ever had, a single set of meanings. Rather,
from its inception democracy has offered people a flexible, ambiguous language of legitimacy and morality that has multiple, and at times contradictory
referents.

The social particulars through which democracy as ideal is manifest in any
given set of circumstances are grounded in context-specific conditions of socio-
political and cultural inclusion and exclusion. As has been widely noted, these
are usually cloaked in a language of universalism. But as a number of authors
have observed (cf. Mehta 1990), the inclusive, generalising claims of democracy
are not to be taken at face value. They are rather best understood as a cipher or
code that is used to distinguish between those who are and are not to be considered worthy of participation in specific kinds of decision-making processes.

In other words, the particular form that democracy takes in any given set of
circumstances is best understood as a claim about who is and is not regarded as
adult, rational, competent, trustworthy, etc. As the highly variable and context-
specific nature of these normalising claims suggests, democracy is not a single
thing. Indeed, the fact that democracy is and has been so many different things,
but that people generally treat it un-problematically as if it were a single thing,
is part of the 'magic' by which democracy is continually reproduced as an ideal.

If we are to understood people's changing relationships to democracy as
an ideal, I suggest, it is useful to conceive of democracy as a language of political legitimacy. In arguing that democracy is productively understood in these
terms, I am not claiming that the people who use democracy as a legitimating
tool necessarily believe in its legitimacy. Nor am I suggesting that those who
respond to these claims, positively or negatively, do so on the basis of belief. I am
interested instead in the circulation of democracy as a quasi-obligatory political
language *regardless* of belief. I am concerned with where democracy circulates
and where it does not, and who employs different understandings of democracy
and towards which ends.

If we are to understand people's changing relationships to the ideal of democracy, I suggest, it is useful to view democracy as an inevitably and forever failing
enterprise that many (but not all) people have been determined to make succeed.
Furthermore, I argue, this is true not only for the present but has always characterised democratic social orders, and stems from the inevitable disjuncture

between the ideal and the practice of democracy. Among the most interesting aspects of this disjuncture are the reference points that people employ to characterise it – points of reference that I refer to by the term 'time and space effects' (Nugent 2001). As this term is intended to signal, whenever people engage in the mundane process of assessing their life circumstances, and do so by drawing upon the principles of democracy, they also *locate* themselves and others with respect to democracy, temporally, spatially and socially. Some constituencies regard democracy as proximate, whether in time, space or social location. Others view democracy as distant. But virtually all engage in the same process of positioning, regardless of where they consider democracy to be located, and regardless of whether or not they view this location in positive or negative terms.

As the foregoing suggests, however, it is not just that people in much of the world tend to establish their temporal, spatial and social position with respect to democracy. In the process, they also make judgements about the adequacy or acceptability of that position. Thus, people do not simply conclude that democracy is distant, but rather *too* distant, not just that it is proximate, but *too* proximate – regardless of where it is regarded as being located. People's assessments are at once assessments, moral judgements and also calls to action, whether on their part or on the part of others, whether they are for or against democracy.

Indeed, implicit in the evaluations that people make of their location with respect to democracy is the need to *change* that location, whether for themselves or for others. Some groups may seek to bring democracy nearer, whether in time, space or social space. Other groups may be determined to keep it at bay. Still others may seek some combination of the two. And still others may attempt to put democracy 'behind them' – to relegate it to their past rather than their present. What so often remains ill-defined, however – and what varies so widely according to context – is the 'it' in the relationships to which people position themselves. And what remains so consistent is the positioning process itself. The fact that so many people continue to locate themselves with respect to democracy suggests that they have a very difficult time imagining themselves or their world outside of a democratic frame of reference – even as they reject it. This appears to be the case even if people regard the age of democracy as coming to an end.

The continuing salience of democracy as a key metaphor by which people assess their everyday lives is indicated by the following: even those who regard democracy as passing away rarely if ever view this development in neutral terms. Rather, the eclipse of democracy may be regarded as a cause of regret, danger or decline, or as a cause of relief, hope or optimism. Symptomatic of the lingering power of democracy-as-(fallen?)-ideal is that its waning is regarded by most people as a *watershed* – whether as one of crisis or opportunity. Indeed, democracy remains a kind of moral compass by which people in much of the globe take their bearings, chart their way, assess their position and evaluate that of others. The principles of democracy act at once as lines of longitude and latitude, temporal markers and cultural signposts, in a social imaginary in which democracy is the key term of reference. What might lie beyond the limits of the democratic imaginary? Although a variety of options are being posed, there is as yet no clear answer. Some people appear to approach this question with real trepidation, and others with great optimism. Few, however, remain indifferent to the question itself.

As suggested by the role of democracy in framing complex moral and political imaginaries, the process of locating oneself with respect to things democratic involves more than spatial, temporal and social positioning. It involves more than moral judgement and call for change. Such observations about the positioning process, while accurate, beg the question of why people feel so consistently compelled to use democracy in making sense of their everyday lives. I suggest that democracy is so extensively employed in contemporary debates about legitimacy all around the globe – both positive and negative – because people's relationship to democracy is above all else *affective*.[5] Indeed, as suggested by even a cursory examination of global political affairs, debates about whether this or that set of political circumstances is democratic, should be democratic, could never be democratic, must never be democratic, etc., are associated with the most powerful affective responses imaginable. Such judgements are not uncommonly used to embrace or demonise, to welcome or to turn away, to mark the limits of the human community.

The foregoing suggests that a distinctive set of processes comes together in the everyday construction of democracy. I refer to these by the term 'democracy effect'. Several components of the process by which democracy effects are produced are relevant to the present discussion. First, as already noted, people tend to position themselves socially, temporally and spatially with respect to the ideal of democracy, as mediated by their everyday experience of political life. Complicating their efforts to do so is the fact that this ideal remains largely ill-defined, even though most people are wholly convinced that they know precisely what democracy is. Second, people conclude that the practice of this (unattainable) ideal is partial, out of reach, out of place or inappropriate.

Third, because democracy as practice (and as practised where particular constituencies are located) tends to be incomplete, partial, inappropriate or out of place, people are driven to imagine forms of political practice – democratic and non-democratic – that would be more complete, or more fitting with respect to their own circumstances. Furthermore, they imagine these new, improved or alternative forms of political life, democratic and non-democratic, as practised in temporal, spatial and social contexts other than the ones in which they themselves are located. In other words, people tend to assume that democracy and its others are, should be or will be practised *elsewhere*.

Fourth, people's assertions about what democracy is, where it is, where it isn't and where it should be are best understood as masks of political practice (cf. Abrams 1988). These assertions conceal in the very process of pretending to reveal. This is because democracy is above all else a legitimating claim, one that inevitably misconstrues particular interests as general interests.

Fifth, the vernacularised constructions of democracy and non-democracy that emerge in particular times and places are both creative and integrative. People tend to combine unrelated rights, rituals and practices into a single, seamless whole that they regard as Democracy (with a capital D). Rarely are they able to recognise the different components of their vernacularised form of political practice as separate, or to regard their specific hybrid as the odd and arbitrary construction that it is. This is especially true of the form of political practice associated with the 'advanced democracies'.

There is a final component of the process that produces democracy effects to which I would like to draw attention. This concerns what it is that binds the various components together into a single effect. I will argue that the force that binds is affect. Indeed, as I have argued implicitly throughout the chapter, and as I show in the section to follow, the entire process of generating the temporal, spatial and social imaginaries associated with democracy is grounded in and saturated by affective considerations.

APRA's Priests of Democracy

In the following sections of the chapter I draw upon ethnographic materials from the Chachapoyas region of northern Peru during the middle decades of the twentieth century to bring out these points about the democracy effect.[6] I am interested in particular in how the disjuncture between ideal and practice generated contradictory imaginaries regarding democracy, each of which was informed by its own time and space effects, its own affective registers.

As I will show, because different constituencies understood and engaged democracy in contradictory ways, Chachapoyas was simultaneously pre-democratic, partially democratic and post-democratic – a situation that has much in common with the contemporary moment in many parts of the world. In Peru, a system of liberal representative democracy, which had been in place for approximately a century, reflected the interests of established, elite social groups. Noteworthy about the practice of liberal democracy was the continual, ongoing violation of its most basic principles by the liberal order's main proponents – a set of circumstances that amounted to a continual state of exception. Even so, those who had a powerful interest in representative democracy defended it fiercely, even as they violated its tenets on an ongoing basis. They also declared much of the subaltern population unfit for participation in democratic life.

The democratic imaginary of those who were ensconced in the liberal order represented Peru as a mix of pre- and partially democratic – as on the road to being a full democracy. For them, their country was 'appropriately democratic' – in the sense that those who were regarded as being capable of democratic participation (i.e., those granted the right to vote) were allowed to participate. They argued that the great mass of the population, however, was not yet ready for democracy – that they were pre-democratic. As a result, it was necessary to hold full democracy at bay, until such time that the masses were able to partici-pate responsibly in democratic political life. Those who temporarily (?) had to be held at bay included all women, all indigenous people, all those who could not read or write, and all those who had not amassed a given amount of property

(Nugent 1997). In short, as has been true of the advanced democracies through-out much of their histories, in Peru's classed, racialised and gendered form of liberal representative democracy, those who were considered not yet (?) ready for democracy included almost everyone.[7]

There was, however, a second democratic imaginary competing with the first for public space and recognition. This alternative understanding was advanced by a political party called APRA, which sought to bring together many of the very social groups that were excluded from the country's liberal, representative arrangements. According to this alternative understanding, Peru was both pre- and post-democratic. By the 1930s, APRA argued, the country had arrived at a historic watershed with respect to democracy. The system of liberal representative democracy, which had been in place for a century, had shown itself to be incapa-ble of addressing the concerns of the country's majority. Liberal democracy did little more than protect the position of wealth and privilege enjoyed by a tiny elite, who had abused their position of public trust. It also denied the great mass of the population the opportunity to participate in political life, to benefit from the rights and protections guaranteed to all Peruvians, or to partake of even the most basic necessities of life. In this sense, the party claimed, Peru was post-democratic.

APRA also argued, however, that Peru was pre-democratic. Responding to the failures of the liberal order, the party envisioned a form of alternative democracy that had yet to be established – one that had little in common with the liberal system of government in place at the time. The party organised many of its activities to make this form of democracy a reality. Symptomatic of the pre-democratic conditions that prevailed at the time, the party claimed, was the fact that APRA was forced to do so from a position of illegality. For both the party and its vision of a transformed Peru were regarded with great hostility and suspicion by governing groups. Indeed, APRA was a proscribed political party, which was forced to conduct most of its activities underground.

In the pages that follow I draw upon these contrasting visions of democracy to explore the temporal, spatial and affective imaginaries associated with this contested term. My analysis emphasises: (1) the multiple meanings associated with democracy, each of which is represented as the authoritative meaning; (2) the process by which people *locate* themselves, in terms of time, space and affect, with respect to democracy; (3) the fact that people's reflections on democracy, and their efforts to locate themselves with respect to it are often accompanied by efforts to *change* that location; and (4) the fact that scepticism about the actu-alisation of democracy, and efforts to reform and revise it, are inseparable from the idea of democracy. In other words, I am concerned with the generation of a particular kind of democracy effect.

Structural Transformation and Alternative Democracy

The Apristas of Chachapoyas were categorical in their rejection of what advo-cates of liberal representative democracy regard as the core of a legitimate political order – voting and elections. A century of experience had taught them that electoral democracy did little more than reproduce the privileged position of the landed elite, and the highly stratified and exclusionary social and racial order that they oversaw. Democracy, the party argued, could not be established by means of the institutions of representation but rather on the basis of generalised participation. True democracy was contingent upon the involvement of all the people in performing the work upon which social reproduction depended. It depended equally on all the people contributing to the group decision-making processes that allow collectivities to determine their own fates.

But the authentic democracy that the Apristas were so determined to establish depended on more than just the participation of all the people. It also depended on the *equal* participation of all the people. As long as there were privileged groups of people who held inordinate amounts of wealth and exercised disproportionate amounts of power, the contribution of all the people to the process of social reproduction could not be equal. This in turn meant that it was impossible for a truly democratic social order to come into being.

Euro-American democracy was based on an origin myth that harkened back to ancient Athens. The Apristas, however, rejected Athens as the birthplace of *their* democracy. Instead, they looked back to Peru's pre-Columbian past (specifically, the Inca Empire) as inspiration for an indigenised form of democracy that could help redeem the country's future:[8]

> The Inca Empire was based on *equality*. A single call from a *cacique* [a local elite] would bring out all the people to work together to build terraces, redirect rivers, harvest the fields. This was the period of *democracia salvaje* [savage democracy] ... We were united at this time, and we were equal, so we were democratic, but we relied on systems of violence. Brutal punishments were used then, especially for the lazy person, the one who thought he was better than others, who refused to work like the rest. The caciques would grab people like this and march them to the top of a fortress, lie them down on the wall of the fortress and – Pa! – smash their heads in with a large rock. This was how they carried out justice. This was how they protected their democracy.

APRA believed that the realisation of democracy depended on establishing radical forms of equality and inclusion – social patterns they attributed to the Inca. In order to establish material equality among the general population, the Party of the People (as APRA called itself) advocated the nationalisation of land, industry and other kinds of economic activity. APRA also called for the creation of self-governing workers' cooperatives in these nationalised economic domains, to ensure broad political participation on the part of the general population.

The party also intended to combine this cooperative-specific structure of participatory democracy with elements of representation, but in a way that addressed the shortcomings of liberal, representative democracy. APRA planned to make its democracy as participatory as possible at regional and national scales by establishing a nested hierarchy of cooperative, decision-making bodies.

Regional federations would be made up of the representatives of individual cooperatives, who would serve two- to three-year terms before stepping down to allow another cooperative member to take their place. All cooperative members would rotate in and out of this leadership position, thus ensuring broad participation in the decision-making process.

APRA also built in other safeguards to prevent cooperative representatives from distancing themselves from their constituencies. The representatives of the various cooperatives that were to meet in regional federations would not have independent decision-making power. All they would be authorised to do would be to carry messages that conveyed the will of their cooperative to the federation assembly. They could not make decisions on their own. Furthermore, they were to be in regular contact with their cooperative in order to settle questions that came up in the federation assembly. Any cooperative representative who failed to do so would be replaced.

Following this same structure of rotation and accountability, representatives of regional federations were to gather in a National Economic Congress. This was to be the major decision-making body for the country as a whole. It was to establish national policy, even as it did so in a way that was sensitive to regional and local concerns. The National Economic Congress was to replace the existing Senate and the House of Deputies, while cooperative representatives were to replace the elected positions of Senator and Congressional Deputy. These latter institutions and positions were regarded as being at the very centre of Peru's false democracy, as doing little more than helping to reproduce the country's exclusionary and discriminatory socio-political structure.[9]

Individual Transformation and Alternative Democracy

These structural changes, however, while necessary, were also seen as insufficient. They were viewed as long-term, rather abstract goals, which could only be established after more fundamental reforms had been undertaken. If structural change was to be successful, the Apristas believed, it would have to be preceded by individual change. It would first be necessary to ensure that the people who were to be a part of APRA's new, egalitarian structures were prepared for life in the democratic society the party sought to form. While it was important to alter the organisation of Peruvian society, more important still was to alter what the Party of the People thought of as the psychology and mentality of the Peruvian people. In other words, APRA sought to cultivate a new kind of democratic subjectivity in its followers. The party sought to do so through highly disciplined work on the minds, bodies and emotions of young Apristas. Efforts to harness and discipline affect were central to this process. As the party sought to prepare its followers for participation in the democratic society of the future, it looked to them to exemplify in the present the kinds of democratised attitudes and behaviours that APRA believed would be the basis of the transformed society the party was so determined to establish.

As was true of the oligarchic powers that dominated Peru's liberal order, the
Party of the People believed that the people were not yet ready for democracy.
Unlike the oligarchy, however, the Apristas did not believe that people's lack of
preparedness was a function of their race or their gender, their illiteracy or their
poverty. In other words, it was not only subaltern groups who were unprepared
for democratic life. According to APRA, virtually everyone had to be readied for
democracy. Among the most damaging legacies of the region's highly stratified,
aristocratic form of rule was that the entire population had been deeply affected
by a cultural politics of *difference*. The region's traditional form of rule did more
than force people to accept lives of humiliation and abuse. So scarred had the
populace been by the physical and symbolic violence of elite domination that
the invidious distinctions of the traditional, aristocratic order had lodged themselves deep in people's emotions and psyches – distorting their entire system of
values and their life aspirations.

APRA saw it as the party's special task to seek out and destroy any and
all manifestations of difference, no matter where they were found. The party
approached this problem with nothing short of missionary zeal, treating virtually any expression of distinction as a form of depravity or moral outrage that
simply *had* to be effaced from the earth. Indeed, in order to effect conditions
of equality, APRA sought to monitor and regulate a wide range of behaviours,
attitudes and emotions. To take but one example:[10]

> A person should always behave in a respectful, polite manner with respect to others,
> and not spit, in a scandalous manner. If you want to spit, you first exercise yourself,
> and go outside and spit. Can I be called a caballero if I spit right in front of you, at your
> very feet? I would not be a caballero. Rather, you are the real caballero, and I am a mere
> cholo. Why? Because I spit at your feet. This is the democracy of individual behaviour.

It is not difficult to understand why the party took such an extreme position
with respect to assertions of difference. APRA saw itself as locked in a battle of
world historical proportions with the most repressive and backward of social
elements imaginable. Nothing less than justice and democracy for the masses
hung in the balance. Difference threatened to undermine the unity upon which
the success of APRA's war with the old order depended. It therefore could not
be tolerated in any form.

New Disciplines of the Mind and Body

Considering what was at stake, APRA believed that its assault on difference
could not be undertaken by just anyone. Rather, it could be entrusted only to
the most worthy of individuals. Only people who had demonstrated beyond any
doubt that they were prepared to make the enormous material and emotional
sacrifices required of them could be trusted to lead APRA's assault on difference.
Only those who had been specially trained could be allowed to wage the party's
war on difference for the promotion of democracy.

In an effort to prove themselves worthy of being included in this noble effort, in the early 1930s a vanguard of young Apristas subjected themselves to years of secret training at the hands of more experienced party organisers – training that was intended to make them into new kinds of subjects. During their training these 'novices' learned essential new disciplines of the mind, body and emotion that were intended to free them of the cultural weight of aristocratic rule. Being educated in this manner was intended to ensure that the apprentice Apristas no longer felt any fear of the elite, were no longer in awe of aristocratic pretensions, and no longer coveted the wealth or power of the region's dominant families. Indeed, one of the central goals of APRA's indoctrination process was to produce highly disciplined subjects who would be wholly committed to the principles of democracy, equality and freedom for which the party stood.

The training of this elite vanguard of Apristas was both broad and rigorous. To learn new disciplines of the mind, party organisers had the novices read, discuss and critique major works of political and economic theory that had bearing on the problems of Latin America. Party organisers were careful to place special emphasis on the ability to explain the strengths and weaknesses of different doctrines to simple, untutored folk, who would be the audience for the novices once they had finished their training.[11] Leaders also constantly tested and assessed the abilities of their novices to communicate effectively to such people.

To assist their novices in developing new disciplines of the body, organisers taught the novices to avoid the excesses considered typical of youth – sex and alcohol in particular. They encouraged good hygiene, regular sleeping habits and moderation in alcohol consumption. They taught the young Apristas to do callisthenics daily, upon waking, helped them organise soccer and volleyball teams, and insisted that they practice and compete on a regular basis. Party organisers also carefully monitored the conduct of their charges in these areas, and had them monitor one another's conduct as well. APRA leaders even went so far as to establish an underground court system, and brought to trial novices who failed to remain true to the party's disciplinary demands.

APRA organisers sought to make their novices as 'cultured' as possible. Becoming a cultured individual, party leaders believed, had two components. One of these was based on education, the other on action. Regarding the relation between education and culture, aspiring party leaders had to acquire the knowledge and master the skills needed to defend themselves and also to promote social justice. Towards that end, they had to learn the 'arts of defence' (Nugent n.d.). That is, they had to master self-defence techniques, and become proficient in the use of firearms and explosives. The novice Apristas also had to master the 'arts of deception' (ibid.). They had to internalise disciplines of the mind, body and emotion that would allow them to evade the police, and to mask party activities so that they would be unrecognisable as such to the authorities. Aspiring party leaders also had to learn the 'arts of communication' (ibid.). They had to have a thorough grasp of the works of Marx, Proudhon, Gonzalez Prada and Gandhi (among others), and be able to explain them succinctly and spontaneously to a variety of audiences.

But education was only one aspect of becoming a cultured individual. Of equal importance was the ability to act on the basis of lessons learned. If they were to lead the party's assault on difference, and in the process advance the democratisation process, the future APRA leaders had to discipline and develop their emotions. They had to cultivate the courage and integrity necessary to face the dangers involved in challenging injustice. To help them do so, party organisers involved their apprentices in 'missions' that required them to perform important tasks for the party – from delivering secret messages to Apristas in other towns to spreading party propaganda in the dead of night, from gathering intelligence from the police and other government functionaries to organising new party cells. The missions were graded by level of difficulty and danger, and organisers were careful to expose their fledgling party leaders to progressively more risk. In this way leaders were able to gauge the degree to which the novices were able to master their fears, and to develop the courage necessary to assume positions of party leadership.

As the Aprista vanguard deepened their training, and confronted situations of increasing danger and risk, party organisers carefully evaluated their novices' progress, paying special attention to each person's strengths and weaknesses. They did so to see who would be best suited to lead each of the ministries, or secretariats of which the party was composed (in the mid-1930s, for example, there were eight separate ministries, including defence, culture, organisation, propaganda, etc.). After training these apprentices in new disciplines of mind, body and emotion for half a decade, and observing their behaviour in increasingly trying circumstances, party leaders decided that their novices had matured to the point that they could assume direct control over the party apparatus. It was at this point – when the process of enculturation was complete – that these individuals began to refer to themselves as *sacerdotes de la democracia* [priests of democracy]. Referring to one another as priests was a sign of deep respect that only the most committed Apristas used with one another.[12]

It is these priests of democracy – who had done the most to develop a new form of democratic subjectivity – who were entrusted with the difficult task of preparing the masses for broader democratic transformation. In the long years of persecution that the Apristas were forced to endure it was these *sacerdotes* who held the party together – who continued to organise in secret, to recruit new members, to develop Aprista activities and to disrupt government efforts to extort peasant labour. It was these priests of democracy who regarded Peru as having arrived at a post-democratic moment with respect to the false, liberal democratic structure that was in place at the time. This post-democratic state, however, was simultaneously seen as a pre-democratic state with regard to an authentic, participatory form of democracy. It was these same priests who sought to move Peru from its pre-democratic state toward a truly democratic future.

In sum, APRA believed that among the biggest obstacles to establishing democracy in Peru were the systems of voting and liberal representation. This set of arrangements, the party asserted, played a crucial role in perpetuating a social order based on exclusion, inequality and discrimination, all of which had to be eliminated if a true democracy was to be established in Peru. To bring about such a democratic order, it would be necessary to establish material equality among the general population – by means of a radical redistribution of the means of production. It would be equally important to ensure that all were able to participate in the egalitarian, group-based decision-making processes upon which real democracy depended – by establishing a nested hierarchy of cooperative associations, in which cooperative representatives remained accountable to their constituencies in a direct and continual manner.

But much more would be required if the Party of the People was to move Peru towards a democratic state. In the peculiar form of the democracy effect that emerged at the time, APRA believed that individuals of all backgrounds – rich and poor alike – would have to be purged of the distorted values and aspirations of the region's corrupt, hierarchical and exclusionary (but liberal democratic!) social order. What was called for therefore was nothing less than a cultural revolution. Such a revolution, APRA argued, would inculcate in people new needs and desires. It would instil in them new patterns of individual and group behaviour, new affective repertoires and new standards for evaluating the behaviour of self and other. Only in the aftermath of such a revolution in subjectivity and affect would the population be ready to participate in a truly democratic society.

Conclusion

In this chapter I have suggested that democracy is best understood as a contested field of legitimating claims rather than a set of institutions, conditions or social accomplishments. Several bits of evidence point in this direction. First, democracy is associated with a very wide range of institutions and social conditions, which are not consistent from one context to the next. Indeed, the very same conditions that are regarded as the epitome of democracy in one set of circumstances are not uncommonly seen as profoundly undemocratic, whether in that same context or in others. Because of the variation of things considered democratic, it is unclear what the referent of this term is.

Second, I have argued that because democracy is at once an unrealisable ideal and a powerful principle of political legitimacy, there is a tendency to view concrete manifestations of democracy as missing something. This is all the more so the case because of the way that democracy seeks to legitimate itself. Democracy relies on principles of inclusion and egalitarianism for its legitimating power. In its liberal representative form, however, not only has democracy been highly exclusionary. It has also been essential to the reproduction of inequality.

Third, I have sought to draw attention to what I have referred to as the 'democracy effect'. By this term, I signal the cultural processes by which democracy is constructed in the course of people's ongoing evaluations of their everyday lives. My analysis has focused in particular on the terms that people employ to characterise the disjuncture between the ideal of democracy and its expression, as this is manifested in particular times and places. As I have suggested, people tend to locate themselves with respect to democracy, in time and space. They tend to place democracy as distant or proximate, and in the process pass judgement on the adequacy or acceptability of their own position, as well as that of other social groups. They may regard democracy as too close, or too distant, in time, space or social space. They may even view democracy as something they are now past, something they have, or should put behind them. What is revealing, however, is that, upon examination, the 'it' in relation to which people locate themselves turns out to be many different things rather than a single thing.

Finally, I have drawn attention to the affective dimension of the process by which democratic and post-democratic political imaginaries are constructed. Passions run deep, I have suggested, as people position themselves and others with respect to democracy and post-democracy, regardless of whether people regard these in positive or negative terms. Indeed, affect may be thought of as the 'binding agent' that holds together these political imaginaries – as the glue that cements together particular constructions of democracy and post-democracy.

Notes

1   As is true of the other components of democracy, this final one comes in a variety of shapes and sizes.
2   It is worth emphasising that the extension of voting rights to the bulk of the population is a very recent phenomenon, even in the 'advanced' democracies.
3   This is not to say that the vote cannot be used to affect any aspect of economic life, but rather that the distribution of property is not available for consideration by means of voting.
4   It is of course true that democracy is not everywhere invoked in ordinary, mundane assessments of legitimacy.
5   The notion of affect is a highly contested one (see, for example, the important but contrasting formulations of Massumi [1995] and Sedgwick and Frank [1995]). I use the term affect to refer 'to those forces—visceral forces beneath, alongside, or generally other than conscious knowing ... that serve [variously] to drive us toward [or away from] movement ... thought and extension' (Gregg and Seigworth 2010: 1). I am particularly interested in the contingent and context specific nature of affective structures. In this regard, I have found Raymond Williams's work on 'Structures of Feeling' (Williams 1977) to be especially useful.
6   The following section of the chapter is based on written materials published by APRA during the period under consideration, primary documents from this period, and interviews with elderly informants who were participants in the democratisation processes. While these sources do not agree on all points, they do on a great many. There is a broad similarity in how they represent APRA's views of democracy.
7   Similar points could be made about the vast majority of countries that have embraced liberal representative democracy – including the 'advanced democracies'. Most of these countries have for most of their histories considered the bulk of the population unsuited for participation in political life. For example, at the time it was written, the Constitution of the United States regarded most (85%) of the population as not ready

even for liberal representative democracy, and limited the vote to white male property owners aged twenty-one and over (less than fifteen per cent of the population). It took 130 years for a full half of the (white) population to gain this right, when the franchise was extended to women in 1920. But it wasn't until the 1960s that African-Americans (who made up eleven per cent of the population) effectively gained the right to vote.

8   Interview with Nicolás Muñoz Valenzuela, 19 August 1985.
9   The Apristas of Chachapoyas took a variety of stances with respect to the question of a president who would be elected by popular vote. In the short term, the Party of the People recognised the need for elections, and despite APRA's illegality, had by far the best machinery for turning out voters.
10 Interview with Máximo Rodriguez Culqui, 5 September 1985.
11 In their secret night-time meetings, and in preparation for their trips to the countryside to organise among the peasantry, novice Apristas received extensive training in public speaking. They were taught to view themselves as an audience of peasant viewers/listeners would view them. In addition to learning to convey complex political ideas in simple language, aspiring party leaders were instructed in how to use their bodies and their presence as tools of communication. Indeed, they were shown how to use each part of their bodies as effectively as possible: how and when to modulate their voices, when to use their hands and arms, when to sit and when to stand, when to pace, even how to hold their heads.
12 The Apristas of Chachapoyas articulated a broader discourse about the role of religious belief and practice in establishing social justice. They did so by invoking egalitarian principles found in the Bible, and using them to attack the Catholic Church. They taught that Jesus was the first communist, that he had based his life on sharing, on helping his neighbours, and on ignoring differences in wealth, status and power that sought to elevate some people above others (see Nugent n.d.).

References

Abrams, P. 1988. Notes on the Difficulty of Studying the State. *Journal of Historical Sociology* 1, no. 1: 58–89.
Alvarez, S., E. Dagnino and A. Escobar (eds). 1998. *Culture of Politics, Politics of Culture: Re-Visioning Latin American Social Movements*. Boulder: Westview.
Chakrabarty, D. 2000. *Provincializing Europe: Post-Colonial Thought and Historical Difference*. Princeton: Princeton University Press.
Diamond, L. 2008. *The Spirit of Democracy: The Struggle to Build Free Societies Throughout the World*. New York: Times Books.
Fraser, N. 2014. Democracy's Crisis. <http://www.publicseminar.org/2014/11/democracys-crisis/#.VZbVkkhPxy9> (accessed 21 July 2015).
Gregg, M. and G. Seigworth. 2010. An Inventory of Shimmers. In *The Affect Theory Reader* (eds) M. Gregg and G. Seigworth, 1–25. Durham: Duke University Press.
Habermas, J. 1989. *The Structural Transformation of the Public Sphere: An Inquiry Into a Category of Bourgeois Society*. Cambridge, MA: MIT Press.
Hardt, M. and A. Negri. 2012. *Declaration*. Jackson: Argo-Navis.
Juris, J. 2012. Reflections on #Occupy Everywhere: Social Media, Public Space, and Emerging Logics of Aggregation. *American Ethnologist* 39, no. 2: 259–279.
Keane, J. 1998. *Civil Society: Old Images, New Visions*. Stanford: Stanford University Press.

Kupchan, C. 2012. The Democratic Malaise: Globalization and the Threat to the West. *Foreign Affairs* 91, no. 1: 62–67.

Linebaugh, P. and M. Rediker. 2000. *The Many-Headed Hydra: Sailors, Slaves, Commoners, and the Hidden History of the Revolutionary Atlantic*. Boston: Beacon.

Massumi, B. 1995. The Autonomy of Affect. *Cultural Critique* 31: 83–109.

Mehta, U. 1990. Liberal Strategies of Exclusion. *Politics and Society* 18, no. 4: 427–454.

Nugent, D. 1997. *Modernity at the Edge of Empire: State, Individual and Nation in the Northern Peruvian Andes*. Palo Alto: Stanford University Press.

———. 2001. Before History and Prior to Politics: Time, Space and Territory in the Modern Peruvian Nation-State. In *States of Imagination: Ethnographic Explorations of the Post-Colonial State* (eds) T. Blom Hansen and F. Stepputat, 257–283. Durham: Duke University Press.

———. 2008. Democracy Otherwise: Struggles Over Popular Rule in the Northern Peruvian Andes. In *Democracy: Anthropological Approaches* (ed.) J. Paley, 21–62. Santa Fe: SAR Press.

———. n.d. *The Encrypted State: Fear, Fantasy and Displacement in the Peruvian Andes*. MS, files of the author. Unpublished.

Paley, J. 2008. Introduction. In *Democracy: Anthropological Approaches* (ed) J. Paley, 3–20. Santa Fe: SAR Press.

Polanyi, K. 1944. *The Great Transformation*. Boston: Beacon.

Robinson, W. 1996. *Promoting Polyarchy: Globalization, US Intervention, and Hegemony*. Cambridge: Cambridge University Press.

Roseberry, W. 1994. Hegemony and the Language of Contention. In *Everyday Forms of State Formation: Revolution and the Negotiation of Rule in Modern Mexico* (eds) G. Joseph and D. Nugent, 355–366. Durham: Duke University Press.

Sedgwick, E.K. and A. Frank. 1995. Shame in the Cybernetic Fold: Reading Silvan Tomkins. In *Shame and its Sisters: A Silvan Tomkins Reader* (eds) E.K. Sedgwick and A. Frank, 1–28. Durham: Duke University Press.

Williams, R. 1977. *Marxism and Literature*. Oxford: Oxford University Press.

Wolford, W. 2010. *This Land Is Ours Now: Social Mobilization and the Meanings of Land in Brazil*. Durham: Duke University Press.

Wood, E. 1988. *Peasant-Citizen and Slave: The Foundations of Athenian Democracy*. London and New York: Verso.

———. 1994. Democracy: An Idea of Ambiguous Ancestry. In *Athenian Political Thought and the Reconstruction of American Democracy* (eds) J. Euben, J. Wallach and J. Ober, 59–80. Ithaca: Cornell University Press.

David Nugent is Professor of anthropology at Emory University.

2

Democracy and the Ethical Imagination

Henrietta L. Moore

The benefits of democracy are often held to be self-evident through their opposition to despotism and tyranny. Historically for the United States and Europe, the opposition that defined the 'democratic' was first monarchic despotism and later ideological tyranny. In contrast, representative democracy is good government precisely because it involves the open airing of different opinions, both between citizens themselves, and between representatives and those who elect them. Democracy is what frees citizens from the fear of leaders, and in principle should act as a mechanism for levelling competition for power, while providing a space for dissenting political minorities. However, democratic ideals are under sustained pressure because the contexts in which democracies operate are changing. New forms of identity politics and multicultural states with diverse citizens raise questions about how diverse interests should and could be represented, and what exactly representation might mean. What constitutes public deliberation and how should processes of public deliberation lead into decision making and policy implementation? Many citizens of the world live in democracies, but how many of them really believe that anything they as citizens think or want makes much of a difference?

Ideas about representation and deliberation invoke framing devices – both cognitive and affective – based on living metaphors of great emotive resonance and historical depth. Consequently, cultural models underlie the character, nature and experience of representation and deliberation, and act in many contexts as powerful conduits for new and emerging political narratives which can be genuinely innovative while powerfully engaged with the past. These narratives, like the models themselves, are culturally and historically specific, but in modern democratic nations they frequently work over the common themes of belonging, voice and authority/legitimacy. Much of the displeasure and dissent towards democracy around the world focuses on the intersections between these three nodal points, animating certain expanding and contracting figures or terrains of reference that both shape material structures as well as forms of political subjectivity. Some of the narratives that shape these figures or terrains are explicitly discursive and well worked out, while others are gestural or epi-grammatic, drawing on forms of experience, orientation and disposition with differing scales and temporalities (Stewart 2007).

Political narratives of all kinds inevitably involve stories about sharing and thus entail accounts of oneself in relation to others. In this sense, they are dense sites for the ethical imagination (Moore 2011). The ethical imagination may be minimally defined as the forms and means through which individuals imagine their relations to themselves and to others. Consequently, it can be envisioned as both the mechanism and the process through which individuals produce dif-ferent kinds of knowledge and specific ways of connecting to the world, to them-selves and to others. New relations and forms of knowledge produce in their turn new forms of desire, hope and satisfaction, as well as new forms of failure, pain and trauma. The ethical imagination – understood as ways of experienc-ing, feeling, thinking and living the relation to self and of self to others – works to animate the fantasies, practices, ideologies and institutions that organise people's worlds. However, the ethical imagination should not be taken as a fixed mechanism, process or structure, but rather as a form of engagement, a lived relation, that may be very explicitly worked out or labile, inchoate, partial and temporal. It inheres both in affect and in cognition, in performative agency and in institutions. While it is engaged with normative practices and distribu-tions of power and resources, it is also open to possibilities, to new encounters, to new ways of thinking and feeling, simultaneously reliving old histories and producing new fantasies. It is the fundament of subjective, social and political transformation.

The political is a particularly dense site for the ethical imagination, where questions of how we deal with each other are part of a larger problematic about how we understand what it means and entails to share the world with others, both those close to us and those very far away, our intimates and those we will never know. This makes the ethical imagination one of the primary sites of cultural invention precisely because it deals with the self in its relations with others, both proximate and distant, and with the historical potentialities for social transformation that are thrown up in our many and varied encounters. In such contexts of encounter, the ethical imagination is brought into play by the advent of new information and new ideas, new ways of being and acting, new forms of representation and their mediation. However, it does not always involve conscious thought and is not always based on a privileging of language and ostensible meaning. While we must always have regard for the kind of inter-pretive talk the ethical imagination makes possible – new languages of descrip-tion, new frameworks, etc – we need to attend equally to the importance of affect, performance and the materiality of the body. Attachment, identification and fantasy are vectors of the ethical imagination and often proceed through forms of unknowing and types of incomprehensibility.

By focusing on specific connections and forms of relation as they are lived, imagined, maintained and transformed, we can make some progress in understanding how people are actively working towards and experiencing the potentialities offered by changing political circumstances and social transforma-tions. If the ethical imagination is understood as the forms and means through which individuals imagine their relations to self and to others, we can immedi-ately grasp that such processes underpin much of what we mean by the political. There is currently an ongoing and well recognised crisis in democracy and in the character of the political – not just in how we share this world with others, and in how we imagine ourselves in relation to others, but in the very character of political agency, in how we recognise ourselves as political agents and what we believe political agency is about.

In the next sections I discuss examples drawn from my research in Kenya and – more briefly – France to elaborate these points. The comparison is instructive because it suggests that certain contradictions in the construction of political subjectivities and the terrain of the political are common both to established and more recent democratic systems. While electoral politics and post-election violence in Kenya might appear distant from disputes over gay marriage in France, unravelling such events through the lens of the ethical imagination reveals how social imaginaries about belonging, voice and citizenship draw on deep historical experience as well as the potentiality of new forms of encounter as people make and remake themselves in relation to one another. The deep anxieties expressed in both France and Kenya about political representation and inclusion draw on distinctions of ethnicity, religion, gender and culture that are simultaneously taken as self-evident and yet the boundaries of which are constantly shifting – sometimes explicitly outlined but more often proceeding through forms of fantasy, attachment and unknowing.

Democracy in Kenya

In Kenya, citizenship is based on ideas about community and belonging, where to belong is to have rights relating to the provision of care, historically indexed through the holding of land, its cultivation, and the consumption of food pro-duced thereon (Lonsdale 2008). This more nuanced understanding of citizen-ship rather than simplistic references to tribalism and ethnic ties is crucial for understanding the history of democracy and associated violence in Kenya (Lonsdale 2014). Between late 2007 and early 2008, following a contested result in the December election in which the incumbent President Mwai Kibaki was declared the winner, widespread violence broke out in a country generally con-sidered the most vibrant democracy in the region. Clashes between supporters of rival candidates hardened into ethno-regional conflict that left over 1,300 people dead and an estimated 350,000 people displaced. The majority of these deaths and displacements took place in the Rift Valley, a cosmopolitan region to the north and west of the capital Nairobi, and which has a long history of tensions over land, displacement and resettlement going back to the colonial 'White Highland' farmers (Berman and Lonsdale 1992). Nakuru and Naivasha, two of the main towns in the Rift Valley and centres of large-scale agriculture with high migrant labourer populations, saw the worst of the street fighting (Anderson and Lochery 2008). Eldoret town further to the north of the region was the site of the horrifying burning of the Kiambaa Pentecostal Church in which at least thirty people were killed, many of them Kikuyu women and children (Human Rights Watch 2008: 43).

In February 2008, with many international observers suggesting Kenya was on the brink of civil war, the presidential rivals eventually signed a peace agreement brokered by the former UN Secretary General Kofi Anan. In a power-sharing deal, Mwai Kibaki (Kikuyu) kept the presidency and his longstanding rival Raila Odinga (Luo) was appointed to the new office of prime minister in a grand coalition government. The Commission of Inquiry into Post-Election Violence (known as the Waki Commission) urged Kenya to create a hybrid national/international special tribunal to investigate criminal accountability and prosecute those most responsible. Its prescient chair announced that if the government did not do this then a sealed envelope containing information implicating senior figures in the orchestration of the post-election violence would be passed to the International Criminal Court (ICC). The government agreed to set up the tribunal, but the relevant bill failed on three separate occasions to pass in parliament. As a result, the information was forwarded to the Office of the Prosecutor (OTP), then Luis Ocampo, and in December 2010 the names of six senior individuals were announced. Of the 'Ocampo Six', Case 1 featured three figures associated with Kibaki's Party of National Unity (PNU) and Case 2 included three figures linked to Raila Odinga's Orange Democratic Movement (ODM).[1] The most senior of these were Uhuru Kenyatta and William Ruto, the running mates of Kibaki and Raila respectively. Their cases at the ICC were to be significant in the strategy and performance of their later coalition, which saw them subsequently elected president and deputy president of Kenya in 2013 (Lynch 2014a).

Michael Mann (2005) has argued persuasively that the murderous ethnic cleansing we have seen in various parts of the world is the product of the modern era of democracy, and more specifically that it is the result of an aspiration for 'rule by the people' which converts *demos* into *ethnos*. This is rather a simplification for Kenya – see below – but it is true that since the first multiparty elections in 1992, all democratic elections with the exception of 2002 and 2013 have been accompanied by serious violence in the Rift Valley. This is in large part because of the significance of the Kalenjin[2] vote in deciding elections in Kenya depending on who they side with (Lynch 2008; 2011). In 2007, the subgroups of the Kalenjin accounted for a majority in twenty-eight out of fifty constituencies in the Rift Valley, which itself accounts for almost a quarter of the nation's seats (Lynch 2008). Historically, this has meant that those in power have had an interest in stirring sentiment in the Rift Valley. For example, President Moi, himself a Tugen, and his supporters declared the Rift Valley a 'KANU zone' in the 1990s, and played the ethnic card very hard to try and suppress political opposition. In 1992, supporters of the then ruling party KANU and President Moi deployed state resources to stir up conflict against their opponents who were predominantly immigrant populations who had been allocated land in the province in the 1960s.

Majimboism, or regionalism, has been a feature of politics in the Rift Valley since the last years of colonial rule. Revived in the 1990s, the term became associated with a radical ethno-nationalism that promotes *majimboism* as the means to expel all non-indigenous people from the Rift Valley and return its ancestral lands to local Kalenjin and Maasai communities (Anderson 2010). In 2007, Raila Odinga did not actively back expulsions, but his support for *majimboism* was popularly interpreted as a call to get rid of outsiders and restore land to those who claimed to be indigenes. The fact that many of those attacked – who were predominantly Kikuyu – had been living in the Rift Valley for fifty years mattered little. As one of the survivors of the Kiambaa Church burning said, 'They were calling us by our names'. 'I don't know why they would do this. We were friends.' 'We knew them well', another said, 'They were people who came to our houses to drink tea' (Bloomfield 2008).

The Kenyan constitution recognises the rights of every citizen to live and own property anywhere in the country, but it coexists with the socio-political realities that membership of an ethnic community grants access to certain rights, particularly with regard to land ownership, and that clan membership remains the only means for poor people to access land. Civic rights might have opened the door for acquisition of land, but they are in conflict, as Mamdani (1996) has noted, with the rights granted by ethnic citizenship. This is what frames the discourses of 'foreigner-indigenous', 'outsider-indigenous' in places like the Rift Valley and many others around the globe (Geschiere 2009). In 2007/2008, around the Rift Valley town of Eldoret, many Kalenjin politicians played on ethnic tensions to mobilise political support among their kinsmen, and one Kalenjin councillor reportedly told supporters that, if elected, the ODM would 'remove the roots' of local Kikuyu communities 'so there would be only one tribe there'. Another prominent Kalenjin politician acknowledged to Human Rights Watch that some ODM politicians were saying 'we have a snake we have to get rid of', a clear metaphor for the Kikuyu (Rawlence et al. 2008: 36). Largely as a result of this ethnic rhetoric, many Kalenjin supporters believed that once elected, ODM would find a way to redistribute most or all land owned by Kikuyu to them. Human Rights Watch reported that they interviewed several Kalenjin involved in anti-Kikuyu violence who said they were merely doing by force what they had been denied a chance to do through the ballot box. Local elders and ODM organisers in many communities around Eldoret called meetings where they declared that electoral victory for Kibaki would be the signal for 'war' against local Kikuyu (Rawlence et al. 2008: 37).

What this reveals is the way the ethical imagination, understood as a means of affectively and cognitively imagining one's relations to others, can animate a sense of ethnic belonging that does not necessarily sit comfortably with democratic tenets of representation at the ballot box. While it is correct to argue that what was new about the post-2007 elections was the magnitude and level of violence, the reality is that Kenya has a long history of the deployment of political violence as an integral feature of democratic elections, where political success is associated with access to resources and the withdrawal of resources – notably land and 'development' – from others (Boone 2011). Kenyan voters have always rewarded politicians who could guarantee *maendeleo* (literally, development, but usually understood as patronage of state resources). Furthermore, in the minds of voters and politicians alike, ethnic calculations have always outweighed any general political policies or ideological considerations. In many ways, the euphoria of pluralism created unrealistic expectations of change in the era of multiparty competition which, far from redistributing resources, concentrated them in the hands of those who were political winners. In a larger context of impunity and a lack of faith in institutions such as the judiciary and the police, democratic politics understood as winner takes all quickly became a zero-sum game over resources – both at an elite level and for non-elites worried about loss of land and opportunities for 'outsiders' (Mueller 2008). In such an environment, it is easy to see how ordinary people's understanding of their political agency can lead to disillusionment with the constraints of the democratic process and its capacity to deliver.

Yet the recent 2013 elections would seem to contradict any trend. The foreign media descended, hoping for violence, only to be disappointed. The general consensus is that the National Cohesion and Integration Committee (NCIC) and other 'democratic innovations' – from those originating in the new constitution and international aid to those arising in civil society community organisations and on the ground – played a major role in preventing violence.[3] For the most part Kenyan citizens heeded calls for peace, participated calmly in the elections as Kenyans, and were not destabilised by the closeness of the vote, accusations of vote rigging and fraud, or the final legal challenge made to the outcome by the outgoing prime minister. Political campaigns were generally peaceful, with politicians urging their followers to keep the peace. However the NCIC continued to urge caution right up to the inauguration of Uhuru Kenyatta on 9 April 2013, because they recognised that the result showed a country almost evenly split, that emotions and tensions were high, and discussions in social media were hardening along ethnic lines.

The political reality is that in the run-up to the elections in March, fierce bargaining drove the formation of alliances, coalitions and new parties. Raila Odinga, the incumbent prime minister and leader of the CORD alliance tried everything possible to swing the Kalenjin vote his way. In February 2013, it was revealed that he had signed an MOU with Kalenjin leaders promising key positions in an elected CORD government to the Rift Valley, including chief cabinet secretary, and to promote agriculture and income growth in the region – thus following the usual pattern of promising access to power and economic resources in exchange for votes (Too 2013). In the rival camp, the man now elected as deputy president, William Ruto, ran as a member of a party only created in January 2013 for elections in March. His United Republican Party (URP) ran on a joint ticket with Uhuru Kenyatta's National Alliance (TNA) and signed a pre-election coalition deal that guaranteed the division of election spoils between them.

This 'Jubilee Alliance' between Uhuru and Ruto effectively allied the Kalenjin and the Kikuyu, whose murderous rivalry in 2007/2008 was largely responsible for the killings and displacements in the Rift Valley. The alliance undoubtedly played a major role in preventing violence, but it also continued the close link between electoral success, power, control over resources and land and settlement issues. Certainly in the Rift Valley, Ruto's ability to deliver URP votes was closely linked to local perceptions that electoral success for the alliance would guarantee not only the delivery of resources, but the righting of old wrongs relating to land and settlement issues.[4] This was clearly signalled when illegal settlers, evicted from the Embobut forest in Elgeyo-Marakwet in 2009, moved back in only days after the inauguration. One settler made the point succinctly: 'We are only carrying out small-scale farming activities to sustain our families as we wait for the Jubilee Government to honour its resettlement promises' (Kibor 2013).

Understanding the terrain of democratic process – and its apparent demise into violence – in Kenya clearly demands an appreciation of the nature of community, belonging and the mapping of these affinities onto territorial space or land. Yet tracing these processes through the lens of the ethical imagination highlights that these are not fixed categories and that the violence cannot be attributed simply to the blind following of ethnic loyalty. The processes through which individuals make themselves in relation to others is open-ended and charged with possibility. Voice and authority emerge as forms of engagement, negotiated in an uncertain context of shifting, fragile alliances and constant speculation over who might be best able to protect individual and collective interests. As people experience forms of potentiality and opportunity, democracy itself becomes something to be evaluated: perhaps worth investing in under certain circumstances, but something that might be regarded as offering limited returns should other circumstances prevail.

Giving Voice to the People

Prior to and during the 2007 election, inflammatory statements and songs broadcast on vernacular radio stations and sent via SMS and emails shaped popular rhetoric at party rallies. Kass FM is the Kalenjin radio station, and is widely listened to in the Rift Valley. Joshua Arap Sang, a presenter for the radio station, is still facing charges at the ICC in The Hague. Call-in shows are popular, but difficult to police, since the presenter has little idea of what the caller plans to say and the language is often metaphorical and thus hard to censor directly. In 2007 Kalenjin callers were heard to make negative comments about other ethnic groups, referring to them as 'settlers', and exhorting their fellows to 'reclaim our land' and 'reclaim our birth right' (Nderitu 2008). Such statements were popularly understood as a call to evict non-Kalenjin from land thought to be part of Kalenjin ancestral lands. References to the need for 'the people of the milk' to 'cut grass' is a similar call since the Kalenjin call themselves people of the milk and contrast their interest in animals with the agricultural traditions of the Kikuyu, and cutting grass is a euphemism for clearing the Kikuyu off the land (Nairobi Chronicle 2008a). Likewise complaints that the 'mongoose has come and stolen our chickens' is a reference to a usurper who has disrupted domestic life and established ways of living through theft.

Denigration of the other, and likening them to animals, is nothing new in the context of hate speech, but ahead of and during the 2007 election it reached unprecedented heights in the Rift Valley, as well as elsewhere. A substantial proportion of the population of Kenya – typically the poorest, the most politically marginalised, those who feel the most aggrieved and excluded from Kenya's economic success – have for most of the country's history had access only to media controlled by a government they distrust. In 2004, a new law was passed liberalising the media, and this paved the way for a wave of new local language radio stations to be established, targeting listeners from the main ethnic communities. Suddenly, and largely accidentally, talk shows became an outlet for public debate and an expression of voice that had been suppressed for decades. Many of these voices were angry, disaffected and set on change. Such outlets are arguably a good thing if tensions can be defused through public debate, but the reality in 2007 was that defamatory speech was used to fan the flames of violence.

Kenyan legislators, judiciary and civil society organisations recognised this, and from 2010 onwards, began to take steps against hate speech, with some high-profile cases. Ahead of the vote on the new constitution in August 2010, three MPs were arrested for hate speech. In 2012, three Kikuyu musicians were also charged, and another MP was arrested for incitement and hate speech in September. In October 2012, the government introduced strict guidelines to control hate speech ahead of the elections in 2013. The guidelines allow for the monitoring of messages sent via mobile phone as well as content disseminated on social media networks to ensure no offensive or inciting messages are posted on Twitter or Facebook. The guidelines also require politicians to submit campaign text messages and political advertisements for vetting at least two days before they are sent, aired or broadcast to the public. Anyone who sends threatening, insulting, abusive or inciting messages capable of stirring ethnic hatred using their mobile phones, as well as those who violate the political advertising rules, could face a penalty of one million shillings ($11,700), a jail term of up to three years, or both. The National Cohesion and Integration Commission, the Independent Electoral and Boundaries Commission, the Communications Commission of Kenya (CCK), the police and the mobile telecommunications industry all worked together to develop the guidelines and were largely successful in enforcing them during the election period. This followed an earlier joint initiative by the government and telecom companies to introduce a text service allowing citizens to report hate speech ahead of the 2010 referendum on the new constitution. This wholly positive move signalled new forms of collaboration between legislators, institutions developed to protect democratic processes and business interests.

However, citizen protest against the perceived venality and incompetence of politicians also uses animal imagery and language drawn from the experiences of rural households: 'when the hyena is the judge, the goat will not have justice'. Graffiti appeared all over Nairobi in 2011, much of it brilliantly acerbic and very provocative, accusing politicians of fomenting ethnic division and conflict, and of amassing riches at public expense. In such images, politicians were consistently portrayed as vultures, living off the flesh of the public.[5] In June 2012, youth protestors in Nairobi carried replicas of coffins with the words 'bury the vultures' written on them alongside signs saying 'wanted: competent leaders' (Elkin 2012; Wanja 2012). Graffiti art has continued to play a role in the political life of cities. Its practitioners see it not only as an outlet for public opinion, but as a way of drawing attention to key issues such as corruption in the police and government officials, a way of holding those in power to account and asking 'What is my vote doing for me?' (Ruvaga 2014). In the run-up to the March 2013 election, the peace train project involved painting a huge mural carrying peace messages on the entire side of a ten-car commuter train passing through Kibera, where serious violence had occurred in 2008 and train tracks had been torn up.

Authority, or, the Politics of the Foreskin

Colonial and post-colonial politics in Kenya have consistently governed through the animation and elaboration of discourses of masculinity, provision and belonging (Lonsdale 2008). Authority in the era of multiparty democracy in Kenya draws on historically established roots linking ethnic identity and character to preferential access to resources and advancement that were developed in the colonial and early post-colonial periods. Yet it is evidently the case that notions of authority have over time developed new languages, new constellations of ethnic identification and new forms of conflict. It is in this sense that ethnic loyalties and identities are not simply the cause of conflict in the modern state, but the consequence of a form of democracy that enlivens them and elaborates them into new cultural forms that have subsequently come to define the terrain of the political.

A good example is what Kenyans with their usual gift for language call 'the politics of the foreskin'. In violence around Nakuru town in 2008, Kikuyu were reported to be attacking and forcibly circumcising Luo men (IRIN News 2011). These brutal actions have certain historical antecedents, starting with claims made by Jomo Kenyatta, independent Kenya's first president, for the political and leadership superiority of circumcised men, and his rivalry with Raila Odinga's father in the first decades of the post-colonial state. While the Kikuyu and Kalenjin circumcise, the Luo do not. The language of Raila's political opponents was consistent in the period 2005–2012. In the period leading up to the 2007 elections, concerns of ethnicity, adulthood and authority were brought into focus through language around circumcision. 'Those who are not circumcised should be taken for a circumcision ceremony'; 'Raila is an outsider. He is from the lakeside. Some people have not crossed the bridge. I cannot work with him as he has not passed through rites of adulthood'; 'An uncircumcised person cannot keep confidences'; 'Should the draft constitution pass, Parliament should add a section that demands every man of age to get circumcised'; 'A campaign on circumcision should be launched by the government' (KNHCR 2006: 46–47).

The issue of circumcision draws on powerful cultural attitudes to authority that are reformulated anew in each generation. For the Kalenjin, circumcision is linked not only to adulthood, but to rational thought, oratory and the ability to participate in managing the affairs of the community. No uncircumcised man could speak at the *kokwo* [the assembly of male elders], nor could he be trusted with ritual secrets, which in any event he would not know. As an uncircumcised man, his bravery was not tested, his word could not be his bond and he could not manage a household or lead others. Circumcision for the Kalenjin links speech both to community representation and to deliberation on which the future of the community depends. This provided something of a contradiction in the 2007 elections, when William Ruto was urging the Kalenjin to vote for Raila against the incumbent Kikuyu President Kibaki, since as a Luo man Raila is not circumcised. At a campaign rally in Marakwet District in the Rift Valley in 2007, Raila responded to this by saying 'what is important is to be "circumcised upstairs"', asking people, 'Which is more important, to be circumcised in the mind or in the flesh?' I heard young Marakwet men repeat this readily on many subsequent occasions saying, 'I want to vote for Raila. He's circumcised upstairs', meaning that he is educated, knowledgeable about the world and capable of being a leader (Nairobi Chronicle 2008b).

In the run-up to the 2013 elections, the politics of the foreskin again animated public discourse and imagination. The Kikuyu musicians arrested for hate speech in 2012 drew on anxieties about leadership, ethnic voting and the political circumstances surrounding the ICC indictment of the then presidential hopeful Uhuru Kenyatta. The language of the songs was especially interesting because it drew on both cultural and Christian metaphors and imagery to determine the rights to political office.

Song 1: *Uhuru ni Witu [Uhuru is Ours] – Kamande wa Kioi*
Greetings people of the house of Gikuyu and Mumbi.
I bring you a message from all Kikuyu musicians.
This is a message from God.
Uhuru is the Moses of the Kikuyu nation.
He is meant to move Kikuyus from Egypt to Canaan.
Do not agree to be divided. Let all votes go to him.
He is ours.
He is anointed by God, poured oil on.
Raila, there is a call.
Go to Mama Ngina's house, a king has been born there.
Once there ask where Uhuru is seated and pour oil on him.
Just like Samuel did for David in the Bible.
Stop chasing the wind Agwambo, go to Icaweri and anoint Uhuru.

You thump your chest about Hague, is Hague your mother's?
There is a curse from God.
Philistines who do not circumcise cannot lead Israel.
When Abraham stressed God, he was told to go get cut, even you General of Migingo, your knife is being sharpened.
(Kiarie 2012)

Song 2: Hague-Bound – *Muigai Wa Njoroge* and *Muhiko*
Question: If it was you who is being pushed to The Hague what would you do?
Answer: I would call my family and divide up my property and then ask my mother to pray for me.

Question: What if you knew that Hague you are being pushed there by an uncircumcised man who wants to push you there and take over your wife and all your wealth? A man who can do anything to ensure you are in problems.
Answer: There it is better to die. Things for a man are not governed by an uncircumcised man. I would kill him. It's better they increase my charges.

Question: What would you tell your crying supporters as you are being shipped to Hague?
Answer: I would tell them to pray for me and know I am being persecuted for my love of my community.

Question: When you get to Hague how you would ensure the white man does not cheat you?
Answer: I would ask for proceedings to be done in Kikuyu.

Question: When on the dock what would you be thinking of the uncircumcised man who is the source of your predicament?
Answer: I would ask God to forgive him. I would also ask that he gets circumcised so that he matures mentally. I would also ask Kenyans to be very wary of that man.
(Kiarie 2012)

The authority to rule – legitimacy – is framed in Kenya by particular understandings of provision and protection allied to ideas about masculinity and its appropriate performance. Interestingly, as the election drew near at the close of 2012, NCIC and CCK, as well as campaigners, MPs, public figures and faith leaders all spoke out consistently against hate speech and incitement to violence, linking successful and peaceful elections to political maturity and the emergence of 'issue-based' rather than 'ethnic-based' politics. Discussion of ethnic differences – including the politics of the foreskin – disappeared from most public discourse to be replaced by discussion of national unity, autonomy and sovereignty. This development was certainly assisted by two things: the representation of Kenya in the international media (see below) and the issue of the ICC and the indictments of Uhuru and Ruto. Clever management of the ICC situation allowed Uhuru and Ruto to be repositioned in the public mind not as criminals, but as individuals being pursued by a hostile international body because of their determination to protect their communities' interests when they were threatened in the 2007/2008 violence (Mueller 2014; Lynch 2014a).

This meshed Kenyan sovereignty with the legitimacy of leaders who protect and provide for their communities, linking citizenship once more to land, and power to provision.

The ethical imagination, the way of living the relation to self and to others, works to animate the aspirations, ideologies and practices that shape our world. New possibilities and new encounters are filtered through older histories and extant ways of being, generating – among other things – new political narratives and affiliations. The deployment of ancient proverbs and cultural practices such as circumcision in contemporary political concerns suggests the way that notions of political authority are understood through much older connotations of adulthood and seniority. Similarly, the Jubilee Alliance's ingenious reframing of the ICC as a neo-colonial interference appealed to a much older sense of historical injustice. The narrative resonated with a broad range of Kenyans since it explicitly invoked a long history of colonial intervention and racially biased assumptions of intellectual capacity.

The Future of Democracy: 2007 versus 2013

Public political sentiment in Kenya has always been vocal, but its form and conduits are changing. New political narratives are emerging at street level as well as among elites, which innovatively rework tired tropes of narratives received both from political elites and pinned on Kenya from afar. Street protests in Nairobi as well as the recent proliferation of online commentary and critique reveal new forms of citizen voice starting to perforate Kenyan politics. Such new encounters are charged with possibility, opening up new transnational horizons, including explicit as well as more inchoate affiliations with citizen-led mobilisations around the world. Central to this nascent critical sphere is a dissatisfaction with the forms and faces of democracy as it manifests in Kenya.

After the election violence in 2007 and right up to just before the elections in 2013, the actions of politicians were widely regarded as shameful. One newspaper article provides a fair summary:

> MPs owe us apologies for poor leadership, reneging on promises and agreements, hubris, deception, dishonesty, nepotism, tribalism, corruption, violence, hatred, grand larceny, fraud, theft-by-servant, blatant self-interest and callous use of the electorate for their own ends, utter disregard for what's good for the country, failure to do their duty, awarding themselves huge emoluments while ordinary folk languish in poverty (and then sickeningly turning round and calling them 'my people') – right down through a whole litany of crimes and offences to the dross at the absolute bottom: behaving like the dregs of society, rolling in the gutter, engaging in street brawls and punch-ups, and wilfully damaging public and private property. They owe us an apology for being utterly without shame. (Elderkin 2012)

These are strong words, but despite such public dissatisfaction with the faces of democracy, in October 2012 Kenyan MPs voted to award themselves a two billion shilling ($22 million) send-off package ahead of the dissolution of parliament in January 2013 in preparation for the elections. The outcry and the outrage were palpable, and thousands of Kenyans used Facebook and Twitter to accuse MPs of selfishness, following which, fortunately, President Kibaki declined to write the send-off package into the law.

However, once back in power after the elections, in April 2013 MPs continued to lobby for salary increases. On 12 June 2013 civil society organisations staged a large protest in Nairobi against the 'MPigs" demand for increased pay. Protesters drove a herd of pigs covered in blood to the entrance of parliament, citing the greed of politicians with people's life blood on their hands. Calling themselves 'Occupy Parliament', protesters blocked the main entrance to the National Assembly for almost four hours waving placards, dancing and singing. Their point was a straightforward one of how basic commodities had doubled in price, well beyond the reach of ordinary citizens, while MPs were awarding themselves ever higher salaries. They chanted *'Bunge sio biashara, bunge ni utumishi'* [Parliament is not a business enterprise, it's a public service], and 'you can jail the revolutionary but you cannot jail revolution', making explicit reference to the Arab Spring.

As this material indicates, one of the major changes between 2007 and 2013 was the emergence of the citizen voice or the voice of the people. Since the introduction of undersea fibre-optic cables in 2009, fast internet services have proliferated, smartphones have taken off and it is now easy and relatively cheap for Kenyans of all backgrounds to connect to the internet via their mobile phones. For the period July–Sept 2014, the Communications Authority of Kenya (CA, formerly the CCK) estimated internet penetration at 57.1 per cent, up from 41.6 per cent at the time of the 2013 elections, and a dramatic rise on the mere 9 per cent penetration rate estimated at the point of the December 2007 elections (CA 2015: 22; CCK 2014: 26; CCK 2008: 16) Kenya now has the highest rate of internet use in sub-Saharan Africa, primarily thanks to its extensive mobile data network and 3G penetration (Mwende 2014). The widespread use of social media has produced a palpable sense of citizen voice in politics, even if it has not yet translated into direct reform or control over political outcomes. It has also been supported by institutional, government and business management of both mainstream and social media.

The new role of this citizen voice is clearly apparent in online commentary around the 2013 elections. It started with the release of a CNN video on 1 March 2013 – three days before the elections – which purported to show Kikuyu 'tribal members' preparing for violence in the Rift Valley. It is a peculiar video – almost like a spoof – which features a few men with cobbled together weaponry (including guns made from old pipes and bullets acquired 'from the police') supposedly 'preparing' for election violence.[6] They roll around in some trees, and do not fire the weapons – it is unclear if they would even work. One man seems to be wearing a woman's wig, and several are covered in white chalk or clay – presumably intended to look 'tribal'. The white dust would be important later as one of the memes that developed on Twitter. The CNN commentary describes Kenyan elections as 'always' marred by violence, and there is the usual sense of inevitability, the implication of irrational Africans resorting to savage means. According to the report CNN had spoken with 'tribal leaders' (of whom one is meant to be one of the men in the trees) and they were preparing for battle.

The report sparked a backlash on Twitter with the hashtag #someonetellCNN mocking the CNN video. Ironic and comedic tweets and especially images continued to be tweeted during the elections, highlighting the peaceful nature of Nairobi and the country more broadly. The video itself was directly satirised in many instances, with one of the most popular images one of a young toddler with a stern expression, his face covered in white flour, with the words 'Ready for CNN' underneath.[7]

The second social media meme developed on election day itself (4 March 2013) when, at around 7 a.m., France24 anchor Stuart Norval tweeted 'BREAKING Gun shots fired in #Nairobi #Kenya as huge crowds fall over each other to vote. Dramatic pictures on @France24_en in 15 min'. Needless to say, the dramatic images never emerged, but the hashtag #picturesforStuart did. This was a witty meme to provide Stuart with images that he suddenly seemed unable to produce on air. A slew of tweets and images piled up showing 'dramatic' scenes across the country, such as people snoozing in voting queues, calm quiet streets, images of peeled fruit and gnawed chicken bones as examples of 'violence', and of opposing politicians joking with each other.

One of the most retweeted tweets of the whole election summed up the mood of a disgruntled Kenyan public keen to wrest the image of the election out of the hands of foreign media sources and assert their own version of the day. It came from Calestous Juma, a Kenyan professor at the Kennedy School of Government at Harvard: 'BREAKING: foreign reporters clash in #Kenya amid growing scarcity of bad news'. This was deemed hilarious by many Kenyans and was retweeted with a huge range of ironic images appended.

Much of the international media seemed oblivious to this and continued waiting for the ethnic violence that was supposedly brewing. Sample headlines included:

'Election peaceful, but Kenya is still deeply divided by tribalism' (Reuters)
'Kenya: Tribal Rift and Risk' (*The Guardian*)
'Kenyans vote in presidential election as violence flares' (*The Guardian*)
'Kenyan inspector general bans post-election demonstrations' (*Allafrica.com*)
'Seven Per cent Kenya Growth Likely If Peace Remains' (*Allafrica.com*)

But some news outlets did pick up rather well on the shift in voice of the 2013 elections compared to 2007, notably *The Washington Post*.[8] An op ed for Al Jazeera by a Kenyan Harvard law student Nanjala Nyabola suggested that Twitter had enabled Kenyans to wrest their 'national narrative' away from foreign journalists, giving them a chance to raise their voices in a way that was not possible in 2007 with lower internet/smartphone accessibility. She linked the rise of Twitter to literacy levels in Kenya:

Obscured by the 'underdeveloped Africa' narrative, it is easy to forget that Kenya has one of the highest literacy rates in the global south (UNICEF estimates as high as 87%) ... Poor people always have ideas; literacy allows them to articulate these ideas in the language of those in power. Technologies like Twitter allow them to broadcast these ideas to a wide audience, to court support for these ideas and to form networks with like-minded individuals. (Nyabola 2013)

While turnout was approximately 87 per cent, it is well recognised that only about 45 per cent of Kenyans over eighteen years of age are registered to vote, so in reality less than half the eligible electorate voted in 2013. Most Kenyans are members of poor rural and urban households and their voices were not heard for the most part. However, there seems to be general agreement that the key difference between 2007 and 2013 was the widespread desire for peace, expressed across the country and in all walks of life in Kenya. The alliance between Uhuru and Ruto undeniably diffused the potential for violence (Lynch 2014a; Mueller 2014). There was also some evidence of renewed faith in demo-cratic institutions – including the Kenyan Electoral Commission – and in the rule of law – especially the impartiality of the Supreme Court, a new creation under the 2010 constitution. However, research suggests that peace was hard won, and that despite the avoidance of mass violence, the election of 2013 was not necessarily experienced by Kenyans themselves as non-violent or wholly peaceful (Elder et al. 2014; Lynch 2014b; Mueller 2014). Intimidation, corrup-tion, ethnic tensions and unresolved historic disputes over land and resource allocation produced and continue to produce ongoing rancour, and a sense that some communities and individuals have benefitted at the expense of others. For the moment, democracy seems to be back on track in Kenya, and not because it has found new purchase and purpose, but because it has delivered politics as usual – albeit peacefully.

As we have seen, politics is a dense site for the ethical imagination. In Kenya, new contexts of encounter, such as street protests and social media, have in dif-ferent ways opened up new kinds of knowledge and critique that have enabled well-worn narratives to be subverted and alternative voices to emerge. Forms of relation worked out in this globally connected sphere, which link Occupy and the Arab Spring to Kenyan MPs' greed, may well generate affiliations, hopes and desires that will prove crucial for how Kenya imagines its future. Yet despite this, for the poor majority in Kenya, belonging continues to be primarily animated by a sense of community that is mapped onto territory: it is indexed by access to and relationship with land and resources. The link between ethnicity and political voice that has been a long running concern in Kenyan politics has not declined since the last elections, and has in some sense been entrenched by the new devolved powers of county governance, which echo the calls for regional *majimboism* of previous years. Ideas about representation then, continue to be framed by historically situated moral communities, and imagined relations between those both proximate and distant are based on powerful metaphors of trust, betrayal and character.

France and the *Manif pour Tous*

Across the world it seems, we hear these clear calls for more democracy, for a recognition of political agency and political subjectivity in the context of disillusionment with governments and global systems more generally. These calls and claims are not all of the same character. I suggest that this is necessarily so because all discussions of democracy and the character of political agency are first and foremost cultural claims – that is ethical judgements about self-other relations. Attachment, identification and fantasy are vectors of the ethical imagination and make use of cultural metaphors of great resonance and depth – seen in the Kenyan references to foreskins, farm animals and 'cutting grass' – which do not need to and indeed rarely do operate within the realm of explicit language and conscious thought. Moreover, such metaphors are animated through engagements with others and so we find, as in the scenes from Nairobi cited above, references to Occupy and the Arab Spring in contexts that in many ways bear little resemblance to the political well-springs of those original movements. References to the Taliban, Occupy and the Arab Spring can in some instances be reflective of sustained intellectual and political engagement with ideologies, social movements and programmes for political change, but in the vast majority of cases, I suggest, they are better seen as more inchoate and productive forms of encounter that drive identification and affect. They are attempts to create spaces, to derive particular understandings of ourselves as subjects and agents in history, to make sense of the orientation of the subject towards political change.

There is no doubt that sometimes the symbolism and semantics is explicitly manipulated – this is often what we cynically intend by referring to something as 'political'. But this observation provides little understanding of the forms of identification, projection and affect that drive political subjects, that make a difference to their engagement with politics, as a way of imagining and re-imagining their relations to themselves and to others. One of the key drives in the contemporary moment is the issue of political agency, or more properly speaking the recognition of the capacity for political agency. The demand to be heard, to be recognised, has a long history in democratic politics, but in its many contemporary manifestations, it is a demand to be recognised as a political subject and a political agent rather than as an undifferentiated other: Muslim, African, immigrant, terrorist and so on.

We see this very clearly at work in debates about gay marriage in France in 2012 and 2013. For many on the left across Europe, it was hard to fully comprehend the scale and character of protest in France against gay marriage. What is clear is that it was not – and is not – a simple matter of the usual fault-lines, Right versus Left, conservative versus progressive. The debate is complex, divisive and full of contradictory positions: Catholic gays who are pro-homosexual marriage, psychoanalysts of the Right and the Left who are vehemently against it on the grounds that it erodes sexual difference, some feminists in favour of medically-assisted conception for women and others opposed because they feel it introduces the spectre of the market place – of 'wombs for rent'. Many issues were and are at stake, including love, desire, pregnancy, filiation, biology, symbolism, education and nationalism.

Within this complex scenario, a self-styled non-violent movement against gay marriage emerged, calling itself *Le Printemps Français* [The French Spring]. Its website makes use of historical figures who won great battles against arbitrary power, including Antigone and Gandhi. They claim to be the voice of ordinary people and civil society; their opponents view them as right-wing and dangerous. Their manifesto contains straightforward claims:

> Despite the historic protests in Paris and the provinces from 17 November 2012 to 24 March 2013, despite a petition of 700,000 signatures, despite the millions of demonstrators, the government has forced the law through and continues its ideological struggle for a 'unnatural' society. This contemptuous attitude is accompanied by repression worthy of a police state. Women, men, children, seniors, elected officials and politicians, journalists and ordinary citizens are beaten, gassed, bludgeoned by the forces under the command of the regime. (Printemps Français 2013a, my translation)

Government representatives made calls in 2013 to ban the organisation on the grounds that it had been hijacked by the far Right and was inciting violence. The organisation took a different view:

> The French Spring regrets the falsely solemn and worried appeals of the government and its representatives calling for peace, calm and order: several millions of protestors against the homosexual marriage law have protested several times in Paris and in the provinces without any incident which would justify their dispersal. Such calls are an additional provocation for movements which are declared as non-violent and have proved themselves to be so on many occasions. The only violence is that exercised by the state, which has imposed its law, which wants to impose a gender revolution in schools, which refuses to listen to the anxieties of French citizens from all political persuasions, viewpoints and religions, and which continues to increase police provocations and intimidating language. (Printemps Français 2013b, my translation)

The claim of these French citizens is not just that they are not being heard, but that their views and opinions are deemed to be outside the terrain of the political: inadmissible, incompatible with a modern state. The website of *Le Printemps Français* contains a number of testimonies, including the following letter from Marguerite N.:

> Mr President of the Republic, I come to you with what little I have: a young French person, young professional, engaged to be married, a young woman of just twenty years. A young idealist, passionate, in love with her country and with the life she has been given. ... Today, I am living in distress like so many young people. Distress at seeing my liberty restricted to benefit an unjustified equality, by a liberty hijacked, by a fraternity betrayed. ... If your government has decided to use special cases to create general laws, then I come to you with the same request. I am engaged to be married and I would like my religious marriage to be recognised in the eyes of the

state without having to pass through a civil marriage. Civil marriage no longer represents anything of what I believe to be the fundaments of this unique and wonderful bond which unites a man and a woman for life, and which legalises for better and for worse the children who result from this union. ... I do not want to sign a contract of marriage with the state thinking that my marriage and my future parenthood are equal to those of two men or of two women. Because that is not my opinion and I ask you to respect it. (Printemps Français 2013c, my translation)

The complaint of the French Spring is that in their view sexual democracy serves to justify – in democratic terms – the rejection of others. Their identification with the Arab Spring is far from cynical because their point is that police brutality is being used to keep them out of politics, to deny them political agency, to make out that their views do not have a place in French society. The scale of the protest in France against same-sex marriage demonstrates how deeply metaphors of belonging tie the sexual relation of marriage to the values of the republic and its reproduction. When the attachments that tie individuals to their sense of self and to the collective life that makes sense of their life in its relation to others are threatened or fractured, then a sense of dispossession rushes into the subject and into the public sphere.

Conclusion

A focus on the ethical imagination reveals the ways in which various spatial and temporal boundaries – social taxonomies – divide the world up and make it intelligible. These taxonomies draw on metaphors – often of belonging, voice and authority – that animate both public discourse and personal orientations and dispositions. They underpin the attachments – rational, linguistic and affective – that connect political subjects to themselves, to others and to the life of the collective. The terrain of the political is invested with personal attachments and this accounts in part for the dismay, resentment and violence that so often erupts as individuals and groups feel themselves to be dispossessed or excluded. Such feelings of exclusion tie the subjective lives of individuals to state policy, public discourses and ultimately violent traumas, and are as evident in the French Spring as they are in the Kalenjin urge to 'cut the grass', even as each of these is projected through different and historically-specific social imaginaries of what politics is all about; a republic on the one hand, a winner-takes-all quest for resources on the other. The power of boundary-making taxonomies is that they come to be perceived as part of the make-up of ordinary subjectivities, and when political narratives emerge that reshape those contours individuals may experience a range of emotions from discomfort through anger and fear, to violent assault.

The fantasies and experiences that make up individual subjects are tied through processes of attachment and identification to the instabilities of collective and personal life. This finds the processes of representation and deliberation that lie at the heart of democratic participation permanently marked by an interrogation about what counts, which is ultimately about the threat of exclusion. The public democratic sphere is thus powerfully shaped by processes of inclusion and exclusion, by an ongoing series of questions about what counts as the terrain of the political and who counts as a citizen. At the level of the individual subject this is experienced as a series of expanding and contracting attachments and identifications, an ongoing series of politicised narratives about what attaches them to themselves, to others and to the world. When these attachments are denied, leached of affect or cease to offer comfort, or when their familiar benefits are threatened, even withdrawn, then violence is often the result.

Democratic politics promises forms of inclusion, but these are inevitably permanently threatened by processes of exclusion, power and resource distribution. The result is a form of politics that while premised on the powerful impact it must necessarily have on the markers and categories of experience and subjectivity, always runs the risk of animating processes that erupt into dissent and disruption. Participation in the public sphere of politics is fundamental to democracy, but by setting the grounds for inclusion in that sphere the lineaments of potential exclusion are necessarily exposed.

Notes

1   In September 2011 charges were confirmed against William Ruto, Joshua Arap Sang, Uhuru Kenyatta and Francis Muthaura. Immediately after the March 2013 elections, the charges against Muthaura were dropped, amid claims by the OTP of intimidation, bribery and the death of key witnesses (c.f. Mueller 2014; Lynch 2014a). In December 2014, charges against President Kenyatta were also dropped, officially due to lack of evidence but again amid claims of witness intimidation and governmental obstruction regarding the handing over of key data, particularly communication records.

2   The Kalenjin make up approximately eleven per cent of Kenya's total population. The label encompasses a number of subgroups (who were administered separately in the colonial period): the Nandi, Kipsigis, Keiyo, Marakwet, Tugen, Pokot, Sabaot and Terik. Though it should be borne in mind that these affiliations are somewhat fluid and other groups are sometimes included. See Lynch (2011) for a detailed history.

3   The NCIC arose out of the National Dialogue and Reconciliation Agreement signed in Nairobi on 1 February 2008 by the government, Party of National Unity (PNU) and Orange Democratic Movement (ODM) delegations, and witnessed by Kofi Annan. See <http://www.cohesion.or.ke/>.

4   In 2013, Jubilee took twenty-three MPs' seats out of thirty-one in counties in the Rift Valley region. The counties are Uasin Gishu, Nandi, Elgeyo-Marakwet, Trans Nzoia, West Pokot and Turkana.

5   For an excellent photoseries of the Nairobi graffiti, see <http://www.bbc.com/news/17548225>.

6   The video can be seen at <http://edition.cnn.com/videos/international/2013/02/28/elbagir-kenya-armed.cnn?iref=allsearch> (accessed 23 January 2015).

7   In fact this was a resurgence of an older hashtag, which first appeared in March 2012 following a CNN report on the Al Shabaab bus station attack in Nairobi. The video, published under the banner 'Violence in Kenya', implied that the violence was both

widespread and ethnically motivated, when in fact it was a terrorist attack. CNN's David Mackenzie eventually apologised and the video was ultimately pulled.

8   See <http://www.washingtonpost.com/blogs/worldviews/wp/2013/03/04/kenyans-mock-foreign-media-coverage-on-twitter/?print=1> (accessed 23 January 2015).

References

Anderson, D. 2010. Majimboism: The Troubled History of an Idea. In *Our Turn to Eat: Politics in Kenya since 1950* (eds) D. Branch, N. Cheeseman and L. Gardner, 23–52. London: Transaction Publishers.

Anderson, D. and E. Lochery. 2008. Violence and Exodus in Kenya's Rift Valley: Predictable and Preventable? *Journal of Eastern African Studies* 2, no. 2: 328–343.

Berman, B., and J. Lonsdale. 1992. *Unhappy Valley: Conflict in Kenya & Africa. Book 2: Violence and Ethnicity*. Oxford: James Currey.

Bloomfield, S. 2008. A Chilling Tour of the Kenyan Church that Became the Scene of Mass Murder. *The Independent*, 3 January.

Boone, C. 2011. Politically Allocated Land Rights and the Geography of Electoral Violence: The Case of Kenya in the 1990s. *Comparative Political Studies* 44, no. 10: 1311–1342.

Communications Authority of Kenya. 2015. Quarterly Sector Statistics Report: First Quarter of the Financial Year 2014/15 (July–Sept 2014) <http://ca.go.ke/images/downloads/STATISTICS/Sector%20Statistics%20Report%20Q1%202014-2015.pdf> (accessed 23 January 2015).

Communications Commission of Kenya. 2008. Communications Statistics Report Second Quarter 2008/09. <http://ca.go.ke/images/downloads/STATISTICS/Sector%20Statistics%20Report%20Q2%202008.pdf > (accessed 23 January 2015).

———. 2014. Quarterly Sector Statistics Report: Fourth Quarter of the Financial Year 2012/13 (April–June 2013). <http://ca.go.ke/images/downloads/STATISTICS/Sector%20Statistics%20Report%20Q4%202012-13.pdf > (accessed 23 January 2015).

Elder, C., S. Stigant and J. Claes. 2014. *Elections and Violent Conflict in Kenya: Making Prevention Stick*. Washington: United States Institute of Peace.

Elderkin, S. 2012. All Members of Parliament Owe Kenyans an Apology. *The East African Standard*, 6 November.

Elkin, B.M.M. 2012. Bury the Vultures. <http://www.warscapes.com/conversations/bury-vultures> (accessed 6 February 2016).

Geschiere, P. 2009. *The Perils of Belonging: Autochthony, Citizenship, and Exclusion in Africa and Europe*. Chicago: University of Chicago Press.

Human Rights Watch. 2008. Ballots to Bullets: Organised Political Violence and Kenya's Crisis of Governance. *Human Rights Watch* 20, no. 1: 1–79.

IRIN News. 2011. Kenya: Plea to ICC over Forced Male Circumcision. <http://www.irinnews.org/report/92564/kenya-plea-to-icc-over-forced-male-circumcision> (accessed 6 February 2016).

Kiarie, A. 2012. Kenyan Musicians Probed Over Hate Speech. <http://www.genocidewatch.org/images/Kenya_2012_06_28_Kenyan_Musicians_probed_over_hate_speech.pdf> (accessed 23 January 2015).

Kibor, F. 2013. State Warns 3,000 Illegal Settlers. *The East African Standard*, 11 April.

KNHCR. 2006. The 2005 Referendum Monitoring Report: Behaving Badly. <http://www.knchr.org/portals/0/reports/behavingbadly.pdf> (accessed 23 January 2015).

Lonsdale, J. 2008. Soil, Work, Civilisation and Citizenship in Kenya. *Journal of Eastern African Studies* 2, no. 2: 305–314.
———. 2014. *Moral Ethnicity and Political Tribalism*. Roskilde: IDS Occasional Paper 11.
Lynch, G. 2008. Courting the Kalenjin: The Failure of Dynasticism and the Strength of the ODM Wave in Kenya's Rift Valley Province'. *African Affairs* 107, no. 429: 541–568.
———. 2011. *I Say To You: Ethnic Politics and the Kalenjin in Kenya*. Chicago: University of Chicago Press.
———. 2014a. Electing the 'Alliance of the Accused': The Success of the Jubilee Alliance in Kenya's Rift Valley. *Journal of Eastern African Studies* 8, no. 1: 93–114.
———. 2014b. Trust, Reconciliation, and Sustainable Peace: The Case of the Rift Valley. In *Kenya's Post-Election Agenda* (ed.) ICJ-Kenya. Nairobi: International Commission of Jurists.
Mamdani, M. 1996. *Citizen and Subject: Contemporary Africa and the Legacy of Late Colonialism*. Princeton: Princeton University Press.
Mann, M. 2005. *The Dark Side of Democracy: Explaining Ethnic Cleansing*. Cambridge: Cambridge University Press.
Moore, H.L. 2011. *Still Life: Hopes, Desires and Satisfactions*. Cambridge: Polity Press.
Mueller, S. 2008. The Political Economy of Kenya's Crisis. *Journal of Eastern African Studies* 2, no. 2: 185–210.
———. 2014. Kenya and the International Criminal Court (ICC): Politics, the Election and the Law. *Journal of Eastern African Studies* 8, no. 1: 25–42.
Mwende, J. 2014. Kenya Has 22.3m Internet Users. *Kenya Business Review*, 5 November.
Nairobi Chronicle. 2008a Vernacular Radio Fuelled Ethnic Clashes. <https://nairobichronicle.wordpress.com/2008/08/04/vernacular-radio-fuelled-ethnic-clashes/> (accessed 23 January 2015).
———. 2008b. Raila, Circumcision and the Luo. <https://nairobichronicle.wordpress.com/2008/10/07/raila-circumcision-and-the-luo/> (accessed 23 January 2015).
Nderitu, T. 2008. When Radio Spreads Violence: Free Speech Questioned in Kenya. <http://www.towardfreedom.com/30-archives/africa/1217-when-radio-spreads-violence-free-speech-questioned-in-kenya> (accessed 23 January 2015).
Nyabola, N. 2013. Kenya Tweets Back: #someonetellCNN. <http://www.aljazeera.com/indepth/opinion/2013/03/20133684021106816.html> (accessed 2 March 2015).
Printemps Français. 2013a. Manifeste. <http://www.printempsfrancais.fr/467/manifeste/> (accessed 2 March 2015).
———. 2013b. Premier mariage gay – le point de vue du Printemps Français. <http://www.printempsfrancais.fr/1716/premier-mariage-gay-le-point-de-vue-du-printemps-francais/> (accessed 2 March 2015).
———. 2013c. Lettre de Marguerite N. <http://www.printempsfrancais.fr/2549/lettre-de-marguerite-n/> (accessed 2 March 2015).
Rawlence, B., C. Albin-Lackey and A. Neistat. 2008. Ballots to Bullets: Organized Political Violence and Kenya's Crisis of Governance. <http://www.hrw.org/reports/2008/kenya0308/kenya0308web.pdf> (accessed 23 January 2015).
Ruvaga, L. 2014. Kenyan Graffiti Artists Spray for Political, Social Change. *Voice of America*, 6 August.
Stewart, K. 2007. *Ordinary Affects*. Durham: Duke University Press.
Too, T. 2013. Secret CORD, Kalenjin Leaders' Pact Revealed. <http://www.standardmedia.co.ke/?articleID=2000077031&story_title=secret-cord-kalenjin-leaders-pact-revealed&pageNo=1> (accessed 23 January 2015).

Wanja, P. 2012. Meet Pauline Wanja: Bursary Recipient. <http://blogs.civicus.org/worldassembly/2012/07/24/meet-pauline-wanja-bursary-recipient/> (accessed 6 February 2016).

Henrietta L. Moore is the founder and director of the Institute for Global Prosperity, and Chair in philosophy, culture and design at University College London.

3

Why Indonesians Turn Against Democracy

Nicholas J. Long

When Syamsuddin,[1] a middle-aged Malay with a laundry business, installed cable TV, it marked a fundamental transformation in our relationship. No longer would we sit in his front yard to sip coffee and discuss the latest neighbourhood goings-on; our conversations were relocated to an airless back room, each of us facing not the other but a twenty-one-inch screen. I rather missed the outdoor location, but Syamsuddin was in no doubt that the change was for the better. He was, by his own admission, a cable TV junkie and, like many Indonesians I knew, would while away many happy hours watching Animal Planet documentaries or the National Geographic channel. His absolute favourite things to watch, however, were re-runs of the Obama versus Clinton debates that had been staged in the run-up to the 2008 democratic primaries.

Syamsuddin had been hoping that the debates would educate him in the ways of democratic personhood. He explained to me that if Indonesians wanted their democracy to be good, they would have to learn from the people of nations such as the United States, who had been democratic for a very long time. He particularly admired Obama, who he felt could put his opinions across firmly but politely. For Syamsuddin, then, watching these debates was not an exercise in political punditry but rather an exploration of how one might live and act in a democratic state. As he put it, 'I have to learn to think and speak like that!'

Such an enterprise seems to be the hallmark of the project of ethical self-cultivation, at least as the latter has been described in a recent monograph by James Faubion (2011). Emphasising the processual dimension of ethical practice, Faubion insists that anthropologists should pay more attention to the work required to *inhabit* a role, to 'savour it' and live it to its fullest, rather than reducing their accounts of subjectification to moments of linguistic ascription (ibid.: 65–66, 160). By this light, Syamsuddin was working hard, with Obama as his exemplar, to inhabit the subject position of 'democratic citizen' that 'had become him' by virtue of Indonesia's democratization in the late 1990s.

This was in 2008. In 2011 I went back to Syamsuddin's house, hoping to understand in more detail the relationship between democratisation and ethical life. He greeted me warmly and, in front of the TV screen, asked me what I was now working on. I answered 'democracy'.

'Democracy?!' he replied, raising his eyebrows in a disdainful way. 'I can tell you all you need to know about democracy! It's no good. No good! Better to have a caliphate. Or a dictatorship.'

His remarks took me by surprise. 'But last time we met, you seemed so enthusiastic about democracy', I protested. 'We watched Obama together!'

Syamsuddin deflated. 'Oh man,' he said, 'I was hoping you weren't going to remember that. You know, I was so arrogant back then. Man! Man!' He grew alarmed. 'Please tell me you haven't written that I liked democracy in your book! I'm anti-democracy now.'

✳   ✳   ✳

On 21 May 1998, Indonesia's President Suharto announced that he would be stepping down from office. His resignation signalled the end of thirty-two years of authoritarian rule under his 'New Order' regime, and the start of a new phase of the nation's political life – one characterised as an era of 'reform' and 'democratisation' by both Indonesians and outside observers. At the time, as Joshua Barker (2007: 87) notes, many Indonesia-watchers were convinced that 'the New Order would reconstitute itself in all but name or that the country would descend into communitarian violence'. However, the early 2000s were instead marked by 'a surprising degree of democratisation' (ibid.: 88), prompting many to hail the country's transition to democracy as a remarkable success story that 'present[ed] valuable lessons for other countries' (Aspinall 2010b: 20).

A key dimension of this positive story has been the observation that – whatever shortcomings persist at the level of elite politics or within political institutions – there is tremendous public support for democracy, and a repudiation of the violent and repressive styles of government that characterised the New Order. Tony Day (2007: 2), for example, has argued that 'after 32 years of authoritarian rule under Suharto and his New Order, Indonesians are crazy about many kinds of freedoms (*kebebasan*) – freedoms that are subjective and sexual as well as public and political', while Suzanne Brenner (2007: 35) found 'very few' of the Indonesian women she worked with 'would wish to return to the days of authoritarian rule'. In 2013, Indonesia's former Minister for Foreign Affairs, Hassan Wirajuda, concluded that Indonesians had 'reached a point of no return' as far as commitment to democracy was concerned. 'Maybe 5 per cent [of the population] want a return to authoritarian presidents', he elaborated, citing 'a poll taken a few years ago', whereas '72 per cent of people want democracy' (Hartcher 2013).

With such assessments in mind, and drawing on over thirty months of fieldwork in Indonesia's Riau Islands Province (Figure 3.1), this chapter seeks to make sense of a category of people who present a curious ethnographic puzzle. These are people like Syamsuddin who, having once expressed a strong commitment to democratic principles and practices, had now come to view them

Figure 3.1 Map of the Riau Islands

with suspicion or disdain. Two points should be stressed at the outset. Firstly, not all Riau Islanders shared these sensibilities. Many delighted in democracy; others had always been hostile to the idea that it was the best form of government. Nevertheless, there was a significant – and seemingly growing – minority of citizens who were changing their minds about democracy as a political form. Understanding why they were doing so is particularly important given evidence that suggests this may be a broader national trend.[2] Secondly, I am not concerned in this chapter with the question of why someone might be opposed to democracy *per se*, so much as understanding why, having once joyfully participated in the 'eruption of the political' that Byron Good (2012: 528) describes as having followed the resignation of Suharto, and which my informants often described as a 'euphoria', someone might now have come to abandon their faith in democracy and thereby adopt what I would describe as a 'post-democratic' subject position. My hope is that this specific empirical puzzle might also raise some interesting contributions to broader anthropological discussions of ethical self-cultivation, how democracy is inhabited and how political subjectivity articulates with systemic change.

A Brief History of Indonesian Democracy

Although the suitability of 'Western style democracy' for Indonesian culture had been hotly debated since colonial times, with opponents suggesting its emphasis on rules and procedures left insufficient scope for leaders to exercise their *kebidjaksanaan* [personal discretion or discernment] (Tsuchiya 1987), Indonesia was established as a constitutional democracy upon its independence. This decision partly reflected the personal commitments of key revolutionaries to liberal democratic principles (Feith 1963: 313), but also a desire to forge Indonesia as the 'social, economic and political equal' of other nations seen as 'modern' (McVey 1994: 4–5). However, when the early years of independence were beset by problems ranging from spiralling inflation to regionalist insurgencies, the president, Sukarno, was quick to assert that 'Western-style democracy' was to blame.[3]

Thereafter the nation witnessed successive attempts to craft a superior political system. Having suppressed regionalist rebellions in coalition with the army, 1959 saw Sukarno introduce a new system of rule, which he termed 'Guided Democracy'. This was a system of government based not on the principle that 'fifty per cent plus one are always right', which he associated with 'Western individualism', but rather 'real Indonesian democracy', in which decisions were based on consensus and discussion, but steered by the discerning wisdom of a revered and trusted leader (Feith 2007 [1962]: 515; Tsuchiya 1987: 213–215). Parliamentary institutions were marginalised from the political process, with most issues discussed at meetings of the presidentially-appointed National Council and at *ad hoc* conferences of military commanders. Civil liberties, such as freedom of the press, were curtailed. 'To many observers', Feith (1963: 326) notes, 'the new political order looked like dictatorship'.

As the 1960s progressed, however, there was increasing dissatisfaction with Sukarno's management of the rapidly weakening economy, his belligerence towards Malaysia, and his increasing closeness to the Indonesian Communist Party. Following an alleged Communist coup attempt in September 1965, the then military general Suharto was given authority by the president to secure order across Indonesia. Through a series of manoeuvrings Suharto purged the military, government and parliament of pro-Sukarno elements, stripped

Sukarno of the title of president, and installed himself as the ruler of Indonesia. Mass violence broke out across the nation, as alleged communists were massacred in their thousands. The nation having been 'purged' of this ideological 'threat', Suharto claimed that his 'New Order' regime would allow Indonesia to enjoy a 'healthy democracy' (Hooker 1993: 277), which he named 'Pancasila Democracy' after the nation's civic philosophy.

As a system 'originat[ing] from an understanding of family values and mutual cooperation', and in which 'opposition groups found in liberal democracies are unknown' (Soeharto 2003 [1967]: 38–39), 'Pancasila Democracy' bore many resemblances to the paternalistic 'Guided Democracy' that it superseded. Regular elections, referred to as *pesta demokrasi* [festivals of democracy] did take place, but Suharto used his authoritarian powers to interfere with the working of the two opposition parties that he allowed to run against his own Golkar party, ensuring they never posed credible challenges to his power (Slater 2007: 102). All the while, state discourse, including that taught in the national curriculum, emphasised the incompatibility of liberal democracy with the Indonesian national character and cited the 'anarchy' and 'incompetent' governance that Indonesia had experienced in the 1950s as evidence to that effect (Bourchier 1994).

Nevertheless, there were activist voices lobbying for more transparent, liberal and democratic forms of governance: an argument justified both on first principles and on the concept of securing membership in 'world culture' (Crouch 1994; Soetjipto Wirosardjono 1994). When the protests of self-styled 'pro-democracy' activists, together with the devastating devaluation of the rupiah, prompted Suharto to resign, this liberal conceptualisation of 'democracy' became dominant. Substantial reforms were passed to support the prospect of free and fair elections, a dramatic decentralisation programme was implemented in the name of supporting democratisation (this had particular implications for the Riau Islands, which became a new province as a result), and the New Order regime was retrospectively seen – whether affectionately or with horror – as a system that had been 'authoritarian' [*otoriter*].[4]

For the majority of Riau Islanders alive today, then, 'democracy' as they now know it is something that they had heard a great deal about – both positive and negative – without having ever directly experienced it in their lifetimes prior to 1998, and certainly never as a stable political system. This was something that people in the province were acutely aware of, and so, alongside the institutional and civil liberty indicators that have typically been synonymous with 'third wave' democratisations, they also spoke of 'democratisation' when describing the refashioning of the ways in which they related to themselves and others. Issues such as how citizens interacted with and related to the political classes were now open for creative rethinking (see e.g. Simandjuntak 2009), as were questions of how to appropriately articulate and listen to political wishes, and how to inhabit and 'savour' one's new-found freedoms.

Such efforts, exemplified by Syamsuddin's training himself to 'think and speak' like Barack Obama, but also various efforts to 'democratise the workplace', 'democratise the family', or simply become a new form of political subject all represent conscious vernacularisations of democracy – to borrow a phrase coined by Lucia Michelutti (2007) to describe Indian engagements with democratic forms of life. Unlike in the Indian case, however, it would be wrong to say that Riau Islanders' experiments in 'vernacularisation' have necessarily led to democratic ideas being 'embedded in … social and cultural practices [and] entrenched in the consciousness of ordinary people' (ibid.: 639). Such analysis implies a depth and finality that stands at odds with many of my informants' dramatic changes of heart. Instead, I will argue, these vernacularisation processes – which we can also understand as processes of acquiring the 'dispositional competencies and affective and perceptual orientations' that Faubion (2011: 65) sees as a prerequisite to the occupancy of a fully realised subject position – were often presented to me as having short-circuited because of the new relational dynamics and forms of sociality to which they had given rise. Democratic citizenship was then abandoned as an ethical and/or aspirational *telos* as Riau Islanders, while still fundamentally envisaging themselves as liberal subjects entitled to adjudicate between alternative political systems, began to place their hopes in the prospect of alternative political forms.[5]

Theoretically, this phenomenon sets a challenging agenda for the anthropology of democracy. Many fine studies within the subfield have traced the forms of disillusionment and dissatisfaction that emerge from incompatibilities between liberal democratic models of politics and locally prevalent notions of moral behaviour, personhood and leadership (see e.g. Ferme 1998; Hickel 2015; West 2008). However, such a line of argumentation cannot be straightforwardly applied to post-democratic Riau Islanders like Syamsuddin, since it would struggle to explain the intense initial identification with democratic ideals from which they are now moving away. A model is required that is more attentive to the changes in momentum and direction of democratic citizens' unfolding ethical lives and that can account for how affinities and incompatibilities with the ideal of 'democracy' are themselves socially produced.

At present, scholars tend to explain such emergent feelings of dissatisfaction with democracy in one of two ways. The first, which is the dominant approach within political science, argues that citizens are 'disappointed' when democratic statecraft fails to deliver the quality of governance to which they aspired. If economic growth is limited and corruption is high, the efficiency of a strongman or CEO-style technocrat can tempt citizens' aspirations away from democracy (Chang et al. 2007; Diamond 2008; Kurlantzick 2013). But this analysis, as Carothers (2009: 12) notes, struggles to explain why concerns with governance and economic development should come to outweigh the benefits of free speech, a free press and checks on the powers of the military and the police. Yet while Carothers sees this flaw in his colleagues' reasoning as a reason for scholars to temper their democratic pessimism, I see it as an invitation to interrogate more precisely what issues matter most to citizens when they reflect on democratic forms of sociality, and why. Indeed, when we pay closer attention to the concerns that dominate Riau Islanders' accounts of their biographical transformations during the post-Suharto period, we can quickly see that the 'freedoms' associated with democracy may, over time, come to be experienced as less positive than Carothers – or Indonesianists such as Brenner (2007) and Day (2007) – might suggest. I commonly heard Indonesians lament that the self-interest and enjoyment of others, or their own 'selfish' desires, had had a destructive effect upon both political and social relations; others reported that democratisation had made them '*too* free'.

So why should democratic sociality feel so unpalatable? A second approach to democratic dissatisfaction, exemplified by Hansen's (2012) recent ethnography of the South African township of Chatsworth, argues that a transition to democracy necessarily elicits feelings of melancholia. By this logic, the dissolution of a repressive regime (such as that of South Africa's apartheid era) induces a Hegelian 'unhappy consciousness' (ibid.: 12), presenting citizens with the burdensome responsibility of authoring their own sense of self and purpose. The result, Hansen argues, is a 'pervasive sense of loss and displacement' anchored to melancholic behaviours of 'self-reproach and self-reviling' (ibid.: 16). And while in Chatsworth this atmosphere of melancholia is compounded by a sense that nostalgia for apartheid can never be articulated in those terms (ibid.: 12), in other contexts – such as post-Suharto Indonesia, where the memory of authoritarianism is less deeply embedded in a politics of racial inequality,[6] the possibility of voicing authoritarian nostalgia seems immediately more thinkable. Where Hansen's argument makes a substantive advance to the anthropology of democracy is in his willingness to place the affective and psychological consequences of democratisation at the heart of his account. However, his argument is compromised by its assumption – evident in his equivocation of authoritarianism with Hegel's lord-bondsman dyad – that those living under authoritarian rule have such little sense of alternative possibilities that life after liberation necessarily presents an existential burden. It thus struggles to accommodate situations such as Indonesia, where citizens entering the nascent democracy carried explicit, if impressionistic, visions of the democratic subjects that they wanted to become.

Rather than following Hansen in seeing the negative affect of democratisation as an *inaugural* element in analysis, we should instead examine how specific attempts to acquire the competencies and orientations of a 'democratic citizen' may themselves generate unexpected and painful dilemmas. It would then not be the intrinsic burden of self-making, but the successes, failures and challenges that arise from *particular instances* of self-making which generate affects (melancholic or otherwise) that influence both a subject's disposition towards the world and towards democracy, thereby shaping the horizons of its future self-cultivation. This approach to democracy's inhabitation requires a biographically-grounded understanding of subjects' changing engagements with the concept as its referent moved from an imagined prospect to a concretely experienced and enacted form of life. Person-centred ethnography, which examines 'how the individual's psychology and subjective experience both shapes, and is shaped by, social and cultural processes' (Hollan 2001: 48) seems like a promising way forward. However, it raises questions regarding how best to generate ethnographic description that is attentive to idiosyncrasy while still able to make broader claims about a general situation.

Here I draw inspiration from Nancy Chodorow's (1999) analysis of gender as both a 'cultural and personal construction'. Chodorow observes that individual experiences of gender can focus on quite different issues: some of her respondents are preoccupied with body image, others with anger, others with status, yet all these 'personal meanings' of gender are nevertheless recognisable as part of the late twentieth-century American genderscape (ibid.: 88–89). From a whole set of ideas about gender that circulate in discourse, certain elements have come to be 'emotionally particularized' (ibid.: 215) and projectively and introjectively recast over the subject's lifetime through the specific emotionally-charged matrices of relations in which he or she is embedded. In this way, cultural and linguistic categories are given 'personal animation' (ibid.: 76) so as to generate a way of inhabiting a gendered subject position that is uniquely individual but nevertheless recognisably American.

Building on this argument, it seems productive to investigate how similar kinds of personal meanings might also surround political life – a field as saturated with concerns about self-expression, acceptance, membership and status as gender performativity. As such, we might expect to observe uniquely individual but nevertheless recognisably Indonesian flavours to how Riau Islanders inhabit the subject position of 'democratic citizen' – and indeed, how willing they are to continue inhabiting it. Through a more individualised analysis, we can develop richer and more diversely textured understandings of post-democratic sentiment (and indeed democracy's inhabitation) than those afforded by explanations focused on the quality of governance or Hansen's unduly deterministic psychological model. Yet while personal meanings are precisely that – personal, and therefore idiosyncratic – cultural, political and institutional arrangements not only constrain the ideas that might become integral to the subject's sense of self, they also encourage and institute particular forms of sociality – particular emotionally-charged matrices of relations – in which certain personal meanings of political life, self-expression and 'free' action become especially likely to be forged. My approach thus enables a politicised but psychologically accurate account of why subjects may come to find democracy difficult to inhabit even in those cases where they were initially strongly drawn to democratic social imaginaries and value systems.

Fio's Story

The first time I met Fio, he didn't make much of an impression on me. I'd been invited home by his younger brother Iyan – the one their father was disappointed in and who locals said gleamed like a knife, but cut like one, too – and quickly found myself captivated. Iyan was an engaging host, regaling me with tales of dodging wild boar on his motorbike at night, while Yanto, their lodger, offered fascinating descriptions of trapping the boar in the jungle, tying their snouts with twine, and rowing them to market for export to Singapore. And then there was Fio, the oldest surviving sibling, approaching thirty and still not married: a wiry, nervy man who stood on the edges of the group and only laughed after someone else had already begun to.

Fio did tell me one story – of how, as well as setting up a catfish farm, he'd started working on a small island to the south, teaching maths and computing to children under twelve. This wasn't a story of pigs and adventure, just mundane detail: it was a long journey to the island, the boats were only fortnightly, hardly anyone lived there, he didn't know what to do with himself, he went fishing a lot. He showed me some photos. Fio with a fish. And then another one: Fio, trying to smile, but with his brow so furrowed that it looked like a grimace. That's how he was feeling on the journey, he told me. I did think there was something arresting about the picture, but then Iyan began to share anecdotes of his own misadventures when fishing, and I quickly forgot all about it. Then out of the blue, a few weeks later, I received a text message from Fio. He was in Tanjung Pinang for a training seminar and suggested we meet for dinner at his hotel.

Fio had been hoping to order fried catfish – his favourite – but it was off the menu. So we opted for *kwetiau goreng*, my choice, a hearty mix of flat rice noodles and seafood fried with spices and treacly soy sauce. It tasted good to me, but Fio was not touching his food. He seemed uncomfortable, nervous. I asked him what was wrong. He liked me, he said shakily, and wanted to be friends with me, but he was aware that I didn't yet know what he was 'really like'. If I knew 'the truth about him', he feared, I would no longer want to know him.

'When I was younger', he said, his voice almost a whisper, 'I used to be active in … democracy.' I didn't know how to respond. I took a mouthful of food to fill the silence; Fio poked a prawn through the tarry mass of noodles congealing on his plate. He gave me a piercing, earnest look. 'I was selfish then. It was arrogant of me. Now I am focusing on something much better. I'm doing this catfish thing.'

When Fio graduated from senior high school in 2004, the very last thing that he had wanted to do was pursue further education. His mother, however, had had different ideas. She had grown up in poverty on the island of Java and her relocation to Lingga – under the government's ill-fated 'transmigration' scheme – had done little to ease her family's privations.[7] Fio's mother was adamant that her son should not suffer the poverty that she and her husband had, and so she threatened him with a terrible curse.[8] 'She told me that if I didn't get an undergraduate degree, she would disown me as her biological child', Fio told me. 'She really valued education. Well, of course, after I heard that, I had no choice. She was threatening me with the most terrible thing that a mother could. So I went to Sumatra.'

Fio enlisted in an economics programme at a private university in a Sumatran city. It was here that he got involved in the world of political parties, campaigning on behalf of electoral candidates and organising public demonstrations in order to fund his studies. He told me that before starting this work, he had always been a very quiet and reserved person, but he forced himself to change.

However, for reasons that he struggled to articulate, his shift to a more outgoing disposition had made him anxious. He worried a lot during this period and found he always craved human company in order to get a sense of security.

Fio's time at university also afforded him an opportunity to meet idealistic students from across Sumatra who were passionate about forging a more ethical and accountable Indonesia. They focused on trying to achieve concrete improvements within their campus, including reform of the economics faculty, where the dean stood accused of corruption and malpractice, such as requiring a bribe to sign letters confirming students' graduation. Because this was 'happening too often and becoming too apparent', Fio and his friends decided that something needed to be done, and that it would be appropriate to exercise their democratic rights by staging mass demonstrations demanding the dean's resignation. Given his previous experience in coordinating demonstrations, Fio's role was to assemble a mass of students for the protests – something he told me with a guilty look.

'When I did the demo we thought if we came together we'd be able to get change in the faculty', Fio explained:

> A new dean. And yes, we toppled her. But, that's the thing for me. All we did was produce ego and selfishness. We got a bigger ego, rather than improving the faculty members. Maybe that dean could have been a worker who was better than she was. That's what our demo should have been making her aware of! It should have been giving the campus staff advice and feedback so that they would get a new way of thinking and would want to develop what they have.

Reform era Indonesia's culture of public demonstrations has been one of the more controversial aspects of the nation's democratisation. This is partly because of the risk of violence, but also because of the widespread concern that demonstrations might not reflect the desires or opinions of the people demonstrating (typically for pay), but rather the agendas of the demonstration coordinators, themselves presumed to be in the service of self-interested elites who were staging the demonstration in order to further their own political careers by, for example, discrediting a rival (see Bubandt 2014 for further discussion).[9]

My own experience was that demonstrators in the Riau Islands were quick to portray their links with political figures as strategic alliances over which they retained control. In their view, there was nothing wrong with receiving financial assistance from elites to showcase the failings of a rival if that demonstration might also contribute to social justice. However, several friends warned me not to believe such claims, suggesting they were simply a rehearsed defence that elites had prepared for the demonstrators to give to any researchers or journalists enquiring about the demonstration. The general opacity of sincerity in democratic forms of mobilisation was enough for many to eschew an involvement in politics altogether. They liked their social relations to be *jelas* [clear], they said, but in democratic politics everything was *gelap* [murky]. The *kepentingan* [interests] of the powerful could hijack everyday forms of sociality and friendship – something these friends were keen to avoid.

Against this more general background of moral anxieties surrounding demonstrations, Fio's own narrative of discomfort with his actions is all the more striking for its idiosyncrasy. Though he could hardly be described as being proud of his general involvement in democratic politics, what led him to decry his involvement as shameful was not the purchase of his services by local elites. It was the success of a demonstration in the service of a campaign that he considered to be both morally justified and of practical urgency given how important it was for him to secure his own graduation certificate. Rather than being uncomfortable that he had become a vehicle for the interests of others, it was the successful realisation of his own 'selfish' desires that had provoked his anxieties.

Our hotel dinner suggested that these anxieties were profoundly relational. Fio was worried I would judge him – and reject him. That makes sense in the context of a social milieu in which demonstrating is viewed with considerable ambivalence, and I had encountered similar discomfort before. Robet, for example, a politics student at a local university, was quite articulate about his own discomfort at having participated in several student demonstrations. 'I don't want to be anarchistic', he told me (the term has connotations of violence), 'but students need to be critical, and sharp in their criticism!' But while Robet felt uncomfortable about the stigma surrounding an activity he nevertheless felt to be justified, Fio's ambivalence went beyond moral ideologies and social imaginaries of 'the demo', involving much more personal responses to the expression and fulfilment of his own desires.

Looking over my conversations with Fio, a striking theme was that the fulfilment of his political desire – to topple the dean – had not proven satisfying. This was evident less in the reporting of the demonstration than in its repeated juxtaposition with alternatives that were proven or imagined to be more affectively satisfying. His counterproposal of giving the dean 'feedback' was the first such example, but he later drew a contrast between his involvement in 'democracy' and his ongoing attempts to develop a catfish farming business:

> **Fio:** I'm doing this catfish thing, and if a *Dinas* [government department] is interested and wants to help, they can come, they can help, and we'll be able to work together. I think it's better than if I did the sorts of things I used to. And God willing, there's someone from the Department of Farming who's interested! ... They just have to print out their operational data. They want to help, but the money isn't here yet, maybe [next month]. And then I can build up the business, even though I'm only getting fifty per cent [of the profits]. That, for me, has generated a bit of enthusiasm amongst my friends, but also enthusiasm within my own self. I'm doing something and there's also a person – a department – that wants to support what I'm doing.

Here, the prospect of 'working together' with the government by means of receiving an agricultural subsidy, was appealing not only because it promised to provide Fio with money (which he needed, having set up his catfish pond on credit) but also because it 'generated enthusiasm within his own self' [*memberi semangat pada diri Fio*]. There was something affectively satisfying about being involved in relations of mutual care and support, whether those of political sponsorship or relations of feedback, that had been absent from toppling the dean.

How then should we account for the transformative feelings of horror and shame that fell upon Fio, and that seemed to still be affecting him quite viscerally as he projected them onto me? One answer to this question – what I call 'the political ideology explanation' – would emphasise how, under 'Pancasila Democracy', mutual support, working together and cooperation were all widely valorised in national ideology, while 'anarchistic' expressions of dissent were discouraged. Could it be that Fio, still subjectificated by those discourses (or their contemporary parallels), found himself torn between New Order and post-Suharto visions of ethical politics and so eventually came to look back on his actions with regret? Possibly. But this kind of explanation, premised on enduring cultural/political values, simply raises further questions, such as why similar tensions didn't also run through his other demonstrations, why it was the New Order values (and not the democratic values) that won out, and why the event was remembered in such a viscerally disturbing way.

The emphasis that Fio himself placed on selfishness, and its juxtaposition with relations of care and mutual support suggests that a productive alternative perspective might come from an approach that historicised Fio's relationship to his own desires within the context of the emotionally charged relationships that he experienced throughout his life. Certainly, there seems to be sufficient evidence in the life histories that I collected from both Fio and his relatives to suggest that Fio's relationships to his desires had long been problematic for him (and problematised by those around him). There was his history of having been 'very quiet', and his extreme anxiety and 'need to be around people' once he started getting involved in a job that required him to express views as if they were his own. No wonder travelling to a remote island had been enough to shadow his face with a dark frown. There was the way he always let kids in his classroom pop out for drinks and snacks if they wanted, because 'nobody likes a strict teacher'. Even his presence in Sumatra was a result of his suppressing his own desires in order to please his mother and secure his status as the favoured child. Perhaps this pattern is unsurprising. According to his siblings, and by his father's own admission, Fio had been brought up under a parenting style that encouraged the children to disavow their own desires and preferences in favour of what their parents thought would allow them to escape the poverty of the transmigration village.

Indeed, Fio's childhood seems to have exemplified the pattern that Keeler (1983: 155) documented in a classic paper on Indonesian conceptions of shame, in which older children in Javanese families were expected to suppress their own desires (previously heavily indulged) in favour of those of their younger siblings. For Keeler, learning that one should disavow one's desire in this way marks an inaugural discovery of social fear, and the recognition that inappropriate behaviour – one's own or others' – should make a child ashamed. Clinical psychologists in America have also found that patients who were forced to forego their own wishes, in the face of emotional violence on the part of their parents, may grow up to experience deep ambivalences towards their own desires: feeling a strong wish to express them and yet feelings of crippling guilt and selfishness when those desires are fulfilled (Davies 2009, and see Chapin 2010 for a comparative ethnographic case). Fio still claims that his 'biggest weakness' is that he is 'quick to make friends, and then quick to follow them and will do whatever they suggest', a claim that suggests a pattern of disavowing his desires to secure the approval of others continues, almost impulsively, to characterise many relationships in his life. Even his friendship with me involved him putting me in a position of power and judgement over him from a very early stage.

We can thus see how the radical new opportunities for expressing one's desires in a socially approved form that an involvement in democratic politics presented might have proven attractive to Fio and yet left him feeling uncomfortable and guilty upon their eventual fulfilment (particularly, perhaps, after this led to the firing of an authority figure). By contrast, the mode of political engagement that Fio now aspired to was one of 'feedback' and 'working together' where he might be able to express his desires in efficacious ways without disrupting harmonious, hierarchical relationships. It should be stressed, however, that such a reading of the material is not really an alternative to the 'political ideology explanation' described earlier so much as a complement to it, since the parenting practices that Keeler ascribes to 'Javanese culture' were themselves powerfully shaped and reinforced by the New Order, which premised its authoritarianism on 'family values' while simultaneously propagating a much more authoritarian vision of the family than had previously been in circulation (Brenner 1998: 232–257). Several male Riau Islanders testified they had 'ruled' their households 'as if they were Suharto', 'with an iron fist', 'in a military style' or 'with coercion and force'. They had seen Suharto, 'the father of the nation', as exemplifying the kind of firm leadership that they should also enact as fathers, even though many now regretted this behaviour and were struggling to reorganise their family lives in more 'democratic' ways. Of course, not every family will have had this character, and not all such families will have produced subjects as conflicted about their desires as Fio. Yet the promotion of particular family forms and values makes these kinds of psychological dynamics especially likely, adding a further layer of understanding to the analysis of why some Indonesians have a conflicted relationship to democratic practices that involve the open expression of their opinions and desires despite declaring themselves intellectually convinced by 'democratic values'.

Further support for this argument comes from examining how families and childrearing were themselves conceptualised as sites of democratisation, and by examining which vernacularisations of democracy proved most popular and sustainable. Interestingly, the more stable variants typically involved a vision not unlike Fio's preferred sociality, emphasising 'feedback' and 'working together'. While more radical models premised on majoritarian suffrage were practised by some families, one Chinese schoolgirl explaining how her family held 'elections' whenever big decisions like where to go on holiday needed to be made, such a practice – in which the father's 'vote' could be easily trumped by the collective will of his children – was relatively uncommon. The model of democratic kinship that found much wider support kept the father as 'head of household' and ultimate source of domestic authority, but nevertheless involved a significant change in the structure of relations. A *Batam Pos* feature on how to be a democratic family (Ratna Irtatik 2012) cites one Riau Island father, Darno, who explains how he allows his wife and children the freedom to express their desires. As long as he deems these desires to be 'good and proper', he (and all family members) will support them as much as possible. Thus, when his wife decided she would like to start a business, Darno offered his full support – but only once he had decided that this was a good and proper thing for her to aspire to. He describes his style of being a father and husband as one that 'opens opportunities for responsible freedoms', contrasting it with his own 'military-style' upbringing. Clearly, then, how to balance individual desires with deference to established authority stands out as an ethical problem for Darno and his family as they embrace Indonesia's democratisation. More interestingly still, this has been assumed to be of sufficient relevance to the newspaper's readership to be the centrepiece of a feature on how to become democratic.

In Darno's case as much as Fio's, the initial embrace of democracy, and the trajectory of its subsequent vernacularisation or rejection, is explicable not just in terms of values or ideologies that were disseminated under the New Order, but embodied and affectively-charged modes of relating to oneself and others that were instituted during that period and which it could feel deeply uncomfortable to break or shake off, even when one might have intellectual sympathy for alternative 'democratic' values. And for Fio himself, these difficulties had led the very concept of 'democracy' to become one that he now wanted to distance himself from. He told me that he was making sure he would have no more involvement with 'democracy' and would instead focus on developing his business, and that he would be warning his friends against getting involved in democratic life. These powerful feelings that stemmed from just one formal dimension of democratisation had come, at least for now, to inflect his assessment of the entire process of reform.

Maznah's Story

For Fio, political life had become charged with personal meanings that had led him to adopt an outlook with considerable post-democratic potential. But there were also many people who did not only express dissatisfaction with democratic forms of life: they explicitly longed for the reintroduction of a more authoritarian form of politics. These sentiments were sometimes expressed in terms of the desire for a theocracy (usually an Islamic caliphate), but more frequently as a wish to return to 'an authoritarian regime like Suharto's'. This latter phenomenon has often been analysed in terms of a nostalgia for the New Order regime, prompted by the perception that governance was of better quality in the past, especially as regards the management of the economy (Mietzner 2009), while the former is often proposed by its Indonesian advocates as a novel solution to these very same problems (Hasan 2008: 38). However, my ethnographic materials show that authoritarianism need not be desired in its own right. Rather, in a context where radical socialism remains extremely unpopular (a legacy of the killings of communists in the 1960s), authoritarianism may represent the only viable alternative to a democracy that has acquired a personal meaning that makes the status quo psychologically untenable. Once again, to understand this, we must appreciate how democracy can threaten the self by assaulting the unconscious or conscious identifications and relationships that are fundamental to Riau Islanders' senses of who they are.

A Malay housewife in her seventies, Maznah told me that she had 'always been interested in politics'. She wasn't certain where that interest had come from, but suspected it could be traced to the influence of her father. This man, Batin Osman, had been the headman of a small island to the west of Bintan during the colonial period – an island which I will call 'Pulau Empat' to protect Osman and Maznah's real identities. Maznah had been very close to her father during her childhood: she had listened with interest to stories of his work, and sometimes accompanied him on his journeys to meet with Dutch officials or other 'important people'. However, her family was thrown into turmoil in 1942, when Batin Osman was murdered by a Chinese plantation worker who he had intercepted committing a theft. Shortly afterwards, Maznah moved to Tanjung Pinang.

Maznah's first active foray into 'politics' (as she termed it) had been in the early 1960s, when Indonesia was in a state of *Konfrontasi* [confrontation] with Malaysia regarding its proposed expansion to include Singapore, Sabah and Sarawak. 'I decided I would join a group of volunteers', she explained. 'There were four men and two women – me and another – and we spent our time hunting for Malaysian spies in the jungle. I didn't get any wages for the work, but I didn't mind. It was important to do it for the good of my own country. I'm lucky my husband was never a jealous man. If he had been, he might have forbidden me from going into the jungle late at night with four other men!' She laughed, and told me that ever since her jungle outings she had found herself increasingly interested in politics and affairs of state.

When *reformasi* began, she seized the opportunity to get involved in political campaigns to 'try and get the very best for the Riau Islands'. She had helped the former regent of the Riau Archipelago, Hoezrin Hood, come up with a strategy to lobby for provincial autonomy, and she had been an enthusiastic participant in several rounds of electoral campaigning. But here the emphasis was very firmly on the 'had'. We were talking in August 2012, just a few months before Tanjung Pinang's mayoral elections, and speculation over who should and would win the election was reaching a fever pitch. Yet Maznah, despite having been approached by several of the candidates' campaign teams, was refusing to play any role in this election.

'Democracy! I don't want anything more to do with it!' she exclaimed. 'Did you know that at the last gubernatorial election, I did a lot of campaigning for one of the candidates? I attended his strategy meetings, discussed policies with him. One night I stayed at the meetings in Batam so late that I had to be escorted back on a private speedboat.' There was almost a hint of pride as she recalled this – or at least a nostalgic fondness – before her voice hardened. 'But that didn't count for anything!'

In the run-up to the election, the campaign team had made a pledge that if their candidate received a majority of votes on Empat, he would repair a local mosque which was in an extremely poor condition. The walls were crumbling, the roof was leaking, and this was causing great distress to Empat Islanders who could not afford to repair the mosque themselves. Maznah spent several weeks campaigning in Empat and the surrounding islands, and she placed a heavy emphasis on the fact that a vote for this candidate would be a vote to restore the mosque to its former glory. At the election, Empat Islanders voted overwhelmingly in favour of the candidate Maznah was supporting, and she was convinced this was due to her effective campaigning activities, and the fact that she was well known and respected in the region, especially by people who could remember or knew of her father. Several months after the election, however, the residents of Empat contacted Maznah to complain that the mosque was still in a state of disrepair. No steps appeared to have been taken to improve it. Maznah was horrified. 'Nick', she explained, 'you know as well as I do that I'm an old lady now. If I lie, then all my life and everything that I have done in it means nothing.'

There were several reasons for Maznah's distress. Lying, or telling an untruth, was something she considered a serious sin, capable of annulling a life of good deeds (see Long 2013: 77). But it would also damage her reputation, along with that of her father's name. She instantly went to visit the candidate and told him how angry and upset with him she was. A week later, sand started to arrive and within a short period of time the mosque was repaired. The damage had been mitigated, but Maznah still felt very embarrassed about the incident and angry that she had been turned into a liar by her involvement in the political campaign. Her integrity as a campaigner had been placed in the hands of a team who actually did not care about her or the mosque on Empat at all. She told me she was not going to get involved in campaigns ever again, and started warning her children against any involvement in democracy. Not only had the Empat incident forced her to realise how potentially deceitful and insincere political candidates could be, it had also shown her how easily the reputations of good people could be marred by their entanglements in the democratic process. The idea that something of this kind might happen to one of her children or grandchildren horrified her. She would vote – because she felt it was her duty to do this while democracy was in place in Indonesia – but she was hoping that at the next presidential election 'somebody good' would be elected and would then outlaw any further elections so that Indonesia could 'get on with developing' as it 'had under Suharto'.

The Empat Island case is in many ways a classic example of the clientelistic politics that has been claimed to characterise direct elections in democratic Indonesia, but Maznah's story highlights the poverty of reducing the system purely to a series of instrumental and self-interested transactions (cf. Palmer 2010). Certainly Maznah would have received payment for her activities in the governor's campaign team, but her own account shows how she viewed them not only – and indeed not even principally – as a means of securing income, but also as the latest expression of a 'political' sensibility that she had been cultivating throughout her life, and which was closely associated with her memory of her murdered father. Part of the pleasure of campaigning in Empat, I sensed, was that it allowed Maznah to enact the role of a beneficent sponsor and leader looking after the islanders (much as her father would have done, when working as a *batin*), even though as a housewife she was structurally disempowered from doing so unless acting on behalf of others. As with her spy-hunting in the jungle, service to political institutions and organisations became an integral means of securing her own sense of political efficacy. This was the personal meaning that 'doing politics' carried for Maznah, reflecting an individual and emotionally particularised animation of cultural ideas about leadership and the provision of service and resources that have long been in circulation in the Malay world (Milner 1982: 23–24).

Yet the debacle that unfolded over repairing the mosque had served to threaten the very understanding of her political self that democratisation had initially seemed to nurture. As a consequence, democratic politics quickly shifted from being an appealing object of contemplation, one that would allow her to use her influence to improve collective well-being on Empat, to a dangerous endeavour that was threatening to 'good people'. The emotional tonality that the concept of 'democracy' acquired was thus once again coloured both by the personally-motivated ways in which Maznah had sought to experiment with democracy, as well as by events having unfolded in a way that threatened the things that were of most importance to her image and experience of her self: her 'good name', her relations with the islanders of Empat and her perceived obligations to (and identifications with) her deceased father. Maznah's horror – so intense, I think, because it so deeply threatened her core sense of who she was – led her to go further than simply disengaging from political campaigning. Recognising the potential for similar traumatic experiences to befall 'good people' in the future, including those about whom she cared very deeply, she was now actively hoping for the day when democracy could be overturned. But this was not because of the positive features she associated with an authoritarian, election-less regime. She just wanted democracy, as she had come to know it, to stop.

Syamsuddin's Story

There were further cases where the proposed alternative to democracy was desired not simply as a negation of the democratic order, but because the troubles of democracy had prompted an identification with its propositional substance. Syamsuddin, the man with whose story I opened this chapter, had found the forms of sociality engendered by experiments with democracy to be problematic after he joined the local branch of the Islamic Prosperous Justice Party (Partai Keadilan Sejahtera, PKS). He had actually wanted to be involved in political life for a long time, but was too scared to join a party under the New Order. It was possible that another party member might actually be a communist, and he would then be seen as someone who fraternised with communists (in a political party, no less), which would make him vulnerable to imprisonment or assassination. From an early age, then, he had felt that the collectivity of collective political mobilisation could be a danger as much as a benefit. He kept his opinions to himself, and read widely. However, under democratisation, where even communists could express their views freely, such dangers seemed unlikely, and he decided it was time to realise his long-held ambition. Although at the time he joined up he had emphasised that joining the PKS could be a way of improving the Riau Islands (and by extension Indonesia), he later told me that he had chosen to join as 'a kind of personal test':

> Was I compatible with the life of a political person? What was it like to be a political person? I had once heard that in politics there are no friends and there are no enemies. Do you believe that? Well, it's true! All you have is self-interest. And that's not a problem if we're on the straight path. Because we don't want to follow another person when he takes us on the wrong path, just because he is our friend. But does democracy put us on the straight path? No.

As with Fio, then, the lifestyle facilitated by the forms of politics made possible by democratisation was one that involved a distinctive new way of relating to self and others, one that was more radically individualised and anomic ('there are no friends and no enemies') and which led to a heightened sense of one's own 'self-interest'. While it was this very fact that became troublesome for Fio, Syamsuddin's experience was different.

His early experiences with the PKS had been wonderful. The members of the local branch used to gather in each other's houses. Syamsuddin reminisced as to how they used to talk about 'important issues: the weaknesses of Muslims, why so many Islamic countries are trailing behind the West, things like that. We concluded the problem was that they were no longer following the Qur'an and the Sunnah – Islam had become their identity not their religion!' Then it was the 2008 local elections, and the incumbent mayor, Hj Suryatati A Manan, wanted to stand for re-election. Syamsuddin was adamant that she would be a bad choice. 'In Islam, it's very clear,' he explained, 'women cannot be leaders. If you think about it, women, they're a little bit *lembut* [soft]. They're weak. They're emotional. And leaders need to be firm. So of course I said that we shouldn't support her.' But other members of the party wanted to. Endorsing Suryatati would lead to the PKS securing a sizeable amount of money, and – given that she was widely predicted to win the election by a comfortable margin – put the PKS in a very strong position in local politics. 'I tried to explain that this was a sin', Syamsuddin told me, 'but nobody would listen. I didn't want to go to hell – I had to leave. But it showed me how I arrogant I had been. I had thought I could use democracy to help get Indonesia on the straight path. But there is nothing to democracy other than self-interest and majority rule. That's what makes it dangerous.'

Syamsuddin's difficulties with democracy can be traced in part to the changing role of Islam in his life – particularly the influence of an inspirational lecture he had heard from a visiting cleric who had claimed that, at the end of the world, Muslims would be divided into seventy-three groups. Only one of those groups – those who had followed Islam perfectly – would be allowed into paradise. This had made Syamsuddin much more anxious about enforcing an orthodox position on issues such as female political candidacy than he might previously have been. Interestingly, though, Syamsuddin's initial response to this new horizon of understanding had been to try and use democratic structures, and in particular his membership of an Islamic political party, to build commitment to a more orthodox, scripturally-grounded Islam within his home community. This was precisely what the long PKS discussion sessions had been oriented towards. His problem came when his fellow party members broke ranks and, from his point of view, sacrificed their unswerving commitment to the Qur'an and the Sunnah in favour of their own 'self-advancement'. (For their part, other local PKS members asserted there was no theological problem with supporting a female candidate.)

While he disparaged these developments as caused by the self-interest of others, and a flaw of the majoritarian principles at the heart of democratic deliberation – itself a trope that had been regularly aired under Sukarno to justify his Guided Democracy (Feith 2007 [1962]: 515) – Syamsuddin was quite evidently disappointed with more than just the behaviour of his colleagues: he was frustrated with the way that democracy had stripped him of the capacity to impose his own vision of the 'straight path' on those around him. Although he now recognised that it was 'arrogant' of him to imagine that he could have done this, his response was not to adopt a more measured approach or set himself a more modest goal, but rather to phantasmatically identify with the prospect of campaigning for a caliphate, a state where, in his terms, political decisions would be ruled not only by the fallible human 'reason' [*akal*] but by *wahyu*: the wisdom of divine radiance that found its clearest expression on earth in the writings of the Prophet.

Significantly, though, he eschewed any attempt to join a coordinated movement that sought to establish a theocracy, instead deferring the prospect of being involved in such a campaign to an unspecified future date when a 'better organisation' might emerge. 'Right now I'm happy just working on my own', he explained, 'although I haven't given up [on politics] just yet. There actually are groups supporting a caliphate, like Hizbut Tahrir,[10] but they are always staging demos with a black flag. They come from Palestine. I don't like the way they make those demos. They aren't allowed by the Qur'an.' Certainly, Hizbut Tahrir were a controversial group, and Syamsuddin could have had many legitimate reasons for deciding not to join them. Yet I also wondered whether, by preserving himself in a world where he could advocate his own vision of a 'straight path' without encountering any institutionalised dissent, Syamsuddin was better able to realise his fantasy of himself as a political figure than either democracy or the actual reality of theocratic advocacy would allow.

As with both Fio and Maznah, such behaviour is consistent with broader patterns of relationships in Syamsuddin's life – especially in the years since he had assumed his position as head of a household. He found it very difficult to be contradicted. Several of his earlier jobs had come to a premature end due to 'disagreements' with managers (a danger he now avoided by being the boss of his own business), and he was currently at his wits' end trying to deal with his father. The old man, still living in Syamsuddin's home town, had decided to marry a new wife some forty years his junior, and refused to be persuaded as to the disadvantages of such a situation. He was even willing to disown Syamsuddin's sister if she refused to accept the woman as her new step-mother. Syamsuddin found this infuriating. 'My father is so stubborn!' he complained, 'it's always his way, or no way!' At this point, Syamsuddin's wife caught my eye, and commented, in a tone that mixed wryness with weariness, that her husband had grown up to be precisely like his father. In a different way to Fio, then, Syamsuddin also found reconciling his desires with those of others to be an area of difficulty in his life, and in a way that appears to reflect a different response to (as well as a different position within) a family form that exemplifies the ideologies of patriarchal authority that once circulated throughout New Order Indonesia.

The better I got to know Syamsuddin, the more easily I could recognise how motivations and psychological dynamics related to authority and contradiction might be inflecting his encounters with and pronouncements about democracy. Certainly it was events associated with these issues that most readily became lightning rods for his criticism. Yet, unlike Fio or Maznah, who spoke in openly emotionalised tones of the horror and shame that democracy had created for them, Syamsuddin was much more disposed to presenting an experience charged with frustrations and affects in coldly intellectual terms. 'Under a caliphate the public will be able to know they are getting someone who is a good leader', he once explained, 'because they know that the leader will be strict in his religion and thus have control. There wouldn't be general elections in this system, because the people are too stupid – they might elect anybody on any basis.' Here, Syamsuddin rehearsed a line of critique that has been levelled against democracies in all parts of the world, but had become particularly acute in the Riau Archipelago, a region dogged by allegations of 'poor human resource quality' associated with its indigenous Malay culture and fifty years of 'internal colonial' neglect (Long 2013: 173–205). 'A caliphate', he continued, invoking another widely echoed trope, 'would avoid the weaknesses of democracy. Currently people are too free. They have latched onto their freedom and are doing anything they want, but it is wrong to do anything that you want. Life has to be controlled – and this is where the people of Indonesia and especially these Riau Islands are really lacking.'

These are commonly voiced reasons for Indonesians to express alarm about democratisation, and although the extent to which Syamsuddin's fellow citizens really were doing 'anything they wanted' was overstated in his remarks, his analyses of voter quality and the need to set limits on citizens' freedoms are not without intellectual merit. What a person-centred ethnographic perspective allows us to see, however, is the way in which those widely circulating and not unpersuasive arguments may have become especially compelling to Syamsuddin because of the underlying personal meaning that political participation – which included making these very pronouncements – carried for him. If democracy had initially been attractive because it offered him the prospect of articulating his views in the public sphere in an uncompromising fashion, it was now, following his exit from the PKS, the public denouncement of democracy that allowed him to do that very same thing with impunity. Was it, then, my observational skills or my imagination that detected a note of glee in Syamsuddin's voice as he brought one of our conversations to a decisive close?

> I'm anti-democracy now. In fact, I think the democratisation of our state is one of the biggest problems we're facing. You know, Nick, there are some people in the West – and now people here are following suit – who say that democracy is the voice of God.[11] But I disagree. Actually, if you're a Muslim, I don't think democracy can be allowed.

Conclusion: Beyond the Political Consumer

The three cases just presented stand as compelling evidence that Indonesians may turn away from democracy for reasons that are much more complicated and personal than simple evaluations of whether or not they are the recipients of 'good governance' or experiences of 'unhappy consciousness'. Each case exemplifies a subjectivity shaped by imaginaries of how one should relate to others that are relatively widespread in contemporary Indonesia. Each has found the new ways of relating to themselves and others that are either demanded or encouraged by democratic forms of political life to be initially attractive but ultimately unpalatable, and in each case the rhetoric and concepts by which they come to voice that displeasure carries echoes of the language used to disparage liberal democracy in the pre-reform period. We can thus see how distinct elements of a widely circulating and heterogeneous set of Indonesian discourses concerning political life and citizenship have been emotionally particularised in ways that constitute distinct, radically individual, political subjectivities that nevertheless share a post-democratic sensibility and, though their actions and declarations, stoke the sense of democratic malaise within the Indonesian population as a whole. Ironically, then, democracy's success in creating a public sphere in which citizens are able to articulate their opinions is becoming a condition of possibility for its recession.

How, then, should we balance these in-depth but individualised insights against the significant body of survey data (summarised in Kurlantzick 2013) that identifies economic performance and corruption as the foremost concerns for Indonesians when they come to evaluate democracy? This issue is significant for interpreting the Riau Islands material, since 'corruption' and 'the economy' were the most immediately declared reasons that my interlocutors gave for having lost faith in democracy. Yet we must once again return to the question of subjectivity and ask why it is that such lines of argument – by now staples in the public sphere – might prove compelling to any given individual at any given time. As I suggested in my earlier discussion of Syamsuddin, well-recognised tropes may not always be latched onto because of a belief in their intellectual content, but rather/ also because of their emotional tonality for the subject. Of the three Indonesians discussed above, it was perhaps Maznah whose volatility of opinion was the most illuminating in this regard. When speaking on the topic of 'democracy' or her involvement in campaigning, she would slide into invective, denouncing how terrible Indonesia's economy had become since democratisation, claiming that while unemployment had once only affected people of Javanese and Minangkabau ethnicity, now even Malays – her own ethnic group – were struggling to find jobs and being forced to work as manual labourers. Yet on other occasions, when we were discussing her children, or her family's history, she gave high praise to the *reformasi* leaders, especially Yudhoyono, under whose rule 'all of her children had been able to find jobs', and noted the improvements in the standards of living that Riau Islanders were beginning to enjoy. While cases such as Maznah's do not negate the very real economic hardships that some Indonesians had felt in the *reformasi* period, especially given the high levels of household debt engendered by a rapacious credit industry (see also Stavrakakis, this volume), they do reveal that citizens may actively express frustration with 'the economy' while also, on some level, acknowledging that the Indonesian economy is booming and that the Riau Islands Province is doing better even than the national average. In such cases, claims about the weak economy are not the perspicacious indictments of poor governance that they first appear to be. They serve instead as 'idioms of distress' (Nichter 1981), a means of expressing other, less easily or appropriately articulated disappointments with democracy, in a language that would resonate with those who heard it.

The practical implications of this argument are significant in a context where both scholars and major donors in the fields of democracy promotion and democracy assistance (notably USAID and AusAID) are emphasising increased funding for 'good governance' programmes in order to 'consolidate' Indonesia's democratic institutions (Aspinall 2010a). This has been done on the understanding that the poor quality of current governance presents the most significant risk of democratic backsliding, both in terms of statecraft and popular opinion. Yet the material I have presented in this chapter suggests that such an assessment rests on a shallow understanding of the subjective difficulties that citizens have with democracy, many of which are likely to continue regardless of modest improvements in governance.

There are theoretical implications as well. By developing person-centred ethnographies of citizenship and political life that attend closely to the varieties of subjective investments that shape a population's apprehension of democracy and underpin the individual changes of heart that comprise, *in toto*, a broader pattern of 'democratic recession', my analysis not only offers political anthropology a new way of accounting for the feelings of melancholy, ambivalence and sadness that emerge after democratisation, but also a new focus for the study of democratic transitions. Placing at the heart of our enquiries the matrices of intersubjective relations in which subjects come to develop understandings of how to relate their own desires and interests to those of others leaves us better placed to anticipate and understand both the pleasures and pains of incipient democratisation. And while it is important to stress that these are not limited to family contexts, nor to social forms explicitly encouraged by authoritarianism, a provisional conclusion nevertheless seems clear: that the ways in which authoritarian regimes give rise to particular patterns of sociality and, in turn, particular patterns of psychodynamic engagement with the world can help us to understand why the euphoria of democracy is not always as long lasting as we, or our informants, might expect.

Acknowledgements

The research for this paper was generously supported by a British Academy Postdoctoral Fellowship and a Junior Research Fellowship at St Catharine's College, Cambridge. For their valuable feedback on earlier drafts, thanks to Marina Benjamin, Tina Pepler and seminar audiences at Aarhus University, the University of Cambridge, the University of Copenhagen, the London School of Economics and Political Science and University College London.

Notes

1 All personal names are pseudonyms.
2 The full extent of this 'trend' remains unclear. Some studies indicate that Indonesians' support for democracy has never been especially deep (Lussier and Fish 2012: 72–73) and that it has been falling steadily since at least 2003 (Kalinowski 2007: 368), while it is widely agreed that the period since 2008 has been marked by a rise in nostalgia for Suharto and in political support for once-reviled military strongmen. This trend reached its apogee in 2014, when former general Prabowo Subianto (perceived by many as a candidate standing for de-democratisation) almost secured the Indonesian presidency, attracting 46.9 per cent of the vote (Mietzner 2014). However, other studies suggest that even despite high levels of dissatisfaction with democratic institutions, public support for democracy remains stable, and as high as 83 per cent (ibid.: 124).
3 The validity of this claim has been widely debated (see Bourchier and Legge 1994). Although some scholars have argued that constitutional democracy was incompatible with the culture and society of newly independent Indonesia, others believe its decline is better attributed to the inexperience of civilian politicians or its deliberate sabotage by the military.
4 While I am sympathetic to the critiques of the democratic-authoritarian dichotomy (see Merkel 2010: 20), my use of the terms reflects the strong emic distinction drawn between 'democracy' and 'authoritarianism' by Riau Islanders.

5   I draw a distinction between ethical and aspirational *telos* to reflect the fact that some informants still felt a national duty to enact democracy as well as they could, while hoping for immanent political reform.

6   Chinese Indonesians were subjected to sustained racial discrimination throughout the New Order, but the levels of public awareness and remorse on this issue are not comparable to the South African case.

7   The transmigration scheme involved relocating Indonesians from densely populated areas of Java to underpopulated areas elsewhere, where it was hoped they would set up productive farms. In practice, transmigrants in Lingga struggled to establish sustainable farming systems and many have since returned to Java.

8   Mothers' curses are held to be especially powerful in the Malay world because of the tie of shared blood (Carsten 1995: 229).

9   Some Riau Islanders did, however, see demonstrations as a sincere means of articulating 'the people's aspirations' – a key trope of reform (Graf 2010: 29).

10   An international pan-Islamic organisation, founded in 1953.

11   Syamsuddin was probably referring to the ancient proverb '*vox populi, vox Dei*', which was widely popularised during Indonesia's initial period of parliamentary democracy in the 1950s (Feith 1963: 313).

References

Aspinall, E. 2010a. *Assessing Democracy Assistance: Indonesia*. Madrid: FRIDE.
———. 2010b. The Irony of Success. *Journal of Democracy* 21, no. 2: 20–34.
Barker, J. 2007. Vigilantes and the State. In *Identifying with Freedom: Indonesia after Suharto* (ed.) T. Day, 87–94. Oxford: Berghahn.
Bourchier, D. 1994. The 1950s in New Order Ideology and Politics. In *Democracy in Indonesia: 1950s and 1990s* (eds) D. Bourchier and J. Legge, 50–62. Clayton: Centre of Southeast Asian Studies, Monash University.
Bourchier, D., and J. Legge (eds). 1994. *Democracy in Indonesia: 1950s and 1990s*. Clayton: Centre of Southeast Asian Studies, Monash University.
Brenner, S.A. 1998. *The Domestication of Desire: Women, Wealth, and Modernity in Java*. Princeton: Princeton University Press.
———. 2007. Democracy, Polygamy, and Women in Post-*Reformasi* Indonesia. In *Identifying with Freedom: Indonesia after Suharto* (ed.) T. Day, 28–38. Oxford: Berghahn.
Bubandt, N. 2014. *Democracy, Corruption and the Politics of Spirits in Contemporary Indonesia*. Abingdon: Routledge.
Carothers, T. 2009. *Stepping Back from Democratic Pessimism*. Washington, DC: Carnegie Endowment for International Peace.
Carsten, J. 1995. The Substance of Kinship and the Heat of the Hearth: Feeding, Personhood, and Relatedness among Malays in Pulau Langkawi. *American Ethnologist* 22, no. 2: 223–241.
Chang, Y.T., Y.H. Chu and C.M. Park. 2007. Authoritarian Nostalgia in Asia. *Journal of Democracy* 18, no. 3: 66–80.
Chapin, B.L. 2010. 'We Have to Give': Sinhala Mothers' Responses to Children's Expression of Desire. *Ethos* 38, no. 4: 354–368.
Chodorow, N. J. 1999. *The Power of Feelings: Personal Meaning in Psychoanalysis, Gender, and Culture*. New Haven: Yale University Press.

Crouch, H. 1994. Democratic Prospects in Indonesia. In *Democracy in Indonesia: 1950s and 1990s* (eds) D. Bourchier and J. Legge, 115–127. Clayton: Centre of Southeast Asian Studies, Monash University.

Davies, J.E. 2009. Considering 'Self-Ful' Desire. *Psychoanalytic Psychology* 26, no. 3: 310–321.

Day, T. 2007. Introduction: Identifying with Freedom. In *Identifying with Freedom: Indonesia after Suharto* (ed.) T. Day, 1–18. Oxford: Berghahn.

Diamond, L. 2008. *The Spirit of Democracy: The Struggle to Build Free Societies Throughout the World*. New York: Times Books.

Faubion, J. 2011. *An Anthropology of Ethics*. Cambridge: Cambridge University Press.

Feith, H. 1963. Dynamics of Guided Democracy. In *Indonesia* (ed.) R.T. McVey, 309–409. New Haven: HRAF Press.

———. [1962] 2007. *The Decline of Constitutional Democracy in Indonesia*. Singapore: Equinox.

Ferme, M. 1998. The Violence of Numbers: Consensus, Competition and the Negotiation of Disputes in Sierra Leone. *Cahiers d'Etudes Africaines* 150–152, no. xxxviii–2–4: 555–580.

Good, B.J. 2012. Theorizing the 'Subject' of Medical and Psychiatric Anthropology. *Journal of the Royal Anthropological Institute* 18, no. 3: 515–535.

Graf, A. 2010. *Bahasa Reformasi: Political Rhetoric in Post-Suharto Indonesia*. Wiesbaden: Harrassowitz Verlag.

Hansen, T.B. 2012. *Melancholia of Freedom: Social Life in an Indian Township in South Africa*. Princeton: Princeton University Press.

Hartcher, P. 2013. Indonesia's Democracy at a Crossroads. *The Sydney Morning Herald*, 5 March.

Hasan, N. 2008. *Reformasi*, Religious Diversity, and Islamic Radicalism after Suharto. *Journal of Indonesian Social Sciences and Humanities* 1: 23–51.

Hickel, J. 2015. *Democracy as Death: The Moral Order of Anti-Liberal Politics in South Africa*. Berkeley: University of California Press.

Hollan, D. 2001. Developments in Person-Centred Ethnography. In *The Psychology of Cultural Experience* (eds) C.C. Moore and H.F. Mathews, 48–67. Cambridge: Cambridge University Press.

Hooker, V.M. 1993. New Order Language in Context. In *Culture and Society in New Order Indonesia* (ed.) V.M. Hooker, 272–293. Kuala Lumpur: Oxford University Press.

Kalinowski, T. 2007. Democracy, Economic Crisis, and Market Oriented Reforms: Observations from Indonesia and South Korea since the Asian Financial Crisis. *Comparative Sociology* 6, no. 3: 344–373.

Keeler, W. 1983. Shame and Stage Fright in Java. *Ethos* 11, no. 3: 152–165.

Kurlantzick, J. 2013. *Democracy in Retreat: The Revolt of the Middle Class and the Worldwide Decline of Representative Government*. New Haven: Yale University Press.

Long, N.J. 2013. *Being Malay in Indonesia: Histories, Hopes and Citizenship in the Riau Archipelago*. Singapore: NUS Press.

Lussier, D.N., and M.S. Fish. 2012. Indonesia: The Benefits of Civic Engagement. *Journal of Democracy* 23, no. 1: 70–84.

McVey, R.T. 1994. The Case of the Disappearing Decade. In *Democracy in Indonesia: 1950s and 1990s* (eds) D. Bourchier and J. Legge, 3–15. Clayton: Centre of Southeast Asian Studies, Monash University.

Merkel, W. 2010. Are Dictatorships Returning? Revisting the 'Democratic Rollback' Hypothesis. *Contemporary Politics* 16, no. 1: 17–31.

Michelutti, L. 2007. The Vernacularization of Democracy: Political Participation and Popular Politics in North India. *Journal of the Royal Anthropological Institute* 13, no. 3: 639–656.

Mietzner, M. 2009. Indonesia in 2008: Democratic Consolidation in Soeharto's Shadow. *Southeast Asian Affairs* 2009: 105–123.

———. 2014. How Jokowi Won and Democracy Survived. *Journal of Democracy* 25, no. 4: 111–125.

Milner, A.C. 1982. *Kerajaan: Malay Political Culture on the Eve of Colonial Rule.* Tucson: University of Arizona Press.

Nichter, M. 1981. Idioms of Distress: Alternatives in the Expression of Psychosocial Distress: A Case Study from South India. *Culture, Medicine and Psychiatry* 5, no. 4: 379–408.

Palmer, B. 2010. Services Rendered: Peace, Patronage and Post-Conflict Elections in Aceh. In *Problems of Democratisation in Indonesia: Elections, Institutions and Society* (eds) E. Aspinall and M. Mietzner, 286–306. Singapore: ISEAS.

Ratna Irtatik. 2012. Bebaskan Kemauan Anak; Berupaya Agar Istri Senang. *Batam Pos,* 31 August.

Simandjuntak, D. 2009. Milk Coffee at 10 AM: Encountering the State through Pilkada in North Sumatra. In *State of Authority: The State in Society in Indonesia* (eds) G. van Klinken and J. Barker, 73–94. Ithaca: Southeast Asia Program Publications, Cornell University.

Slater, D. 2007. The Ironies of Instability in Indonesia. In *Identifying with Freedom: Indonesia after Suharto* (ed.) T. Day, 95–104. Oxford: Berghahn.

Soeharto. 2003 [1967]. Pancasila Democracy. In *Indonesian Politics and Society: A Reader* (eds) D. Bourchier and V.R. Hadiz, 37–41. London and New York: RoutledgeCurzon.

Soetjipto Wirosardjono. 1994. Interpretation of the Current Scene. In *Democracy in Indonesia: 1950s and 1990s* (eds) D. Bourchier and J. Legge, 243–247. Clayton: Centre of Southeast Asian Studies, Monash University.

Tsuchiya, K. 1987. *Democracy and Leadership: The Rise of the Taman Siswa Movement in Indonesia* (trans. P. Hawkes). Honolulu: University of Hawai'i Press.

West, H. 2008. 'Govern Yourselves!': Democracy and Carnage in Northern Mozambique. In *Democracy: Anthropological Approaches* (ed.) J. Paley, 97–121. Santa Fe: SAR Press.

Nicholas J. Long is Assistant Professor of anthropology at the London School of Economics and Political Science.

4

Opposition and Group Formation
Authoritarianism Yesterday and Today

John Borneman

I. Authoritarianism in the Maternal Register

If any single characteristic defines authoritarianism in all its forms over time, it is hostility to opposition. By contrast, a central feature of democracy is that it must incorporate difference and opposition. Pluralism and social division are presupposed in the nomination 'the people' and in the political recognition of a 'loyal opposition' necessary for democracy to legitimate itself as political form. That pluralism must be performed as disturbance or negation, specifically in regularised elections, which reveal the divisions among the people and even threaten to exacerbate them. After all, the point of the election is to reincorporate divisions into a unity after election day (Lefort 1986; Borneman 2011: 153–165). Periodic dissolution of the whole and irruption of disunity reminds the ruling party or faction that reckoning with an opposition is not merely a ritual ruse but an ongoing feature of rule necessary to produce unity.

In thinking opposition, one is tempted to focus on the grand Opposition movements that brought down the authoritarian regimes in Latin America in the 1970s and East and Central Europe and the USSR after 1989. These movements were indeed historically crucial in opening the way for socio-political transformations, but they are oppositions with which we are familiar. They are Oppositions with a capital 'O'. One can find quite accurate depictions in Wikipedia. Such grand Oppositions could be witnessed in the Middle East and in Ukraine after 2012, though we can hardly be optimistic about their success in those places, as they provoked and strengthened new authoritarian movements as well as the political regimes that they opposed.

There are other kinds of opposition, however: less coherent, more diffuse, more peculiarly cultural in character and thus much more diverse in form and in relation to the social group forms they oppose. They are not only 'weapons of the weak', as James Scott (1985) might have it, nor do they always grow out of the everyday, or the heterodoxy of certain dispositions, as Pierre Bourdieu

(1977) theorised. What they are and how to identify them will be the object of this chapter, which will cast its net wide and focus less on these grand kinds of Opposition, but on those with a small 'o' and on their cultural sources. It will draw primarily from my own my experience and study in two very different states – East Germany (the GDR) and Syria. This comparison hopes to yield insight into the question of contemporary opposition by highlighting the radical difference in the historical traditions within which opposition in both countries has taken and takes form. Moreover, in all cases oppositions appeal not only to different traditions but also to different understandings of group affiliation. Two observations drive this focus: one is that we tend to neglect the culturally variable meanings of opposition because of an idealisation of the forms of grand Opposition that marked experience in the recent Cold War (Borneman 1993). There is, thus, widespread confusion, if not misrecognition, or an inability to bring fully into view, of both today's oppositions and today's forms of authoritarianism. The second is that the primary source for these new gestalts in authoritarianism and opposition is the advanced disintegration of what Max Weber (1978: 212–301) called 'traditional authority'.

The relation of opposition to tradition is often itself framed as an opposition: tradition is conservative, it stands for stability and authority, it militates against change and opposition. Yet the inverse relation characterises our contemporary world: the waning of traditional authority has been integral to pave the way for a new kind of authoritarianism, one that resists more commonplace definitions of politics, authority and opposition. Ever since the introduction of the concept of 'modernity' into the analytical lexicon, which one can date anywhere from the fifteenth to the eighteenth century, scholars from every theoretical perspective have observed challenges to and assaults on traditional authority as well as on the authority of traditions. This claim I pursue is therefore nothing new. Hegel and Marx were perhaps the first Western theorists to foreground how 'modernity' leads to the relentless undermining of all forms of traditional authority, beginning of course with the authority of kinship. Marx argued that capitalism as a form of production frees the individual to work as an automaton, independent of kin relations, integrating him (or her) into a system of formally free wage labour that misrecognises the value of his own labour while converting everything into the commodity form. This freedom that derives from capitalism, I suggest, is the engine that also drives the assault on tradition.

Nowadays, the relentless deconstruction of tradition in all its changing forms is increasingly associated with globalisation (also conceptualised in its relation to capital by Marx). Since the final collapse of a Second World socialist system in the 1990s, globalisation appears as a juggernaut, as an unstoppable process that, to some degree, facilitates the penetrations of all ideologies, markets and goods. This collapse has created the positive conditions for the resurgence of authoritarianism on both sides of the former Cold War divide, of a type no longer opposed to, but counterintuitively allied with, democracy and individualism. Much like fascism was the radicalisation of a potential within democratic form, the new authoritarianism appears to be a radicalisation of democracy when paired with a victorious global capitalism. In this sense, the failure of political or religious authorities to constrain capitalism, or, more radically stated, their total capitulation to the logic of capital accumulation, contributes to the weakening of tradition (Streeck 2014). The hijacking of democratic process is in fact apparent in many contemporary political formations, characterised by Colin Crouch (2004) as 'post-democracy', wherein wealthy elites control the political classes and the terms of debate in which political action is defined.

In those cases where 'tradition' is still marshalled to oppose political authority, it is most often in the name of a regressive if not repressive tradition or closed community. Christian evangelists, the Russian Orthodox Church, ultraorthodox Jews and Islamists are just a few of the many religious movements that seek to reinstate tradition in accord with a regressive, reactionary logic. But appeals for restoration are also made to secular traditions of, for example, nuclear families, social clubs or tribal authorities. In the United States, the argument of the waning of tradition and its relation to secular authority is often framed by the conservative diagnosis of the political scientist Robert Putnam (2000). He argues that the decline in participation in traditional civic organisations (he laments the waning of 1950s forms of communitarian participation) undermines democratic participation. While acknowledging his empirical claim, we might also pay more attention to how new forms of social organisation that have no direct connection to democratic participation, such as increasingly suburban or exurban residential populations (no longer primarily urban or rural), have undermined the formation and reproduction of socially cohesive groups and escaped many of the traditional controls of legal authorities while strengthening authoritarianism (Borneman 2011). We might also counter the thesis of the disengagement from politics by noting for the period that Putnam examines the growth of other forms of social groups and mobilisations, for example, both left-oriented social movements centred around civil rights and minority inclusions, and well-financed right-oriented movements for property rights, religious expression and guns, and against immigrants, minorities, and the poor.

Part of the problem with both conceptions of tradition, Putnam's conservative-liberal and the right-oriented one, is surely the attempt to fix the meaning of the present in the past. Along these lines, Vincent Crapanzano (2001) argues that by insisting all present must be filtered through a literalist understanding of the past, such religious and secular movements close the community off to its 'others' and hence undermine a central condition of democracy as a particular way of organising the political. In any event, it is important to note that under pressures of global capitalism, both new configurations of nationalism and claims to represent a single invariable 'tradition' result in peculiar forms of individualism, and tend to operate today not in the name-of-the-father or symbolic register but in a maternal one.

The heuristic of paternal and maternal registers I take from psychoanalysis, specifically from reformulations by Melanie Klein and Jacques Lacan of Freud's typology of mind. Whereas Freud had concentrated on the role of the paternal in his typology id, ego and superego, Klein shifted the focus to the pre-Oedipal or maternal relation to the child. Lacan, in turn, rethought the Oedipal tension in his triangulation of Imaginary, Symbolic, and Real registers (see e.g. Lacan 1956: 29–52, 1958: 575–584). Scholars of the political field have largely ignored the maternal and concentrated on what Lacan identifies as the name-of-the-father – i.e., rules of descent and succession, political oratory, disciplinary power. Here I would like to focus on how tension between the paternal and maternal (or what Lacan calls the Imaginary) is sustained and resolved in the political field.[1]

The Imaginary of the maternal register – of oneness, unity and fullness – exerts a very strong pull on the psyche, an integrative pull that makes it difficult to say no; it is in fact constructed around the absence of negativity. If, indeed, what we are seeing today is authoritarianism in the maternal register, then the difficulty of articulating an opposition to contemporary authoritarianism is even more understandable. Before analysing the dynamics of opposition and authoritarianism in the two specific cases of East Germany and Syria, I want to suggest one way to anticipate opposition: the identification of disruptions.

II. Four Disruptions

If the forms of opposition are changing, then we must be open to identifying a wider range of disruptions as possible modes of significant opposition than has characterised our recent past. Consider four scenes of recent disruption that might express some of the central characteristics and conundrums of opposition in four different places today. They should not be understood as exemplary for opposition; I chose them opportunistically as a range of sites where opposition might be fruitfully analysed.

Disruption One

The first involves a conversation with an Iraqi scholar teaching in Oman whom I met last autumn at an institute in France. He is a very large, gentle man, quiet, reticent, self-directed, an impulsive buyer, generous, obviously traumatised by his war experiences but able to hold this experience at a distance from himself. He is a married man with three grown children, Sunni – meaning orthodox Muslim – and he has never once tasted alcohol, nor pork, though he does have a taste for 'young beautiful girls', as he puts it. After the fall of the regime, in 2002, he was voted dean of the School of Arts and Design in Baghdad.

'That must have been a very dangerous time', I said. He replied, 'I drove with a pistol in one hand, the steering wheel in the other.' 'That was a time of major looting. The university was looted also, wasn't it?' I asked. He described:

> They took everything, chairs, bathroom fixtures, and all of our computers in the School of Design. I knew who took them, an Islamist group from a neighbourhood nearby. I wrote them a letter asking to return them. They said, 'All you do is dance

and sing there in the arts school. We don't approve of that.' So I wrote another letter, with a make-believe letterhead, stating I was dean of the Islamic School of Design and would like the computers back. They returned the computers.

Disruption Two

My second disruption is the scandal of Pussy Riot. This band of young women with mediocre voices and sense of musicality performed some heavy metal music in front of an altar in a Russian Orthodox church. They wore masks, made aggressive kind of fuck-you arm movements in their dance, mocked Muslim and Christian prayer, and appealed to the Virgin Mary to intervene against Vladimir Putin. For this, they were arrested, tried, sentenced and given long and variable prison terms. Putin was chastened by various world leaders, including former U.S. Secretary of State Hilary Clinton and German Chancellor Angela Merkel – but to no avail. Their performance went viral on the internet, and they became a Russian and international *cause celebre* while imprisoned or in hiding.

Disruption Three

My third example is the writing of graffiti by youths in Syria, which led to their arrest and torture, and unwittingly provoked a countrywide uprising. In early March 2011, in the city of Dara'a, police arrested fifteen children, aged 9 to 15, all belonging to the Al-Abazeed family, for writing a slogan: 'the people want to topple the regime', on the wall of their school. After the children were detained, rumour has it that members of their families approached General Atef Najeeb, the cousin of Bashar al Assad, to ask for their freedom, and the general responded, 'I'll release your children only if you bring me their mothers [to replace them].' Word spread and demonstrations, initially spontaneous gatherings with dancing and taunting of the authorities in the streets, followed immediately all over Syria, except for in the two central cities, Damascus and Aleppo, which followed a year later. Within a year this disturbance had metamorphosed into something else: a full-scale revolution and civil war engulfing the entire country. By April 2013 the situation gave rise to a reactionary yet new political form, the so-called Islamic State in Iraq and Syria, established in western Iraq and eastern Syria, but aimed at a worldwide caliphate.

Disruption Four

The fourth disturbance involves a German scandal that took place in December 2012 and January 2013, caused by the accusation of anti-Semitism levelled at columnist and editor Jacob Augstein by the journalist Henryk Broder. The Simon-Wiesenthal Centre in Vienna had already placed Augstein on its list of the ten worst anti-Semites for criticising Israel and comparing ultraorthodox Jews to Islamic fundamentalists. Broder then accused Augstein of preparing through 'propaganda the next Final Solution of the Jewish question – this time in Palestine'. Augstein has generally followed a politics similar to that of his progressive father, Rudolf, long-time editor of the respected weekly *Der Spiegel* and one of the most steadfast and outspoken supporters of Aleksandr Solzhenitsyn and other East European dissidents during the Cold War. Broder has been highly honoured and respected in Germany for his courage and sharp wit, but he is also well known for his cynicism and, more recently, cheap provocations. The month after this accusation, he apologised 'only' for his 'dramatisation' of events, he emphasised, not for his accusations. In his apology, he argued it was not right to compare Palestinians today with Jews in Germany during the Third Reich: 'A chicken coop is not a KZ [concentration camp], the Muslims are not the Jews of today.'

* * *

These disruptions, disturbances and scandals are examples of opposition to contemporary kinds of authoritarianism. We might think of them as indexing culturally specific sources and sites of opposition in Iraq, Russia, Syria and Germany. It is also constructive to compare them temporally, as a group, to the fundamentally different principled opposition that marked the Cold War, to the scenes of Soviet bloc 'dissidents' leading up to the grand Oppositions of 1989. Take as examples two central oppositional figures who became more important in the years of the waning of the Cold War: the poet and singer Wolf Biermann in East Germany and the writer Aleksandr Solzhenitsyn in the USSR. The governments of East Germany and the Soviet Union denounced Biermann and Aleksandr Solzhenitsyn, respectively, as traitors. Biermann was denounced as a 'class traitor' and forbidden to publish his music or perform in 1963, then stripped of his citizenship in 1976 while on an official concert tour in the West. Solzhenitsyn was imprisoned in a work gulag in 1945, sentenced to internal exile until 1956, and after a period of relative freedom deported to West Germany in 1974 (Borneman 1993).

On the surface, these contemporary disturbances appear less serious, even humorous when compared to the dissidents of the Cold War. Back then, Western governments often protested loudly the persecution of dissidents, at times even sacrificing other foreign policy and exchange goals in order to claim the moral high ground of human rights. Today, governments on both sides of the former divide are themselves persecuting dissidents. Russia's Vladimir Putin has sidelined – through harassment, arrest and murder – journalists and political rivals, basically any figure who might represent some kind of opposition to his authority. In the United States, the prosecutions of Bradley Manning for his release of war documents, and Julian Assange for publicising them through WikiLeaks, are perhaps the most notoriously scandalous part of an attack on informing the public through a free press. Problems of comparability aside, attacks on opposition to the two governments suggest that the stakes today for authoritarianism within governments of all kinds are equally high.

An analysis of these four disturbances in terms of their significance would necessarily take us into four very different cultural contexts. Briefly, the first example involves the inclusions and exclusions of Iraqi Islamists who are moving from Cold War marginality to the assertion of oppositional power. A minor event that remained local in meaning is actually the acting out of a conflict on a small stage that is happening in the entire MENA region. The second is of young female performers' opposition to the Russian President Putin, often dubbed the new czar (much as Mohammed Morsi in Egypt is called the new pharaoh); with the aid of digital virality made possible by the internet, they became an international scandal, an iconic identification for a world audience, but with little consequence within Russia. The third example, of schoolyard play – writing on the wall – exposed an at-the-time unspeakable thought, namely that Syrians could challenge and bring down their authoritarian regime, much like citizens had done in Tunisia, Egypt, Yemen and Libya; it also signals the importance of the register of the mother or the maternal (the mother here is asked to replace the unruly youths in jail) in disruption. The fourth example, of Henryk Broder's accusation of anti-Semitism, is what I would call an opposition in search of something to oppose. It appears Broder's goal is to reduce to silence any possible criticism of (or opposition to) Israel's scandalous 'politicide' against Palestinians (Kimmerling 2002).

III. The Political Field

Regardless of whose definition of authoritarianism we turn to, most build on the important systematising work of Yale political scientist Juan Linz (2000) and include a similar set of interrelated criteria: concentration of power at the top maintained through repressive means, including the police and military as well as the state bureaucracy, submission to authority, unaccountable if not unchecked exercise of power, and intolerance of meaningful opposition. Linz's work, as well as my own, grew out of a consideration of authoritarian rule during the Cold War. These criteria seemed sufficient to represent the political and economic forms of authoritarianism of that time extending from the countries of East Central Europe, to South Korea, Southeast Asia, China and to some of the countries in Africa and Latin America.

As standards or principles for government, they remain extremely useful. But they were formulated solely with a view from the top, and from a narrowly defined political field. If seen phenomenologically or ethnographically, from the experience of people, however, our analytical perspective might change, especially if we want to account for the variability in political fields: the forms of authoritarianism, the modes of relating to difference and division they foster in everyday life, and the diverse ways in which groups of people depart from authoritarian rule and introduce more democratic rule. With these three emphases in mind – variability of, relationships in and departures from authoritarianism, let us narrow on only one criterion identified by Linz, on the intolerance of meaningful opposition. But rather than focus on this intolerance, let us look at opposition itself and ask: From where does the opposition come? And under what conditions is it institutionalised?

IV. Turn Taking

One particular practice is of ultimate importance in institutionalising opposition in a democratic system, and that is the practice of turn taking. It is something quite obvious but analytically fruitful as it exists in every society and parallels can be found at every level of society, from top to bottom. The significance of turn taking is not my discovery. I was first led to contemplate it seriously as a principle in an essay by the system theorist Niklas Luhmann, who posited turn taking as a fundamental principle of democratic rule.

Luhmann (1990: 175, see 167–183) maintains that the 'binary code of government/opposition', which structures democratic political systems, replaced the single, unchallengeable head arrangement of the kingship or feudal estate in Europe. I have elsewhere extended Luhmann's insight to argue that the key principle at stake in *democratic* elections is turn taking, which is driven either by a logic of sacrifice or representation (Borneman 2011). In democratic elections, as opposed to those in authoritarian systems, the ruler or ruling party must regularly risk being replaced. That is, rulers must sacrifice their hold on power to take turns with the opposition. The longer the incumbent person or party remains in power, the less 'democratic' a regime becomes, the more elections are dominated by a logic of representation rather than of sacrifice. Ritual elections become merely displays of the power of representation rather than a means of obligatory turn taking. In a democracy the leader or leading party remains legitimate only to the extent that it maintains itself as distinct from a viable opposition, with which it takes turns in ruling. In other words, in a democracy opposition is not just an inconvenience: the ruler needs an opposition in order to claim legitimacy. Unlike a religious order in which 'the elect' claim to be chosen by a god (to whom the elect claim to have unique access), modern secular elections assume the people elect their leaders in a ritual periodically repeated so that leaders are subject to recall. Authoritarian systems often fake such elections, as the outcome is predetermined, or, if a loss is likely, then victory is fabricated and the importance of the opposition is denied. In short, one of the telltale signs of an authoritarian turn is when the logic of representation becomes the dominant ideological take on politics; in that case the logic of sacrifice becomes a footnote to the ideology of the power of the people.

This principle of turn taking does not belong to the domain of politics alone (where Luhmann initially locates it) nor is it merely practised by adults. As part of any essential socialisation, children must learn turn taking in play, in sport, in music. The alternative to taking turns is to dominate, to single-mindedly pursue one's own interests rather than define oneself in a fluid and ongoing relation to others. In refusing to take turns, one risks being branded as antisocial. Turn taking is a principle that any domestic couple knows well, a constant spectre of fairness and reciprocity that haunts all practice, whether it involves dishwashing, house-cleaning, cooking, childcare or even sexual play. I am not arguing that to practise turn taking is easy or instinctual. It must be learned through experience, and it is very difficult to sustain, as we know from our own relationships and the departments and institutions in which we work. It is more generally a challenge to all patriarchal systems, and more specifically to patrilineal descent systems.

V. Bilateral Descent as Institutionalised Opposition

Rule through male descent alone – more technically, patrilineal organisation in the service of agnatic lineage – arose in the mid-eleventh century in Germany, and around the same time in much of the rest of Europe. Originating in noble families, it became a major organising principle of the feudal orders of medieval societies (Leyser 1968: 32–36; Herlihy 1985: 92; Goody 1983: 223). At the same time, however, it coexisted with the principle of bilateral descent – inheritance through male and female lines – which in most contexts competed with agnatic descent (Leyser 1979). Jack Goody (1983) argues that bilateral descent was one of the most important and distinctive features of European kinship, significant for gender organisation generally, but also as the specific mode (the inheritance of widows) in which the Catholic Church accumulated property.

The introduction of bilateral descent creates a bifurcated source of power that derives from the ability to marshal both male and female lineages to appropriate history, memory and resources for one's own purpose (Goody 1983: 223). Bilateral descent acknowledges difference and division at an ideational level, and hence contains within it the notion of freedom and choice over permanence and fate. At the psychological level, it also presents a challenge to patriarchy and to the name-of-the-father. The woman's power comes from the recognition of a source of authority incommensurable with the man's, and that source has since been institutionalised, in the form of, first, a dowry, inheritance the woman brings into marriage and retains, then bilateral descent generally. This principle shadows power that is concentrated in the name of a single authority. All of this has changed considerably today, in the West especially, as power is structurally fragmented, with many alternative sources. Women and men are often now defined as equals, neither as ontologically incommensurate nor as having supplemental qualities. The introduction of same-sex marriage, for example, makes men and women commensurable and exchangeable, and thus challenges the very grounds on which the principle of turn taking initially drew its strength. The value given to radical equality makes turn taking an expedient rather than a necessary principle, and in this way can undermine the democratic notion of a necessary opposition.

Where I am going with this is that to the dissidents in the GDR who drew on this cultural principle for legitimising the act of opposition, the dissolution of that state marked the end of the particular way in which agnatic descent – the ruling gerontocracy – had fostered intolerance to opposition. Political opposition in Syria also has cultural sources. The question comparatively, in other countries, is what role bilateral and agnatic descent play in legitimating rule and opposition. Syria, as I explain below, like the former GDR, is currently ruled by a leader, Bashar al Assad, who claims legitimacy in part through his relation to his deceased father. Yet most Syrians in everyday life also practise a form of bilateral descent. The relation of bilateral descent to political authority has never been explored, to my knowledge. The dissolution of the Assad rule in Syria, if and when that ultimately occurs, may also mark the end of agnatic descent at the level of rule. Bilateral descent, as an alternative mode of investing authority, may then become more important in informing the political. It might give rise to an idea of the necessity of institutional opposition, which both challenges agnatic descent and makes it possible to legitimate and institutionalise the principle of turn taking at multiple levels of social organisation.

VI. East German Authoritarianism and the Tradition of Opposition

At the level of the political regime, now more narrowly conceived, what is the relation of opposition and of the patriarchal structures of descent to authoritarian rule? Theoretically informative for the relation of opposition to contemporary authoritarianism is an ethnographic comparison of former East Germany with Syria today. First, to the former German Democratic Republic. Founded in 1949 in the Soviet Zone of occupation of Germany, it represented itself as a 'worker and farmer state', a people's democracy that both broke with the 'national socialism', or fascism, of the Third Reich and was opposed to the bourgeois liberal state of the West. The initial democratic impetus and multiparty system of representation was fairly quickly streamlined, with a Soviet-Leninist model Socialist Unity Party (SED) accumulating all power while retaining the formal structure of alternative parties. Outside the relatively free domain of cultural production, progressive voices were silenced and often forced into exile. Even the voice of workers became suspect, culminating in a 1953 anti-Stalinist worker uprising that was brutally repressed.

By 1981, when I entered the country for the first time, the ruling politburo had become the enclave of a male gerontocracy. The one younger member, Egon Krenz, had been the officially dubbed 'crown prince', the designated heir apparent to Eric Honecker, but he was a product of the Kader system and offered no distinctive difference to his elders, and thus did not represent his own generation (Jarausch 1994: 59). Alternative environmental and peace movements found a home in the Lutheran Church, and by 1989 served to spearhead a non-violent revolution, which led to the dissolution of the state in 1990 and the incorporation of its territory and people into the West German state. Other factors, especially economic problems associated with the declining importance of heavy industry and a planned economy, and the obvious superiority of West Germany and the Western European political-economic model, were equally if not more important than the limitations of an overly centralised political authority for the ultimate dissolution of the GDR (cf. Borneman 1992; Fulbrook 2005; Jarausch 1994; Maier 1997)

One factor peculiar to citizens of the GDR, which they shared with West Germans and some other Europeans, was a very recent prior experience of authoritarianism from which they had supposedly departed. I will return later to this prior experience of departure, which implies the development of historical consciousness. For now, I want draw attention to how East German rulers had to distance themselves from the spectre of Nazi totalitarianism and its principle of *Gleichschaltung*. A concept coined in 1933, *Gleichschaltung* means 'coordination', 'making the same', 'bringing into line', in other words, a process to eliminate diversity or pluralism in both public and private life. While the East German government may have welcomed such coordination to facilitate its policies of centralisation and uniformisation, the people had a recent experience that led many of them to be sceptical of sameness and coercive unity. And they could not escape the comparison, even if a repressed recognition that remained unconscious, to a freer West German society and state, which, under Allied occupation, became openly conflictual and pluralistic over time. Citizen scepticism about the goal of sameness along with an ideological embrace of social equality sustained a tension with the authoritarian state's attempt to monopolise and control everyday life, legitimated through the Leninist dogma of the party's leading role. Yet even the ruling Socialist Unity Party officially represented itself as merely the leading political party and not the only one, leaving a space open for the argument of turn taking.

Thus in October 1989 when citizens of the GDR began to mobilise and demonstrate publicly, they looked to several prior generations of critics, especially to those critics of Leninism from the early part of the century rather than to the later critics of Nazi totalitarianism. One of the frequently repeated slogans by regime opponents was a statement by the Communist theorist Rosa Luxemburg, who had been murdered in 1919 in Berlin with the aid of the Social Democratic government. In her criticism of Lenin's doctrine of a dictatorship of the party after the October Revolution in Russia, she had written:

> *Freiheit nur für die Anhänger der Regierung, nur für Mitglieder einer Partei – mögen sie noch so zahlreich sein – ist keine Freiheit. Freiheit ist immer Freiheit des Andersdenkenden.*
>
> [Freedom for only the followers of the regime, for only members of the party – even if they are numerous – is not freedom. Freedom is always the freedom of those who think differently.]

'Freedom is always the freedom of those who think differently' became a rallying cry written on banners and placards held in demonstrations used to mobilise an opposition against the authoritarian rule by the SED. It contains within it a trenchant critique of authoritarianism in any form, but especially of the idea that a ruler, leading party, or dominant ideology might be legitimate without first securing freedom for those who differ, for those people or ideas that are outside the ruling clique or normative framework.

The most important question regarding any departure from authoritarianism is how to avoid producing a similar authoritarianism in what follows. In the chaos of change, it is tempting to dismiss less established voices and turn back to an authoritarian leader or system. But nothing is automatic when it comes to the departure from or reproduction of a political form. In their discomfort with negotiating differences, democracies can easily slide into authoritarianism; authoritarian forms can yield to recognition of pluralism within and to democratic process; monarchies can evolve into constitutional republics, or such republics can also become dictatorships. And reformed or reforming authoritarian systems can readily regress back into authoritarian systems. Not only does each birth produce a different kind of baby, but the set of institutions intended to raise this baby function within an inherited cultural context that carries a particular historical resonance. That context and its influence is what used to be analysed as 'tradition'. When it comes to political form, cultural traditions matter greatly, and, irrespective of actual political form, a culture with an ideology and a history of legitimate and institutionalised opposition always contains within it a democratic reflex.

Scholars and political activists in twentieth-century Germany elaborated such a tradition, and some citizens in both of the German states in the Cold War continually confronted their leaders with this tradition. In the West, for example, this tradition was most apparent in a culture of public demonstration, which achieved its fullest expression during the 1980s: every demonstration seemed to provoke a counter-demonstration. In the East, by contrast, where the regime feared any large public demonstration it had not itself organised, there was in fact an older legal mechanism, the *Eingabe*, or petition, which citizens used to make personal claims on an unresponsive state, ranging from requests to travel in the West, to resolve local conflicts, or access to consumer goods (Borneman 1991: 71–81).

These everyday traditions informed the behaviour of ruling elites in unexpected ways. One of the most perverse was in a meeting of the Central Committee of the GDR politburo on 17 October 1989. The question posed was how or even whether the leadership, which had been radically called into question through mass demonstrations, should continue to rule. Eric Honecker, head of state and party, raised his own hand to vote himself out of office, paving the way for what the Czechs and Slovaks later dubbed a Velvet Revolution. What followed the collapse of these regimes we know well: political parties proliferated and citizens of all backgrounds began to publicly articulate their interests, East Germany was legally re-incorporated into the West through a popular vote and the renamed and later expanded ruling party became in effect one faction in the opposition, in some provinces even entering into ruling coalitions with other parties. In the decades that have elapsed since the dissolution of the GDR, a vigorous multiparty competition has established itself, along with a new protest culture that runs the gamut of right and left ideologies.

VII. Syrian Authoritarianism, Agnatic Descent, the *Umma*

Syria shares with the former GDR two of the central characteristics that Linz attributes to authoritarianism: adherence to the principles of patriarchal rule and affiliation with Leninist one-party-rule socialism through the rule of the Ba'ath Party. It also shares with the GDR one characteristic Linz does not mention: inheritance structured around unequally valued but nonetheless bilateral descent. Here I would like to turn to descent as part of a specific discussion of the relation of kinship to group formation and political authority. Kinship, as I am using the term, means not merely a model of and for the organisation of society and politics, as in Ibn Khaldun's classic elaboration of *asabiyya* [clan or group solidarity]. It is also a model of libidinal desires, that is, for the relations that make the impulse to live and to destroy into collective patterns. Kinship is never simply the organisation of affinities at the level of family and clan, nor is it only the extension of these principles to patron-client relations, nepotism and corrupt networks – although these are, of course, important aspects (cf. Joseph 1999). Kinship teaches us both *how* to organise our relations to the world and how those worlds *should* be organised. In short, kinship should not be seen as a micro-organisation of society apart from the macro-organisation of the state, but as the principles of affiliation and alliance, of identification and differentiation, that endow meaning and grant cultural legitimacy to all social and political forms, including the state.

Although it appears today that the Syrian opposition in all its multiplicity is driven and controlled by men, women initially played an active role in much of the behind-the-scenes organising, and they continue to play a huge if not dominant role in organising refugee life for the half of the population displaced in the current civil war. That so little is made of the turn taking that actually characterises decision making in Syrian families I would attribute to the dominance of paradigms in political science and economics that focus on representations in the public sphere alone, and to general theoretical blindness about the significance of kinship on the part of analysts.

Much like the GDR, the Syrian political regimes of the last half-century tried to eliminate any opposition, though in the recent uprising the regime turned to measures more extreme than in the GDR, such as mass incarceration and mass killing. Since the uprising began in March 2011, the Assad regime has even resorted to firing skud missiles and chemical weapons into, and dropping barrel bombs packed with TNT, rebar, nails and machine scrap on residential neighbourhoods. In both the GDR and Syria, the principle of succession to high office followed the logic of authority in the name-of-the-father: Krenz should follow Honecker and Bashar should follow Hafez. The power of the patriline is merely a cover for the more significant process of nominating, in the sense of the ability to legislate and prohibit, the ability to name, designate, voice, to bring into speech, and the power to appoint, to fill the offices of the institution.

Syria's revolution began like that in East Germany two decades prior, with peaceful opposition and unarmed revolt that spread among neighbouring countries. Yet the conditions for departure from authoritarianism in Syria could not be more different from those in the GDR because the cultural sources for opposition vary. For one, Syrian patriarchy has neither the negative legacy of the Nazis nor a pan-national democratic theorist like Rosa Luxemburg to contend with. For another, the Syrian revolt began under very different circumstances, those framed by the self-immolation of the street vendor Mohamed Bouazizi in early March 2011, in Tunisia, which set off revolts in several other Arabic-speaking countries. This was a sacrifice not in the name of representation but in the name of sacrifice alone: the only adequate compensation for self-immolation would be another sacrifice of equal or greater value, that is, in this case, political immolation: a resignation and regime change.[2]

In Syria, President Bashar al Assad and his ruling Ba'ath Party have, unlike Honecker and the regime in East Germany, instead steadfastly refused to relinquish power, or to engage the opposition groups in any meaningful way. Bashar demanded that the people – diverse groups largely organised by tribe, sect and religion – follow him blindly, in the name of a united Syria. He did this even though he belongs to a minority branch of Shi'a Islam, the Alawites. Malise Ruthven (2011: 3) pointedly characterises this political form as 'a military state controlled by a kinship group bound by tribal loyalties underpinned by a minority faith'. The Alawites make up approximately 12 per cent of the population, while the majority Sunnis make up almost 75 per cent.

Bashar's father Hafez al Assad had seized power in a bloodless intra-party military coup in 1970. And while he created a vast system of nepotism and encouraged a formal and secular peace between groups, he solidified his power through control of the party machinery and expansion of secret police to sow mistrust generally among the populace. In 2000, after his father's death, Bashar inherited the position of leader: first he was appointed as head of the party and army, then elected president unopposed. Bashar, like his father, consistently favoured Alawites, packing the state, economy and military with his own kin, while simultaneously installing a principle of representation and distribution, but not of sacrifice, whereby some members of each social group enjoyed some of the spoils of the system while Assad and his coterie retained all power with no principle of turn taking.

In other words, we have here not only a patriarch but a classic tyrant who claims legitimacy in the exercise of political power through agnatic descent. But that tyrant has no general cultural legitimacy. The Assads did appeal to forms of legitimacy that do not draw from culturally specific norms such as patrilineal descent. For example, the Assad regime was often praised for keeping Syria out of the internecine conflicts that bled the neighbouring countries – Lebanon, Israel and Iraq – of so much vitality. And the regime was praised for offering a home to Syria's various Christian minorities and its Palestinian residents, for the relative stability and freedom from religious and political persecution that these minorities especially valued in light of their treatment by the regimes from which many of them fled.

For the discussion of opposition, the most important difference in the patriarchal rule of Arab countries generally is their lacking the cultural history of the feudal system of medieval Europe, in which a hierarchical order of fathers was legitimated by links between his different instances. In Germany this was the linking of the king to *Gottesvater*, *Landesvater*, *Doktorvater* and *Familienvater*, each resting on the others in a hierarchical order (Borneman 2004). The cultural-political history of Arab countries does not replicate the European feudal system. Arab rulers of the postcolonial order did not build their rule on an order of fathers but instead either created theocratic and monarchic forms, as in the Gulf states and Morocco, with fictive genealogies entitling them to permanent rule, or morphed into secular despots as in Egypt, Iraq, Libya and Syria, where rule involved usurping and undermining local tribal and paternal authorities.

The lack of an order of the father has consequences for the longevity of structures of authority. In Syria, as mentioned, Bashar's father claimed authority as a member of a minority group through an intra-party coup, not through the authority of lineage. And he secured that authority neither by drawing on paternal descent systems nor by strengthening local patriarchs, but by usurping their authority and expanding internal policing. Then he increasingly turned his instruments of state, the entire security apparatus along with the bureaucracy, against the poor and the middle classes, betraying much of the socialist project of the Ba'ath Party, purging it of its founding generation and their ideology (Borneman 2007).

These authoritarian policies further weakened the lineages of families of notables (Batatu 1999). Moreover, the post-1989 collapse of the markets and support systems of the socialist bloc, in the context of weakness and division within pan-Arab alliances and regimes and an ascendant Israeli power, further undermined the ability of local patriarchs and family fathers to secure adequate futures for themselves and their increasingly educated and informed children. Several generations of young men have been forced to try and find work abroad, and many have been successful. In short, even before the youth-initiated revolts began in March 2011, the Syrian authoritarian state had seriously weakened the authority of the father. And because forms of identification with the Assads, and by extension with the authoritarian state they developed, were only lightly, if at all, resting on kin loyalties, the survival strategy of the regime could not draw from the life of local authorities but instead was positioned in fundamental opposition to them.

Despite these repressions by the government and the apparatuses at the regime's disposal, kin groups remain strong and amazingly resilient in Syria, specifically, as they do in all Arab societies. In fact, kin loyalties have always been central to sustaining the various communities that make up Syrian diversity, and they form a cultural base of hospitality and inclusion that is formally at odds with the paranoid, repressive state apparatus. However, these various kin-based communities, though all patriarchal, operate in the register of the maternal, the *umma*, not the father, the *ab*. The principle of unity that unites each is maternal, not an order of the father or law. The concept of maternal register has many connotations, referring at times to descent through the mother and, as I am using the term here, to a set of maternal meanings (nondivision, sameness, care) defined within a particular cultural system.

While in the last half-century people may have retained a strong identification with the Syrian nation, many did not think the regime and its ordering principles represented the national unit. At the same time, what were imagined as primordial communities never lost their glitter; unities were not imagined alongside the registers of division and discipline. After Hafez el Assad's 1982 massacre in Hama, which quashed the revolt instigated by the Muslim Brotherhood, most Syrians reluctantly submitted to the authority of the political regime in Syria, but this did not translate into identification with its leaders. That submission appeared to be at an end in 2011, but the regime fought back, tenaciously, and as of this writing appears to have secured for itself a prominent role in future rule.

In talking of the maternal register, the *umma*, I want to draw attention to the fact that initially the moments of revolt, or movements in what is misleadingly called an 'Arab Spring', could hardly be called uprisings *against* the father or *for* any specific order or leadership that might unite the various social divisions. The general sentiment to get rid of autocracy cannot be equated with a general sentiment to install democracy. To be sure, the conscious motivations of the participants, both active instigators and passive supporters, are extremely varied. What we know is that the protests began largely as youth protests, and included men and women. Following Bouazizi's self-immolation, the protests everywhere were initially peaceful. In Syria, specifically, they appeared to be motivated more by calls for *karama* [dignity], *kefāya* [enough] and *al hurriyyah* [freedom or liberty] than to advance any particular idea of order.[3] *Hurriyyah* is a passion, understood in the register of the mother, a passion in the first instance to be free of the tyrannical father, of the corrupt old order, of the fear on which that order was based, but also to bind and connect, to trust, to feel secure, to unite the masses. Because the focus was not on democracy itself, this binding was imagined without reckoning with social divisions, such as between those who want a strict Islamic state, full of prohibitions, and radical secular democrats who want to shrink religion in public life in the name of abstract freedoms. The absence of the father, the absence of a concern with law and order, is one of the most striking characteristics of the uprisings, and once we acknowledge this fact, it should lead us to rethink the importance of the maternal register in what is happening.

Political revolts are most frequently interpreted solely in the register of the father as being about descent, hierarchical or anti-hierarchical, marked by difference and exclusion, and by the desire to rule over rather than to simply be like each other. Descent in Syria, I have been arguing, had already been seriously disturbed by the regime's delegitimisation of local patriarchs, who were seen as rival sources of authority. The register of the mother, by contrast, remained largely intact. It is another imaginative sphere altogether, one of affiliation, of being alike, of unity and completeness, inclusiveness and nurture. It is the register in which the Muslim Brotherhood operated for years in the Middle East, being both in opposition to the 'corrupt' executives of the ruling parties and offering inclusive care at the local level even to those who disagreed with them politically. Psychodynamically speaking, both vertical ties and horizontal attachments are at stake in any group organisation: the vertical, as relations of descent, are in the register of the father; the horizontal, as relations of affinity, are in the register of the mother.

As authoritarian governments are overthrown and leaders are killed, imprisoned, or driven into exile, forms of affinity, attachment and solidarity are of primary importance in building the new community. In the peculiar balance between maternal and paternal registers, these Arab uprisings share little with European-style popular revolutions of the last four centuries. There was, for example, no comparable 'storming of the Bastille', no event agreed in retrospect to mark the end of authoritarian orders, even though many leaders were eliminated and regimes unseated. In any event, the Euro-American wish for democratic form under the rule of law in semi-autonomous, centralised states is unlikely to be the outcome of these revolutions. While the potential for tectonic shifts in rule in the MENA region are indeed palpable, the trajectory of change will not be dependent on visible political forms because of the disconnect between these forms and everyday orders of cultural legitimacy. Rather, new configurations of authority will be inspired by the local dynamics of group identification, which are fundamentally different from what they were in Europe and America during the Age of Revolution. Group identification, in turn, is a learned behaviour, learned through the practice of kinship relations or kinship analogues.

In Arabic-speaking countries, the primary political community is the *umma*, and new communities, I reiterate once more, are being imagined in the register of the mother [*umm*] and not the father [*ab*]. The *umma* could refer to an imagined community of a country, a city, or a kinship group, or it could be an imagined caliphate, or Islamic polity, extending from southern Spain to Indonesia. It does not specify a particular political form. Although community can be imagined as an ageless source of authority without appeal to descent, my attention to the maternal register should not imply that community can operate without attention to the vertical, to descent systems or leaders, to difference and division. To be sure, the spectral or real return of the father always shadows relations of affiliation and ideas of unity, and is especially present when a community dissolves and seeks to reshape itself after the death of the leader/father. In other words, given the indeterminacy of political form at this moment, there is a distinct possibility of a return to the vision of a patriarchal order and the reassertion of a principle of agnatic descent alone, as appears to have been the failed strategy of the Muslim Brotherhood and Salafis in Egypt, for example, or the military regime that followed.

This said, the imagination of future community is not controlled by those authoritarian rulers still in control at this moment in time. Principles of the *umma* and agnatic descent are both at play, especially among the youths who have led the uprisings. Their visions for the future are also shaped by new pan-Arab imaginings as well as by European and American democratic constitutional orders, which are no longer considered elite nor, as in colonial times, external to the sense of self in much of the Arab world. Since the various uprisings are supported by external forces and countries – in Syria, with Iran and Russia supporting Assad, and with Saudi Arabia, the United States, and member states of the European Community supporting different opposition groups – these countries will likely become internal to identifications of self. Internalisation is an unstable process, as it is often accompanied by an attempt to externalise or place outside the self that which is already within. One sees this in the dream of negating the century-old integrity of countries like Iraq and Syria – because they were illegitimate creations of the colonially imposed Sykes-Picot agreement of 1916. Or one can see it in purification movements, like al-Qaeda, which seeks to eliminate 'the West' in all its forms from any presence in Muslim countries. Al-Qaeda is of course caught in a hypocritical position, dependent as it is on Western banks, profits (especially from drug sales) and munitions.

The degree of internalisation of the West, and how this relationship develops over time, will be especially significant for the imagination and rationalisation of forms of ordering authority in the future in Syria. Syrian opposition groups have felt largely abandoned by the West, as well as by fellow Arabs, but have nowhere else to turn for support. Buttressed by foreign fighters from opposed Sunni and Shi'a camps, some of those groups remain dependent on the West but others depend on alternative Islamist imaginings that, as of this writing, have attained nearly total dominance over the Opposition. Early in the struggle, Bashar al Assad dubbed all members of the internal opposition 'terrorists' and accused external groups who support them of controlling them. His claim had no basis at the start of the uprising, but as the war continued into its third year, it became more plausible. Half of the population have become refugees, leading to a radically different internal dynamics and also to a new composition of the opposition. The opposition is increasingly dominated by foreign jihadis interested in domination with little or no connection to the emancipatory goals of the original local oppositional groups.

Before returning to the principle of opposition and authoritarianism, one other related point about groups, community, and the nation. By 1999, the first time I visited Syria, the Assad regime had successfully created a general paranoia about being watched, a suspicion of difference and a distance from authority, something also described by the political scientist Lisa Wedeen (1999) in her observations in the prior decade. It appeared to me that Syrians had over time come to live with fear, but peacefully, in their separate communities, without sharing much information of any substance or even services with each other. The creation of relatively autonomous communities resembles what we call theoretically caste divisions, but these communities lack the critical elements of caste complementarity, reciprocity and hierarchy. Caste, in classic Indian structural theory, is in principle organised around a division of labour specific to castes, but labour in Syria is not organised by discrete groups. There is, for example, no Christian sect that monopolises sanitation services, no Druze sect that monopolises education, no Alawite sect that monopolises agriculture. Each sect tends to have its own members to perform the different vital occupations, which enables communities to remain relatively autonomous from each other rather than forcing interdependencies. The secular imposed peace of the Ba'ath Party, and its system of redistributing the spoils of the state to selective members of each community, did not break down the borders between communities but actually used the spoils system to create structural suspicions and paranoia within and between groups. The structural suspicions proved useful to the Assad regime once the revolt began, uniting some minority groups behind the ruling Alawites and radicalising divisions among internal groups.

VIII. Changing Terms

I conclude with some final reflections on the changing meaning of some key terms: opposition, authoritarianism, liberalism, democracy, tradition. Some twenty years ago, I began to explore the temporal changes in the relation of opposition to political authority. In an analysis of resistance during the Cold War called 'Trouble in the Kitchen' (Borneman 1993), I compared two dissidents, Wolf Biermann and Sascha Anderson, as signifying temporal and stylistic differences within the authoritarian GDR, and as moving from a modernist virtuous resistance to an authority that claimed love as its base, to a postmodernist resistance that was complicit with authority because the state had become internal to one's self of self, compromising one's relationship to it as an external object. Inclusiveness and cooptation is in fact a defining principle of all socialist or welfare states.

Ten years after the collapse of the international socialist project, at least in its European gestalt, with capitalism and a particular version of democratic-representative politics now triumphant, I analysed the largest European happening – demonstration, parade, party, festival – of the 1990s: the 'Love Parade' (Borneman and Senders, 2000). The collapse of the Cold War ideological binary of communism/capitalism prompted a search for new identifications along with new forms of participation in a democratic and united Germany. This pattern was not specific to Germany, however, as other European nationals found themselves in a similar ideological abyss. Europe as a project, which might have drawn support from this search – indeed, the expansion of the EU into Eastern Europe was one sign in this direction – was instead increasingly questioned from partisan national political, economic and cultural perspectives.

The Love Parade indexed two processes: first, the dissolution of the inherited nineteenth-century political structures in which democratic political parties set the ideological filters and appropriated the schisms of the everyday for their own purposes of interest articulation, and second, the development of nascent forms of

authority and ritual identification under the aegis of an emergent acephalic political authority, that is, an authority based on affect without a single head. Another
decade has passed since I made these observations. Now it seems quite paradoxical that authoritarianism is flourishing alongside these more anarchic forms of
identification, which emerged amid processes of democratisation of families, dissolution of traditional authorities, and quite radical attacks on patriarchal rule.

Max Weber's use of the term 'traditional authority' remains useful to understand this modern gestalt. Weber has often been criticised for dumping everything into this category that did not correspond to his more clearly delineated
concepts, charismatic and bureaucratic authority. Indeed, the extreme cultural
and temporal variability of tradition, a point well documented since by ethnog-
raphers and historians, made it difficult for him to construct tradition as an ideal
type. Yet, much as a Derridean deconstruction of linguistic concepts does not
make such concepts heuristically useless, the contingency of tradition does not
negate its utility. Instead, we are challenged to be more aware of the temporal
and cultural variability of tradition, and to examine its relation to specific social
and political units – for example, empires, nations, tribes, nations, sects, clans,
a proposed caliphate, extended kin groups, nuclear families or the individual
consumer – and the local meanings assigned to these identificatory units.

Emphasising the contingency of the term 'traditional authority' entails
acknowledging the cultural distance travelled since the 1960s, and taking leave of
some of the more popular theorists from that time. As an example, consider Louis
Althusser's (1994: 104) frequently cited 1970 essay, 'Ideology and Ideological
State Apparatuses'. There he identified the school, the church, the state, the army
and the family as interpellating the ideological and repressive state apparatuses
necessary to 'ensure subjection to the ruling ideology'. What is the status of these
institutions and of the 'ruling ideology' today? It would be difficult to argue, even
for France, that institutions such as state or church today ensure subjection to a
ruling ideology. It is not that ruling ideologies do not exist, or that the state does
not have one, but over the last thirty years in most places in the world the particular institutions Althusser identified as 'state apparatuses' have lost much of
their power to inculcate children and adults in the ruling ideology. Certainly new
media has contributed to this decline in centralised power, but so have changes
in parent-child relations and attacks on all traditional authorities.

To the extent that there is still an overarching ruling ideology that contributes to subjection, then it is a market ideology related to consumerism and
individual choice. The efficacy of market ideology cannot be understood as
interpellation of the norms of a single power, nor is it merely the imbibing of a
consciousness from elsewhere. And the ideologists are not priests, teachers and
family fathers but economists, behavioural psychologists, business leaders, capi-
talists and financial experts, professional mediators in visual and print media
– most of whom do not work for a state apparatus. To be sure, families and the
institutions of world religions still struggle for influence over the specific ways of
thinking and understanding the relationships we have with each other and over
the societies within which we live. But the state, insofar as it has an ideological

apparatus, and the political classes, narrowly defined, who are to orient this apparatus, now appear to be subservient to the dictates of mysterious 'market forces'. On the one hand, these market forces are merely interpretations of numbers based on certain assumptions of value. But on the other hand they are real choices of individual consumers. The ideologists who increasingly dominate several academic disciplines also successfully arrogate to themselves the ability to define and explain all empirical realities – from macroeconomic trends to motivations for terrorism – in a more rational, reproducible, controllable form than other disciplines. Their ways of knowing lend themselves to immediate political or economic utility, hence their closeness to policy and politics. But the policy outcome of following their expertise is by no means a clear success.

The immediacy of use is in itself not a criticism of their knowledge; 'usefulness' is an important value. But to subject all knowledge to this metric has the effect of devaluing forms of truly empirical knowledge, such as what anthropologists generate, which is not isolable through a survey or observable without long-term commitment to person and place. Anthropological knowledge, based on actual lived experience over time, is difficult if not impossible to standardise, and therefore does not lend itself to the same kind of utility for policy. 'Scientific knowledge', of the sort from which I distance myself here, has been doubling every ten to twenty years this last century (as measured by numbers of scientists and scientific journals), and it now buttresses certain beliefs about human character and meaning, which in turn inform public policy. Such policy prescriptions are by nature culturally insensitive. The kind of argument I am making is dependent on understanding cultural origins and the contingencies of context. It is slightly different but wholly congruent with those consistently made under the label 'the critique of neoliberalism'.

The term 'neoliberal' is used, at least in anthropology, essentially to refer to the deferral of processes of social and economic valuation to abstract 'markets', to standards of 'efficiency' realised in such concrete projects as the privatisation of state enterprises, the rationalisation of the labour force, and coerced 'structural adjustment' or export-oriented economic restructuring of national economies. While the critique of neoliberalism has drawn attention to a significant global process, it often becomes a set of repetitive claims of victimhood, which do not help us much in understanding the new culturally specific institutional alignments that are both undermining tradition and facilitating authoritarianism, as well as the frequent populist will to submit to these new alignments.

To be sure, neoliberal policies are very real and many are extremely harmful to everyone but the very wealthy. But this top-down frame ignores cultural sources of disruption. As with all policy, neoliberal policies may produce some of the effects they intend, but not all of them. And some of the effects are perverse – the opposite of those intended. Effects lend themselves to ethnographic exploration, as they can best be studied from the bottom up. Moreover, two of the major intended goals – efficiency and the rationalisation of ends – are not negative in every context. That depends on what exactly has become more efficient, and on what happens to the irrational in the attempt to rationalise.

What is particularly unfortunate and misleading, however, is the gloss on liberalism as an economic ideology. The concept of liberalism has had many different meanings over time and place. One association is indeed, as neoliberal critics claim, with *laissez-faire* capitalism, that is, with free markets. Another meaning, originally more central, is limited government. Neither *laissez-faire* capitalism nor limited government can be reduced to the effects of each other. The two values are of course related, but both have their own integrity. In some economic domains, in fact, *laissez-faire* capitalism leads to centralisation and monopolisation, which in turn can make limited government appear ineffectual. Who can afford to invest in government determines, in turn, who government invests in and who it neglects.

Everyday political discourse can also pervert the meaning of the two values, attributing to liberalism a meaning opposite to its intent. In the United States over the last half-century, 'liberal' was the epithet used by political 'conservatives' to deride any kind of planned change that benefited the less well-off parts of the world. In other words, 'liberal' was the label given to activist, not limited, government. The original liberal theorists Adam Smith and John Locke directed their enquiries to the proper and necessary use of government, not to its size or relative activism. They certainly did not espouse an ideology of turbo-capitalism as a means to replace the state's role in domestic welfare. That ideology is relatively new, neither liberal nor conservative, but revolutionary and authoritarian at the same time. It is authoritarian in the sense of the submission to an ideology intolerant of opposition or alternatives to market-driven logics.

Vacating the political sense of liberalism makes it easier to subsume the term under an argument of market efficiency. As Smith and Locke would argue, liberalism is more about the significance of limited government than the size of the state. The argument is about limits on executive authority as a necessary antidote to the compulsive centralisation of power true of most authoritarian regimes. My contribution here has been to explore the sources of opposition as antidotes to authoritarianism, specifically in two different settings. I also suggested that one potential for institutionalising opposition to authoritarianism rests in the practice of turn taking and alternative principles of descent. Much of the contemporary power of an ideology of free marketism is due to the lack of a clear idea of what an articulated alternative or opposition might be. Prior to 1989, socialist projects – the promulgation of utopic schemes of collective organisation, production and redistribution – were thought to provide an alternative to free market ideology. But as we know in retrospect, the socialist states of East-Central Europe, the Soviet Union, China and the Middle East were never able to liberalise their authoritarian political structures. That is, these regimes were never able to set real limits on the exercise of executive power. Liberalism today remains the most useful counter-concept to the authoritarianism of right-wing, nationalist movements.

I have noted much of this in my book, *Political Crime and the Memory of Loss* (Borneman 2011). What I hope to add here are several avenues for ethnographic research on authoritarianism and opposition. Specifically I suggest that we focus on identifying the cultural sources of opposition in disruptions in particular places, and look for the libidinal investments in changing forms of traditional authority. One of these sources lies in practices of turn taking and the articulation of alternative principles of descent in contemporary settings. There are certainly other sources to be identified. Further, I suggest we look into how practices of opposition are institutionalised at different levels of social organisation, and how these levels reinforce or conflict with each other at a time when the institutionalised forms of opposition, globally seen, appear less efficacious than in the recent past and appear in themselves to be waning. To do this kind of research, we must probe beneath surface networks of actants located in assemblages to query instead the motivations and investments of human actors and critically question the efficacy of their actions. It is still essential to investigate how actual human attachments and identifications revolve around unconsciously structured relationships in this global, capitalist and democratic age, and how these structures facilitate certain kinds of group formation that make it difficult to identify and articulate opposition.

Acknowledgements

This chapter was initially delivered with slight modifications as a keynote address at the conference of the SOYUZ Research Network for Postsocialist Cultural Studies, 22–23 March 2013, Harriman Institute for Russian, Eurasian, and Eastern European Studies, Columbia University, New York.

Notes

1   A fuller analysis would also include an account of the Real, that which is foreclosed from speech (such as trauma) but nonetheless has distorting effects on the Symbolic.
2   Much of what follows is drawn from a longer account in Borneman (2012).
3   Explanations for these revolts should and often do vary by country, and as the situation on the ground changes quickly, scholars explain different things. For the 'Arab Spring', by which I mean the initial motivations or triggers, scholars have focused on underdevelopment and changing demographics (Perthes 2011: 24), demands for dignity, freedom and social justice (Asseburg 2011: 3; Perthes 2011: 33–34), access to new social media (Howard and Hussain 2011: 36, 42), and economic liberalisation without political reform (Desai et al. 2011). For an Althusserian argument of the importance of ideological interpellation and the use of humor in the uprising in Syria, see Wedeen (2013).

References

Althusser, L. 1994 (1970). Ideology and the Ideological State Apparatuses (Notes Toward an Investigation). In *Mapping Ideology* (ed.) S. Žižek, 100–142. London: Verso.

Asseburg, M. 2011. Zur Anatomie der Arabischen Proteste und Aufstände. *Aus Politik und Zeitgeschichte* 61, no. 39: 3–8.

Batatu, H. 1999. *Syria's Peasantry: The Descendants of its Lesser Rural Notables, and their Politics.* Princeton: Princeton University Press.

Borneman, J. 1991. *After the Wall: East Meets West in the New Berlin.* New York: Basic Books.

———. 1992. *Belonging in the Two Berlins: Kin, State, Nation.* Cambridge: Cambridge University Press.

———. 1993. Trouble in the Kitchen: Totalitarianism, Love, and Resistance to Authority. In *Moralizing States and the Ethnography of the Present* (ed.) S.F. Moore, 93–118. Washington, DC: American Ethnological Society Monograph Series.

———. 1997. *Settling Accounts: Violence, Justice, and Accountability in Postsocialist Europe.* Princeton: Princeton University Press.

———. 1998. *Subversions of International Order: Studies in the Political Anthropology of Culture.* Albany: State University of New York Press.

———. 2004. Gottvater, Landesvater, Familienvater: Identification and Authority in Germany. In *Death of the Father: An Anthropology of The End in Political Authority* (ed.) John Borneman, 63–103. New York: Berghahn.

———. 2007 *Syrian Episodes: Sons, Fathers, and an Anthropologist in Aleppo.* Princeton: Princeton University Press.

———. 2010. European Rituals of Initiation and the Production of Men. *Social Anthropology* 18, no. 3: 289–301.

———. 2011. *Political Crime and the Memory of Loss.* Bloomington: Indiana University Press.

———. 2012. Und nach den Tyrannen? Macht, Verwandtschaft und Gemeinschaft in der Arabellion. *La Lettre International* 98: 33–48.

Borneman, J., and S. Senders. 2000. Politics without a Head: Is the Love Parade a New Form of Political Identification? *Cultural Anthropology* 15, no. 2: 294–317.

Bourdieu, P. 1977. *Outline of a Theory of Practice.* Cambridge: Cambridge University Press.

Crapanzano, V. 2001. *Serving the Word: Literalism in America from the Pulpit to the Bench.* New York: New Press.

Crouch, C. 2004. *Post-Democracy.* New York: Polity Press.

Goody, J. 1983. *The Development of the Family and Marriage in Europe.* Cambridge: Cambridge University Press.

Desai, R.M., A. Olofsgard and T. Yousef. 2011. Is the Arab Authoritarian Bargain Collapsing? <www.brookings.edu/opinions/2011/0209_arab_economies_desai_yousef.aspx> (accessed 18 June 2015).

Fulbrook, M. 2005. *The People's State: East German Society from Hitler to Honecker.* New Haven: Yale University Press.

Harvey, D. 2011. *The Enigma of Capital and the Crisis of Capitalism.* London: Profile Books.

Herlihy, D. 1985. *Medieval Households.* Cambridge, MA: Harvard University Press.

Howard, P.N., and M.M. Hussain. 2011. The Role of Digital Media. *Journal of Democracy* 22, no. 3: 35–48.

Jarausch, K. 1994. *The Rush to German Unity.* Oxford: Oxford University Press.

Kimmerling, B. 2002. The Politicide of the Palestinian People. *New York Review of Books,* 11 June.

Krugman, P. 2009. *The Return of Depression Economics and the Crisis of 2008.* New York: W.W. Norton & Co.

Lacan, J. 1956. *The Language of the Self: The Function of Language in Psychoanalysis* (trans. A. Wilden). Baltimore: The Johns Hopkins University Press.

———. 1958. *Écrits* (trans. B. Fink). New York: W.W. Norton & Co.

Lefort, C. 1986. *The Political Forms of Modern Society.* Cambridge, MA: MIT Press.

Leyser. K. 1968. The German Aristocracy from the Ninth to the Early Twelfth Century: A Historical and Cultural Sketch. *Past and Present* 41: 25–53.

———. 1979. *Rule and Conflict in an Early Medieval Society: Ottonian Saxony.* London: Edward Arnold.

Linz, J.J. 2000. *Totalitarian and Authoritarian Regimes.* Boulder: Lynne Rienner.

Luhmann, N. 1990. *Political Theory in the Welfare State.* New York: Walter de Gruyter.

Maier, C. 1997. *The Dissolution: The Crisis of Communism and the End of East Germany.* Princeton: Princeton University Press.

Perthes, V. 2011. *Der Aufstand. Die Arabische Revolution und ihre Folgen.* Munich: Pantheon Verlag.

Putnam, R.D. 2000. *Bowling Alone: The Collapse and Revival of American Community.* New York: Simon and Schuster.

Ruthven, M. 2011. The Revolutionary Shias. *New York Review of Books,* 22 December.

Scott, J.C. 1985. *Weapons of the Weak: Everyday Forms of Peasant Resistance.* New Haven: Yale University Press.

Streeck, W. 2014. *The Crisis of Democratic Capitalism.* New York: Verso.

Weber, M. 1978. *Economy and Society: An Outline of Interpretive Sociology. Volume One.* Berkeley: University of California Press.

Wedeen, L. 1999. *Ambiguities of Domination: Politics, Rhetoric, and Symbols of Contemporary Syria.* Chicago: University of Chicago Press.

———. 2013. Ideology and Humor in Dark Times: Notes from Syria. *Critical Inquiry* 39, no. 4: 841–873.

John Borneman is Professor of anthropology at Princeton University.

5

Rejecting or Remaking Democratic Practices?
Experiences during Times of Crisis in Italy

Jan-Jonathan Bock

In April 2009, a strong earthquake hit the central Italian city of L'Aquila, taking the lives of 309 Aquilani. The historic city centre, previously a lively urban space of scenic baroque and renaissance architecture, was left in a semi-ruined state; its houses and monuments were declared to be unstable and hazardous. Tens of thousands of people had to be resettled, first in camps and remote hotel resorts, and subsequently in purpose-built rehousing sites across the periphery of L'Aquila's extensive municipality. The cityscape, routines and relations were rapidly transformed.

In this chapter, I explore the ways in which Aquilani experienced life during the government-declared state of emergency, when the powerful Civil Protection Agency managed local day-to-day life strictly, curtailing citizens' rights and possibilities of democratic participation, purportedly in the interests of speed and organisational efficiency. Urban spaces were transformed without involving L'Aquila's citizens in far-reaching decisions, including an access ban to the historic centre and the construction of permanent rehousing sites for over 16,000 people. Aquilani responded to authoritarian emergency measures – a post-democratic moment in the sense that autocratic expertise and crisis management suspended debate, ordinary rights and local participation – in multiple ways, which I investigate.

Between January 2012 and May 2013, I conducted ethnographic fieldwork in L'Aquila, following, among other initiatives, political grassroots movements that had come into existence in response to the government's handling of the state of emergency. Activists criticised the authoritarian disaster response, demanded greater participation and denounced a lack of transparency in post-earthquake decision-making processes. Eventually they converted their initial anti-government protests into institutional politics and participated in municipal elections.

Thus, a certain type of Aquilani reacted to the disaster and to the subsequent crisis in an unexpected way, using experiences of authoritarian rule to rethink connections between politics and individual or collective existence, to reshape political consciousness and civic engagement. Events and experiences during the emergency period induced some Aquilani to reconsider the impact of political constraints on individual and collective agency, after having endured the repercussions of state disaster management in their private lives. In many cases, subsequent attempts to reclaim a sense of control over personal and communal affairs centred on the possibilities provided by state democracy. This chapter shows that, while some people quietly accepted the imposition of authoritarian rule and the suspension of democratic practices as necessary concomitants of the disaster response, others questioned the proportionality of such measures, actively reflecting on their crisis experiences to reinvigorate values and practices of participatory democracy.

I suggest that emergent democratic practices of citizenship can be understood through the conceptual notion of what Caroline Humphrey (2008) has called a 'decision-event': troubling experiences require people to take drastic decisions to retain the capacity to act, if only for a moment. In the wake of the L'Aquila earthquake, Aquilani faced unnerving transformations of their private lives, and many accepted the need for expert crisis management, and thus a post-democratic moment. Others, however, sought to remake their commitment to participatory democracy, to retain a sense of control over their local world, as a strategy for recovery from catastrophe. This chapter explores a range of responses, with a focus on the remaking of citizenship practices in an arduous struggle of living a self-determined life under circumstances marked by the ongoing effects of catastrophe and authoritarian governance.

The L'Aquila Earthquake

On 6 April 2009, a major earthquake measuring 5.9 on the Richter scale devastated L'Aquila, the capital of the Abruzzo region in central Italy, as well as dozens of smaller communities in the L'Aquila valley. The city is located 120 kilometres east of Rome, in the Apennine mountain range, between the Tyrrhenian and Adriatic Seas, and surrounded by peaks reaching 3,000 metres. Before the earthquake, L'Aquila had been a showpiece of central Italian architecture, predominantly from the eighteenth century. In both 1461 and 1703, powerful quakes had razed the city, depopulating large parts of it (Antonini 2010; Clementi 1998). The Aquilano, as the city and surrounding area are called, is among the most seismically active zones in Europe, and at high risk from powerful earthquakes.

After the 1703 destruction, a new L'Aquila was built, dominated by large baroque and renaissance edifices arranged around picturesque courtyards, churches and squares with scenic fountains (Clementi and Piroddi 1986; Mammarella 1990). Students from L'Aquila's university turned this *centro storico* into a lively, atmospheric urban space dotted with bars, coffee shops and restaurants. While only 24,000 Aquilani, out of a total population of 73,000, lived in the historic centre before the quake – the majority inhabited condominiums and single-family houses in quarters constructed during Italy's post-war economic boom years outside the historic walls – the *centro storico* remained the unrivalled pivot of urban social life.

Before April 2009, Aquilani recall nostalgically, there had been no need to fix dates. In the evening, young and old used to stroll along L'Aquila's main centre avenue, lined by grand buildings and monuments, for aperitifs with friends and colleagues. Aquilani from diverse social and economic backgrounds frequented the historic streets daily, with bars and cafés as the stages of much-cherished social routines of 'cultural intimacy' (Herzfeld 1991).

When the earthquake struck at 3.32 A.M. on 6 April 2009, 309 people died, 1,500 were injured and almost 70,000 people were subsequently evacuated from their homes (Alexander 2010, 2013). While few houses collapsed, many were damaged and declared unfit for habitation by the government, particularly in the historic centre of L'Aquila and those of nearby towns and villages. In response to the large-scale damage, the then Prime Minister, Silvio Berlusconi, launched an emergency response through the national Italian Civil Protection Agency, Protezione Civile, coordinated by its then head, Guido Bertolaso. There was little to no transparency in initial decision-making processes, when billions of euros were allocated for emergency operations. Nonetheless, the foreign press commented positively on the relief effort, describing it as Berlusconi's rise 'from zero to hero' (Popham 2009).

Only days after the catastrophe, the Protezione Civile and volunteer organisations erected 170 evacuation camps on sports fields and other open spaces across the L'Aquila municipality, and urban neighbourhoods across the area were placed under military control. Historic centres were closed off, sealed with metal barriers and security fences, restricting access to the spaces that used to constitute the material backdrop for everyday sociality. L'Aquila's extensive old city was deemed hazardous for residents; the government justified the military presence with the need to prevent looters from entering abandoned buildings. In the interest of public safety, purportedly non-negotiable emergency decisions were implemented by the Italian state. Aquilani lost the ability to access their former homes as well as the monuments and urban spaces they used to inhabit routinely.

Silvio Berlusconi quickly presented a solution to the large-scale damage: an unprecedented rehousing scheme, involving the construction of nineteen resettlement sites with 185 housing blocks across L'Aquila's rural periphery, for over 16,000 people.[1] The Italian prime minister, who had amassed legendary wealth in the construction industry before he revolutionised private television, successfully personalised the state support: relief projects, he claimed, would have been impossible without his expertise.[2] Local criticism of the large-scale resettlement was disregarded, despite many survivors fearing that the rehousing scheme might delay heritage restoration efforts and disfigure the city's rural periphery forever (Ciccozzi 2011). Expertise and top-down management characterised the government's relief effort – not participation, public discussion or transparency.[3]

Figure 5.1 Ruins in L'Aquila's historic centre

Figure 5.2 Peripheral resettlement sites

Post-earthquake evacuation and resettlement initiatives raise important anthropological questions. Exploring experiences of bereavement and the removal of opportunities for everyday social interaction, for example, can inform our understandings of memory practices after extreme events (Cappelletto 2003; Foot 2009; Malkki 1995; Yoneyama 1999), revealing how local identity and sociality intersect with urban spaces (Jiménez 2003; Low 1999; Silverman 1975). In this chapter, however, I approach the ethnographic material differently, highlighting explicitly political dimensions of displacement, suffering and recovery.

Commenting on the emergency period, some Aquilani emphasise that they believed initial promises made by the prime minister and other state representatives to restore both historical buildings and a sense of normality within years. A passive acceptance of measures passed by decree without consulting local institutions (such as the mayor or the city council) resulted from hopeful assumptions that L'Aquila could thus be restored more quickly and effectively.

Informants recalled comments made by Guido Bertolaso, who masterminded the relief operation as the government-appointed Extraordinary Commissioner for the Emergency, that Aquilani should not seek participation in decision-making processes, but should trust him and his experts to manage the crisis better. L'Aquila's population remains divided between those who admire Guido Bertolaso as an exceptional disaster manager, on the one hand, and others who see him as a dictatorial figure, disenfranchising the Aquilani in a moment of shock that left them unable to react collectively to disproportionate emergency measures, on the other (Trapasso 2010).

While the first type of Aquilani accepted expert management and the impossibility of democratic participation in political processes more readily, it is the second type of survivors I explore: these Aquilani reacted imaginatively to the disenfranchisement, reflecting on practices of citizenship and ultimately remaking them. During the prolonged crisis, following the destructive quake, Aquilani began to think about how their democracy had 'run into trouble' (Cook, Long and Moore, this volume), either rejecting it as too slow and arduous a method for reaching important decisions, or (and sometimes even successively) reinvigorating democracy through emergent practices of citizenship, attaching them to novel aspirations for control over local affairs amidst extreme circumstances.

By investigating emergent understandings and practices of citizenship in post-disaster L'Aquila, I seek to trace Aquilani interpretations of events that led survivors to reflect on their relation to state institutions and on political engagement. I argue that novel forms of citizenship evolved in dialectical response to what many Aquilani identified as excessive forms of authoritarianism, disregarding their concerns and desires during the emergency operation. Aquilani involved in political movements and parties used these platforms to demand more transparency and accountability in political decision-making processes. They invested democratic practices with new meanings and aspirations at a time when they appeared under threat, dismissed by many as unable to cope with calamity.

The State and Democracy in Italy

Edward Banfield's *The Moral Basis of a Backward Society* (1958) remains a classic text on modern Italians' attitudes to their state. Banfield suggested that southern, small-town Italians struggle to identify a common good and to engage in democratic processes, being solely concerned with the well-being of their relatives – a cultural disposition he coined 'amoral familism', preventing commitment to non-kin forms of community action.[6]

Much criticism has been levelled at Banfield, for conflating familism and 'the South' without accounting for differences among villages and towns, as well as for disregarding the presence of the family in northern Italy (Ferragina 2009). In academic circles, Banfield's theses have been discredited. Nonetheless, in popular discourse, (southern) Italy is still widely associated with political ineptitude, corruption and backwardness. Also, Banfield's neologism, 'familism', 'struck a resonant chord, not simply as a description of attitudes in the backward and primitive South, but also for Italy as a whole' (Ginsborg 2001: 97). John Foot suggests that, 'as a portrayer of a key feature of Italian ideology and social life, Banfield remains important' (2003: 52).[7] The notion that Italians are incapable of democratic practice, or of the pursuit of a common good, because of their self-centred family adhesion, remains influential (see also Putnam et al. 1993).

Depictions of southern Italy, of which L'Aquila is considered to be a part, continue to reproduce its 'unchanging otherness' with regard to corruption, government failure and political apathy (Saunders 1998: 178).[8] Popular commentators still suggest that a sense of the communal good is of second-order interest: 'The distancing from anything *statale* breeds individualism and an unusual attitude towards law-abiding' (Jones 2003: 17). Colin Crouch (2004) has argued that post-democratic tendencies are particularly powerful in Italy because of the conflation of business and state interests in the figure of Silvio Berlusconi, simultaneously the country's richest man and its dominant political figure. For Crouch, Italy has been a showcase of neoliberal politics, favouring private interests at the expense of state support for public services, which reduces the scope of participation and estranges the populace from institutions. The picture that emerges is one of a deep crisis of Italian democracy.

If Italians have been moulded into 'good' or moral citizens, committing themselves to help others, this is said to happen predominantly in the voluntary care sector, since the neoliberal state educates citizens to take over privatised welfare provisions, by manipulating both Catholic traditions of charity and communist practices of solidarity (Muehlebach 2012). Instead of conceptualising new forms of associationism as a product of a neoliberal ethics, however, I investigate emergent political engagements as endeavours to remake control over local affairs in the wake of a major catastrophe, as aspects of recovery. Rather than accepting historical or cultural determinacy as a sufficient explanation to account for contemporary Italian engagements with democratic statehood, I explore specific causes and narratives that lead Aquilani to seek distance from, or greater intimacy with, possibilities of democratic citizenship, complicating the picture of how contemporary Italians relate to their state.

State of Emergency

Being evacuated from their damaged or destroyed homes, tens of thousands of Aquilani spent the summer and autumn of 2009 in mainly government-administered camps. The details and minutiae of camp life varied, since their handling depended on the organisation responsible (Civil Protection Agency, the Red Cross, or numerous volunteer groups).

In many of the larger camps, however, administered by the Civil Protection Agency, the consumption of alcohol, coffee and Coca-Cola was prohibited, because they were considered to be excitant substances. Identity cards, without which access to the enclosed encampments was impossible, were issued. Often, residents' meetings or group discussions were not allowed, to keep order and to prevent opposition to the authorities. Instead, many survivors were given tranquilisers without medical prescription. Recalling their experiences from the summer of 2009, many now politically active Aquilani describe the crisis management as an experiment of total social control, claiming that the government consciously turned them into 'guinea pigs', testing how far a democratic state could push authoritarian measures before facing popular resistance. For some, it was too far.

At the time of my fieldwork, Alessandro worked for the press office of L'Aquila's rugby club. He was in his early thirties, born and raised in L'Aquila. Politically, he had always sympathised with left-wing politics, he told me, but until the earthquake, he had not been involved in movements or parties. Following the disaster, he had lived in various *tendopoli* [tent cities]. I met him because of his involvement in local activist groups, for which he coordinated cultural events. We developed a friendship, and Alessandro agreed to speak about his experience. He made it clear that his impression of camp life, and of what he described as 'the dynamics of social control', led him to reconsider the importance of political involvement. He explained to me: 'When someone tells you that you are in a state of shock, after such an event and experience, you believe it. And so people just spent their days sitting around in the camps, being quiet, eating and sleeping, because they *believed* they were in a state of shock – and that that is how they should behave.'

Alessandro relived the camp routine: 'The programme for the day – activities, schedules, meal times, and so on – changed every couple of hours, and so people could no longer plan anything; everything changed all the time. People just resigned to the authorities, followed the rules, did as they were told, and stopped complaining. It was total social control.' The rhetoric of emergency had been ubiquitous in post-earthquake L'Aquila. The presence of the army, numerous different police forces, fire fighters, the Civil Protection Agency, the international media and volunteers created the impression of a state of exception, which necessitated authoritarian measures and deference to state institutions to manage the crisis effectively, suspending aspects of the ordinary rule of law (Agamben 2005).

Emergency legislation transformed L'Aquila's centre, as well as urban spaces outside the historic walls, into inaccessible areas. Camp life became a shared experience. For survivors, this meant constant illumination, high fences, tough checks and an overwhelming sense of dependency on state support, for food, shelter and protection. Pre-disaster quotidian practices, such as coming together to gossip, discuss politics, or share a glass of wine, and the ability to move freely around one's city and historic neighbourhoods, were discouraged, and often suspended, through disaster management.[9]

In the camps, retaining a sense of intimacy between spouses or partners was a challenge, as tents were shared between ten to fifteen evacuees. Soon, Aquilani began to drive into unlit streets at night to make love in their cars; others returned for a few hours to their damaged homes for the same purpose. Access to these buildings had been banned, however, and so the very act of returning constituted a breach of emergency legislation, with potentially severe consequences. In coastal holiday resorts, tens of thousands of evacuees had to wear identity cards around their necks. They were forced to have their meals in separate rooms from other guests. Some Aquilani spent up to three years in hotels, and were expected to be grateful for the support while subjected to a kind of treatment that informants described as that of second-class citizens.

While many survivors acquiesced and accepted the imposition of government power, others began to question the authorities. Various grassroots movements were formed, citizens' initiatives grew, and opposition to the state's response became a uniting feature for many dispersed Aquilani. Alessandro, for example, was forced to change camps repeatedly; his questioning led to consecutive evictions. Aquilani often framed camp experiences by referencing Naomi Klein's theory of the shock doctrine, arguing that the Italian state's imposition of costly, unwanted projects on the local population – such as the rehousing sites and the hosting of the 2009 G8 summit in the ravaged city – would have met with local opposition had the government not used the moment of shock to bypass resistance (Klein 2007).

David Runciman (2013) has argued that one of the strengths of democracies is their ability to suspend democratic practices during crises, experimenting with autocratic governance before returning to democracy. This sets democracies apart from autocracies, which cannot allow democratic periods without losing control. What Runciman does not explore, however, are disagreements about whether or not the affected individuals consider suspensions proportionate, and, relatedly, how people react when they perceive autocratic measures to be incommensurate with the need for action. Reconstituting suspended dimensions of democratic life after an experiment with authoritarian rule is not automatic, and not a shared concern of a homogeneous population; instead, it needs activism and resistance, sometimes by a few, sometimes by the many, to break authoritarianism.[10] The aftermath of the L'Aquila earthquake provides a fascinating case study into the groundwork of political subjects to (re)constitute democratic realities.

During my fieldwork, many politically active Aquilani recollected their pre-disaster lives as apolitical, in contrast to their new engagements. In the late 1990s, L'Aquila's mayor had pursued the construction of a tramway, connecting post-war quarters with the centre. Tracks were laid, but many streets were too narrow. The funding expired and the project was abandoned. Still today, however, L'Aquila's streets feature unused tracks and tram stops, and Aquilani often described the pointless infrastructure as emblematic of the administrative incapacity and corruption that used to cause their political apathy.

In their accounts of post-earthquake life, many informants described how their previous disenchantment with politics transformed into novel political engagements. The experiment with authoritarian state management during the emergency period impacted on people's private lives, pushing survivors to reconfigure understandings of citizenship. Through their new political involvement and resistance to state power, they shaped the concrete transition from what Runciman calls an autocratic experiment (back) to active democratic citizenship.

Multiple Responses

A key argument of this chapter is that people respond differently to authoritarian forms of crisis governance. While, for some, experiencing catastrophe triggers reflections on democratic politics as an important dimension of their personal lives, rather than as a distant political plane without consequences, others consent to authoritarian forms of government when disasters overwhelm them.

In May 2012, three years after the L'Aquila earthquake, northern Italy was struck by a series of quakes. Twenty-seven people died and 14,000 buildings were damaged. Over 45,000 people were forced to live in organised emergency accommodation. In June 2012, I visited the area and stayed at a horse farm in a small town in the Lombardy region. One of the farm buildings had collapsed; another one had been declared structurally unsafe. The farm's owner, Tomaso, lamented the financial constraints resulting from the loss of summer camp revenues. Parents had cancelled bookings for their children, fearing aftershocks. Tomaso, however, did not expect much help from politicians:

> This is the great difference between the north – Germany, England, Scandinavia – and the south – Italy, Spain, Greece: we just have no sense of collectiveness or collective responsibility, everyone just cares about himself. No one will help us. The only time things worked in Italy was during the fascist dictatorship, when people were afraid of the police.

Tomaso explained that the buildings least affected by the recent tremors had been built during Italian fascism, when 'things worked', as he reasoned. He concluded: 'Maybe this is the sad truth about the south. Democracy just doesn't work here. People just take what they can, without any fear of the consequences.' For Tomaso, it seemed, Italy's democracy would always be in trouble, because of the country's culture. During crises, however, these shortcomings become more pronounced. Reflecting on his ideal-type, non-Italian democracy, Tomaso sketched a system of objective and fair governance, incorruptibly supporting those in need. Tomaso imagined Italy's fascist past romantically, as a time when 'things worked', with fear levelling the playing field for all.

Merely days after the catastrophe, Tomaso considered democratic Italy's crisis response inadequate. Nobody had offered him support for repairs; no one had told him what to expect from the future. Berlusconi was no longer in office; his successor, Mario Monti, preferred a more sober approach to disaster management. Tomaso longed for decisive political leadership, and even praised the efficiency of dictatorships that had wrecked Europe. Post-democratic disillusionment and resignation, leading to a feeling of hopelessness, are common during crises. Democracies routinely fail to demonstrate strong leadership when facing troubling times – instead, they are successful at negotiating interests, finding compromises and 'muddling through' (Runciman 2013).

In L'Aquila, however, over three years after the earthquake, many Aquilani complained that the government's authoritarian management had not been more successful at 'getting things done' than the purportedly slow democratic procedures that had been surrendered in the interest of efficiency. When I left the city in 2013, the historic centre was still uninhabited and in a state of disrepair. Soldiers continued to patrol the *centro storico*; only limited economic activity had resumed in a few dozen buildings. After the earthquake, Berlusconi had promised that L'Aquila would be restored before 2013. In 2013, however, initial expectations for an unprecedented, well-coordinated return to normality had been shattered, with tens of thousands of Aquilani still displaced and dependent on state aid.

Survivors told me that 20,000 residents had left the city permanently. Those who remained called L'Aquila a *città fantasma* [a ghost town] or a *città morta* [a dead city]. Rat poison boxes were scattered across the historic centre; vermin plagued abandoned houses. From grand hopes for fast recovery, many had lost faith in their future, no longer knowing whether or how historic houses and monuments would be restored to pre-disaster normality.

Furthermore, the personnel of the relief effort had also been discredited, at least in the eyes of government-critical survivors. Guido Bertolaso had come under investigation for corruption in early 2010, accused of handing out contracts to dubious firms in the run-up to the 2009 G8 summit, and resigned later that year (Parboni 2010). Leaked phone conversations showed that Berlusconi and Bertolaso had known that L'Aquila's restoration would take decades, but they had nonetheless promised that the city would be repaired within a few years (La Repubblica 2013). Faced with a lack of recovery initiatives, many survivors criticised the fact that the government's disaster management had been a clever publicity stunt for the metropolitan and international media, rather than the vital crisis response as which it had been presented, and often accepted, in 2009.

In January 2013, a private conversation between L'Aquila's prefect, Giovanna Iurato, who had taken office one year after the earthquake, and a colleague was made public during a trial in Naples.[11] In the phone conversation, Iurato recalled her arrival in L'Aquila one year after the disaster. To win the survivors' hearts, she disclosed, she had visited the ruin of a student hall of residence near the city centre, where eight students had died – it had become a symbol of the tragedy. Standing in front of the ruins, Iurato boasted to her colleague, she had simulated tears while putting down a wreath, to win over the sceptical Aquilani. The plan had worked, Iurato rejoiced: 'immediately, in the newspapers, they were writing about "the prefect's tears"', and she laughed about her cunning strategy of ingratiating herself with L'Aquila's distraught population (Il Fatto Quotidiano 2013).

When the conversation was made public, it unsettled L'Aquila. Giustino Parisse, a journalist who had lost his father and his two children in the earthquake, summed up local anger in a newspaper editorial:

> I knew the former prefect well. And so today my bitterness is even stronger. During a winter night, a year and a half ago, she ate dinner with me and my wife; she shared our simple meal. She asked about our children, she looked at their photos, and she asked us to talk about them. She seemed sincere. Seemed. And that is why today I feel betrayed – betrayed in my feelings. Many people have come from Rome to exploit the earthquake, to make money and to promote their careers. Some of those are still around. Fake ceremonies, fake marches, fake celebrations, fake meetings. Today, we also discover a prefect with a mask. The most horrible one: the one of hypocrisy. Not much can hurt me anymore. Everyone will have to answer for what they do to their own conscience. You as well. I offer you some friendly advice though, ex-prefect: stay well away from L'Aquila. And also from me. (Il Centro 2013)

Experiences of hypocrisy, dissimulation and the exploitation of suffering by government representatives featured in most Aquilani's recollections of post-earthquake experiences. They constitute crucial ways in which local people conceptualised the intersection of political and personal dimensions of crisis, and survivors referenced them to explain their disillusionment with the political system. As one friend put it:

> Many have taken advantage of the situation and exploited the dead – our dead.[12] We feel anger, resentment, resignation and frustration. When you live through difficulties and someone says, 'I'll help you', you want to believe it. Then, when you realise that this person isn't helping you, but tries to exploit you, it really hurts. It leads to resignation and to distrust in institutions. The Aquilani no longer believe in institutions; they are disillusioned.

Most of my informants described at least aspects of the earthquake aftermath, with hindsight, as PR stunts that had served the interests of Roman politicians, but not the local population. Aquilani lamented that those who had pledged to help had ultimately exploited them. Having already entered a post-democratic phase of authoritarian disaster management, scandals exposing that promises were unrealistic and sympathy false estranged survivors from state institutions. It was initially the post-disaster state of emergency, with its top-down suspension of democratic participation and rights, which shaped local processes of alienating citizens from democratic statehood; then, realising how cynically the political personnel of the emergency administration had abused their powers in an hour of need intensified personal disillusionment and gave rise to different post-democratic sentiments.

Thus the imposed state of emergency was not solely responsible for the disappearance of aspects of democratic life and of a system of rights, as Giorgio Agamben suggests (2005); nor did Banfield's amoral familism cause a universal lack of interest in public affairs. Instead, disaster survivors cited concrete, often personal, experiences with officials to account for their disillusionment with, and rejection of, state institutions. Simultaneously, however, other Aquilani used the very same experiences to reconstitute participatory democratic citizenship as part of their recovery.

Emergent Participatory Democracy

The earthquake and its aftermath constitute a series of decision-events, in Caroline Humphrey's reading of the philosopher Alain Badiou's theory of the event (Badiou 2005), i.e., events that mark all members in a given society, 'in the sense that they could no longer assume that only one kind of society was possible' (Humphrey 2008: 363). Humphrey suggests that the conceptual notion of the 'decision-event' permits an analysis of the ways in which 'a singular human being might put him- or herself together as a distinctive human subject by adding to, or subtracting from, the possibilities given by culture as it has been up to that point, through the very process of taking action' (ibid.: 358). In her examination of troubling times in Inner Mongolia, Humphrey focuses on emerging subjects that exist only temporarily, to permit concrete action. For L'Aquila, however, I suggest that such emergent political subjectivities can last beyond the initial moment of action, transformed into enduring understandings and practices of democratic citizenship.

The drastic transformations in private, intimate lives experienced by L'Aquila's survivors precluded for many the possibility of continuing to encounter politics with apathy, shrugging shoulders when the politics of authoritarian rule conditioned everyday life. Some began to constitute the value of participatory democratic politics dialectically, reinvigorating values and practices after having experienced infractions, suspensions and absences during the emergency phase. Local grassroots movements reacted to what activists considered unacceptable infringements and a disproportionately authoritarian reaction, instead demanding participation, transparency and the restoration of the historic centre.

In May 2012, over three years after the earthquake, municipal elections were held in L'Aquila. Two new civic platforms participated, having been formed after the earthquake – Appello per L'Aquila [Call for L'Aquila] and L'Aquila Che Vogliamo [L'Aquila That We Want]. Only recently founded, they nonetheless won two seats in the city council, gaining over ten per cent of the vote. The two platforms – under the electoral system analogous to political parties – resulted from experiences of loss and of crisis management in the earthquake aftermath. Their followers illustrate how affective experiences can shape aspirations to seek greater democratic participation.

In response to authoritarian forms of governance during the relief effort, some Aquilani had founded a number of autonomous evacuation camps, refusing aid from the Berlusconi-led administration. These campaigners staged protests in L'Aquila and Rome, invited critical thinkers to offer outsiders' per-spectives on transformations in the city, denounced the G8 summit by display-ing the famous 'YES WE CAMP' lettering, and broke emergency legislation by forcing their way into the inaccessible historic centre to remove debris, helped by thousands of survivors, almost one year after the earthquake, in early 2010.

A number of these grassroots initiatives then founded Appello per L'Aquila as a proper political platform, in order to participate in the 2012 elections. One of Appello's prominent faces is Cecilia, who teaches at L'Aquila's university. Before the earthquake, she explained, she had not been involved in politics, but afterwards, she wanted to influence what was happening in her city. The experience of total outside control had shocked her: 'I wanted to be involved myself. I no longer felt comfortable delegating decisions to others after what had been happening to my city.' Cecilia emphasised that the government handling of the emergency effort had shaped her transformation from an anti-political academic into an aspiring local politician. During the election campaign, she worked endlessly for Appello per L'Aquila, giving interviews to newspapers, local television stations and facing the electorate in a number of open meetings.

Cecilia described certain core values – participation and transparency – as constitutive of her understanding of democratic politics. Appello's leading can-didate, Ettore, who became a city councillor, represented these values for her: he was the founding member of a website called Openpolis, which seeks to enforce transparency in political decision-making processes through wide-ranging public participation, enabled by publishing official documents online – practices described by Openpolis as 'the most ancient and purest form of democracy'.[13]

Cecilia's experience illustrates how the authoritarian state of emergency led to a reflection on values, ideas and practices regarding political lives in L'Aquila. New aspirations – such as accountability, transparency and participation – were chosen following reflections on specific experiences during post-earthquake authoritarian governance. Politics could no longer be conceptualised as con-fined to a dimension separate from ordinary life; the impact of political deci-sions on a community, as well as on intimate, personal lives, had been concrete.

The second civic platform that participated in L'Aquila's 2012 municipal elec-tions was L'Aquila Che Vogliamo [L'Aquila That We Want]. Its figurehead is Vincenzo Vittorini, a surgeon who lost his wife and daughter in the earthquake. Vincenzo had remained under the debris of his collapsed multi-storey home for many hours, before fire fighters rescued him. His teenage son survived, away on a school trip. Soon after the tragedy, relatives of the 309 victims founded La Fondazione Sei Aprile Per La Vita [The 6 April Foundation For Life], with two central aims: to remember the victims, and to lobby for safety in the reconstruc-tion process.

'Why is it', Vincenzo asked me rhetorically a few weeks after he had gained a seat in the city council, 'that earthquakes bring down houses in Italy? In Japan, they have much stronger quakes, and nothing collapses. Because they have a culture of safety! We need that same culture here.' We were sitting in a small café outside the regional parliament of the Abruzzo region. Since L'Aquila's

Figure 5.3 Vincenzo Vittorini addresses supporters at a rally during the 2012 election campaign

Figure 5.4 Appello per L'Aquila supporters discuss incoming election results in their headquarters

historic city hall had been rendered inaccessible by the earthquake, local councillors met here to debate municipal politics. Parts of the historical building were still propped up by extensive scaffolding; the façade was cracked in numerous places.

After the earthquake, the bereaved relatives had initially tried to influence politics as a lobby group, Vincenzo recalled, 'but we didn't achieve anything. No one wanted to listen to us, and no one took us seriously.' Frustrated with the difficulty of trying to achieve political change, Vincenzo and others from the foundation sought direct participation in decision-making processes: 'When we realised that the local administration would not guarantee safety standards in the reconstruction process and learn from past mistakes, we decided to create our own political party, L'Aquila Che Vogliamo.'

For Vincenzo, rethinking the intersection of a purportedly private existence and political processes resulted from experiencing the devastating failure of politics in his family life. Just like Cecilia, Vincenzo insisted he had not been politically involved before April 2009. Losing his wife and daughter forced him to rethink connections between intimacy and public institutions, since individuals or families cannot implement building standards and lead the fight against organised crime involvement in the construction industry. Vincenzo insisted that the state must support these causes. This created a moral impossibility of maintaining detachment from institutions:

> So, the earthquake was an extremely tragic event. OK. Now, we have to make sure that this event can initiate a positive process that will permit us to make this a better city, to improve. Houses can get damaged in earthquakes, but buildings mustn't collapse. Only collapsing buildings kill people.

Vincenzo's turn towards the possibilities offered by participatory democracy and transparency resulted from pragmatism, rather than idealism. Nonetheless, his example illustrates the complex ways in which some Aquilani envisioned, and engaged with, democratic opportunities after the quake. 'There will be other earthquakes here. We must make L'Aquila safe for the future', Vincenzo concluded. 'No father should ever have to find his daughter underneath a collapsed house. If we don't learn from this, their death will have been in vain.'

Vincenzo's reflections on safety connect intimate vulnerability with institutions of the democratic state. He believes that democratic participation can establish vital control mechanisms, preventing further tragedy. Vincenzo illustrates one way in which Aquilani engage with the possibilities of democracy: as a political strategy enabling citizens to remake their world, as a particular dimension of disaster recovery. For him and others in L'Aquila Che Vogliamo, the death of family members constituted the kind of decision-event that forces people to act. This is one possible avenue in which Aquilani conceptualised the effects of state institutions in their lives; in response, they sought to reconstitute individual and collective capacities for control over local lives through participatory democracy.

Campaigners behind Appello Per L'Aquila hoped to guarantee the non-repetition of the authoritarian suspensions of what they conceptualised as crucial practices of citizenship: critical debate, transparency, accountability and public participation. The relatives of the earthquake victims were motivated by a moral imperative to influence state institutions. Both groups pursued future-oriented political visions rooted in intimate experiences regarding the intersection of private lives with the work of state authorities and public politics. By participating in elections – presenting visions for L'Aquila's future to Aquilani voters – both Appello Per L'Aquila and L'Aquila Che Vogliamo illustrated an enduring belief in the transformative power of democracy, and in the maintenance of at least local state institutions such as councils, mayors and public officials.

Members of affected populations respond to moments of post-democratic authoritarian rule differently: some acquiesce passively, others romanticise nostalgically the fascist past for its purported efficiency, and a different set of people might fill the notion of democracy with new meanings and practices. Engagements with participatory possibilities of democracy during times of crisis are complex. For some Aquilani who found such infringements disproportionate, their experiences were decision-events demanding action. Local campaigners became engaged in long-term participatory democratic politics, shaping institutions from within, with significant support from the city's electorate.

Italy's Expert Government

I suggest that examining the ways in which post-earthquake Aquilani reflect on practices of democratic citizenship and on the role of institutions helps us understand developments across Italy. In November 2011, after having been Italy's dominant political figure for almost twenty years, Silvio Berlusconi resigned from the office of prime minister. Under pressure from 'the markets' and European leaders, Italy was expected to require emergency loans from the so-called 'troika' of international institutions (IMF, ECB and European Commission). Crisis talk was ubiquitous. Without elections, Italy's president, Giorgio Napolitano, thus appointed Mario Monti, a former European Union commissioner and the president of Milan's prestigious Bocconi University, to head an emergency expert government.

In parliament, Monti and his *governo tecnico* relied on a bipartisan majority to pass legislation drafted by expert ministers. No major party dared to withhold support. Throughout 2012, Monti's government enacted painful cuts, initiated structural reforms and attempted to reduce Italy's budgetary deficit. Despite not having been elected, Monti and his government enjoyed widespread popular support. A newspaper poll in March 2012, after three months in office, gave Monti's expert government a fifty-one per cent approval rating; by contrast, only eight per cent of respondents expressed trust in political parties. International newspapers speculated that for Italy's traditional political elite 'the party's over' (The Economist 2012).

The rhetoric of an economic emergency, the threat of an Italian default and pressure from European partners suggested that there was no alternative to Monti. Opposition was weak and silent. Legislation was whipped through parliament. Time was pressing and decisions had to be taken swiftly, it was argued – just as in L'Aquila. Expert crisis management was widely accepted, and even welcomed, across Italy. Italian newspapers reported interest rates on government bonds daily, warning that the collapse of state finances was a possibility. Effective debate about alternatives was limited, and when it surfaced, it barely changed the government's austerity trajectory.

Monti's cuts echoed the effects of structural adjustment policies imposed on Greece, Spain, Ireland and Portugal: over the course of one year, one million Italians became unemployed. In early 2013, unemployment reached twelve per cent. Thirty-nine per cent of Italians below the age of twenty-five were without a job, the third-highest rate in Europe. However, polls showed that Italians predominantly blamed past governments for the difficulties, rather than Monti or the euro crisis (Censis 2012). Previous administrations, in the eyes of Italians, had failed to govern the county adequately, to use resources wisely, to respond to global challenges, to reduce the deficit and to prepare Italy for the future. While this sentiment led to the acceptance of an unelected government, in a similar fashion to many Aquilani, the personal effects of crisis led Italians to rediscover participatory democracy.

The success of the MoVimento Cinque Stelle [Five Star Movement] – the landslide winner of the February 2013 Italian parliamentary elections, which marked the premature end of Monti's time in office – was a reaction to a crisis of Italy's representative democracy. Despite having been founded as recently as 2009, the Five Star Movement, led by a charismatic former comedian, Beppe Grillo, rose to twenty-six per cent in the 2013 national elections, taking almost nine million votes. The MoVimento proposed a radical break with the traditional party system to reinvent participatory democracy, drawing on social media involvement and the internet. It became the largest single party in the Italian parliament.[14] The MoVimento's goal was to oust the traditional political personnel, ending what MoVimento campaigners castigated as entrenched corruption and nepotism.

The MoVimento's candidates were chosen in online referenda, and all of them had something in common: no previous experience with party politics. They did not try to compensate for this lack of experience, however, but instead flaunted their status as outsiders as a sign of distinction in a system widely considered corrupt and remote from voters. After the elections, the average age of the new MoVimento's parliamentarians was thirty-five (much below the average for MPs), and many of them were women.

The MoVimento's election manifesto opposed what campaigners denounced as Italy's political ills. Its goals included: the abolition of privileges for parliamentarians, banning serving MPs from having second jobs, reducing parliamentarians' salaries to reflect the average income, banning candidates convicted for criminal offences, a restriction to two terms in office and the obligation to table legislation proposed by citizens' initiatives. Through rhetoric and content, the MoVimento presented itself as a virtuous alternative to a political reality associated with vice, sleaze and corruption. A 'Code of Conduct' for all MoVimento parliamentarians included a passage prohibiting cooperation with other parties. If MPs dissent, they are routinely asked to leave the movement and join other parties. This authoritarian style has brought much criticism to Beppe Grillo – but the MoVimento's ranks have remained largely closed.[15]

Interestingly, the MoVimento has proposed a break with the current system while retaining key features. It does not seek extra-parliamentary opposition, but participates in national, regional and local elections. During the course of Monti's expert government, as Italians began to feel the effects of the cuts, the polls saw a steady rise of support for the MoVimento. Local branches were founded across the country with unprecedented speed. Young people, especially, found a promising alternative to traditional political realities in an active platform that combined a profound rupture with the retention of state institutions and practices of representative democratic politics, celebrating the public good, transparency, participation and accountability – which campaigners described as proper democracy.

Conclusion

The literature on (southern) Italy, particularly by Anglo-American authors (Filippucci 1996), has routinely portrayed Italians as the West's unchanging Other: corrupt, family-orientated, incapable of collective action and unfit for democracy. Investigating concrete engagements with democratic possibilities during times of crisis, however, produces a more complex picture. Prior to the earthquake, a lack of interest in participation regarding politics and state institutions existed in L'Aquila. After the earthquake, however, the authoritarian crisis management at the hands of Silvio Berlusconi's Civil Protection Agency gave rise to a variety of responses: while some Aquilani accepted the autocratic rule as necessary and surrendered hope in democracy's capacity to improve their lives, others used the same experience to invent novel practices of participatory democracy. Following the 2012 Emilia-Romagna earthquake, a horse farmer imagined the fascist past nostalgically, describing Italy as unfit for democracy – particularly so during times of crisis and personal difficulty. Some Aquilani echoed the sentiment, and individual disillusionment added to the seeking of distance from state institutions and the ideal of democracy, adding dimensions of personal disappointment to the state of emergency's post-democratic top-down management.

The heavy-handed disaster relief operation dismantled an imagined boundary between public politics and private lives. Intimacy was reworked through camp life, from which escape was arduous. Everyday sociality – moving around freely, meeting friends and relatives, and discussing current affairs in public, urban spaces – became difficult, if not impossible. Experiencing the absence of certain routine practices – such as participation, transparency, communication and civic duty – during authoritarian governance induced some Aquilani to reconstitute these values as the core aspirations for their emergent political engagements.

For the relatives of the victims, bereavement turned cynical detachment into an untenable form of citizenship in the face of the devastating consequences of failed governance. Facing post-democratic disillusionment, some Aquilani sought to remake the value of participatory democracy, revealing complex interactions between autocracy, crisis and democratic citizenship. Similarly, the national economic decline, which led to the widespread acceptance of a non-elected emergency government under Mario Monti, did not constitute a permanent rejection of democratically elected state institutions. The winner of Italy's 2013 parliamentary elections was neither the traditional political class, nor an expert elite (Mario Monti participated in the elections with a newly-founded centrist party, and gained around eight per cent), but a grassroots movement that proposed a radical break with the current political system and advocated greater transparency, participation and democracy.

The unelected expert government under Mario Monti did not constitute the watershed event that estranged Italians from representative democracy, with its slow reaction time and need for compromise. Rather, crisis moments can permit people to reflect on interactions between political and personal dimensions of governance, between private lives and state institutions. Only through personal and collective engagement do transitions from states of emergency and crisis to political normality occur. Crises can thus constitute the decision-events that make people act differently, designing novel life trajectories. One decisive possibility of agency amidst circumstances of top-down crisis management and the rhetoric of exceptional measures in contemporary Italy, documented in this chapter, is located in emergent citizenship practices, often still conceptualised as participatory democracy.

Notes

1   It was creatively called 'Progetto C.A.S.E., an acronym for 'anti-seismic, sustainable and eco-compatible complexes'. *Case* is also Italian for 'houses'.

2   For an overview of Berlusconi's transition from the self-made construction magnate to a private television monopolist, see Paul Ginsborg (2004).

3   Berlusconi did not fail to compare his government's dedication to the city's plight with past political failures in disaster response (Dickie et al. 2002).

4   The July 2009 G8 summit had originally been organised for La Maddalena, a small island off the coast of Sardinia. After the L'Aquila earthquake, however, the Berlusconi administration moved the meeting of world leaders to the ravaged city, purportedly to bring attention to its plight.

5   Informants' names have been changed, with the exception of the leaders of political movements.

6   For a discussion of stereotypes of 'the South' see Dickie (1996: 27–30), Gribaudi (1996), and Schneider (1998).

7   Sydel Silverman (1968), in response to Banfield, has argued that familism is not a cause of poverty, but rather its result. In a study of family firms in the wealthy Como area in northern Italy, Sylvia Yanagisako (2002) has shown that a focus on the family's well-being can be a key factor in local businesses' success, rather than an impediment to prosperity.

8   Geographically located in the centre of the country, L'Aquila is associated with southern Italy because of its historical role as part of the Kingdom of Naples (1282–1816) and of the Kingdom of the Two Sicilies (1816–1861).

9   This view of camp life as an experiment in total social control is captured in Sabina Guzzanti's critical documentary Draquila (2010).

10   I am using the terms autocracy/authoritarianism and autocratic/authoritarian interchangeably.

11   The prefect represents the Italian national government in a specific town or city, communicating local concerns to Rome, and thus is an important state representative.

12   The literal translation from the original Italian would be, 'many have eaten our dead' [*tanti hanno mangiato i nostri morti*], which expresses frustration and moral outrage better than the English idiom.

13   See <www.openpolis.it>.

14   Because of an election law that favours coalitions and awards an automatic majority of fifty-four per cent of seats to the largest coalition, however, the MoVimento did not actually constitute the largest MP group in the Italian parliament. A left-wing coalition led by the Partito Democratico [Social Democrats] was the largest faction, hence awarded a majority bonus. The new Prime Minister, Enrico Letta, served until spring 2014, when he was replaced by Matteo Renzi, who staged a coup within the Partito Democratico.

15   This discussion of the MoVimento Cinque Stelle is necessarily preliminary and limited, and I do not attempt to offer a comprehensive, detailed analysis of its contribution to, or legacy for, the Italian political system. Rather, I seek to draw attention to interesting parallels between the political realities in L'Aquila and across Italy, regarding a double movement of crisis and expert management, on the one hand, and growing civic awareness and involvement, on the other. This insight also results from my informants' assertion that L'Aquila and its crisis constitute a mirror of pan-Italian developments and challenges.

References

Agamben, G. 2005. *State of Exception* (trans. K. Attell). Chicago: University of Chicago Press.

Alexander, D.E. 2010. The L'Aquila Earthquake of 6 April 2009 and Italian Government Policy on Disaster Response. *Journal of Natural Policy Research* 2, no. 4: 325–342.

———. 2013. An Evaluations of Medium-Term Recovery Processes after the 6 April 2009 Earthquake in L'Aquila, Central Italy. *Environmental Hazards* 12, no. 1: 60–73.

Antonini, O. 2010. *I Terremoti Aquilani*. Todi: Tau Editrice.

Badiou, A. 2005. *Being and Event* (trans. O. Feltham). New York: Continuum.

Banfield, E. 1958. *The Moral Basis of a Backward Society*. New York: Free Press.

Cappelletto, F. 2003. Long-Term Memory of Extreme Events: From Autobiography to History. *Journal of the Royal Anthropological Institute* 9, no. 2: 241–260.

Censis. 2012. *Segnali di Reazione degli Italiani: in Moto Processi di Riposizionamento nel Sociale e nell'Economia*. <http://www.censis.it>, 7 December.

Il Centro. 2013. Il Terremoto e l'Ipocrisia del Prefetto. <http://ilcentro.gelocal.it/regione/2013/01/20/news/il-terremoto-e-l-ipocrisia-del-prefetto-1.6383857> (accessed 10 July 2015).

Ciccozzi, A. 2011. Catastrofe e C.A.S.E. In *Il Terremoto dell'Aquila. Analisi e Riflessioni sull'Emergenza* (ed.) U. d. S. Dell'Aquila. L'Aquila: Edizione L'Una.

Clementi, A. 1998. *Storia dell'Aquila. Dalle Origini alla Prima Guerra Mondiale*. Rome/Bari: Laterza.

Clementi, A., and E. Piroddi. 1986. *L'Aquila*. Rome/Bari: Laterza.

Crouch, C. 2004. *Post-Democracy*. Cambridge: Polity Press.

Dickie, J. 1996. Imagined Italies. In *Italian Cultural Studies* (eds) D. Forgacs and R. Lumley, 19–33. Oxford: Oxford University Press.

Dickie, J., J. Foot, and F. Snowden (eds). 2002. *Disastro! Disasters in Italy since 1860: Culture, Politics, Society*. New York: Palgrave Macmillan.

The Economist. 2012. The Party's Over. *The Economist*, 3 March.

Il Fatto Quotidiano. 2013. Terremoto dell'Aquila, il Prefetto Rideva e Fingeva Commozione per le Vittime. <http://www.ilfattoquotidiano.it/2013/01/19/prefetto-iurato-rideva-e-fingeva-commozione-per-vittime-del-terremoto-dellaquila/474340/> (accessed 10 July 2015).

Ferragina, E. 2009. The Never-Ending Debate About the Moral Basis of a Backward Society: Banfield and 'Amoral Familism'. *Journal of the Anthropological Society of Oxford – Online* 1, no. 2, 141–160.

Filippucci, P. 1996. Anthropological Perspectives on Culture in Italy. In *Italian Cultural Studies* (eds) D. Forgacs and R. Lumley, 52–71. Oxford: Oxford University Press.

Foot, J. 2003. *Modern Italy*. New York: Palgrave Macmillan.

———. 2009. *Italy's Divided Memory*. New York: Palgrave Macmillan.

Ginsborg, P. 2001. *Italy and Its Discontents: Family, Society, State*. New York: Palgrave Macmillan.

———. 2004. *Silvio Berlusconi: Television, Power and Patrimony*. New York: Verso.

Gribaudi, G. 1996. Images of the South. In *Italian Cultural Studies* (eds) D. Forgacs and R. Lumley, 72–87. Oxford: Oxford University Press.

Guzzanti, S. (dir.). 2010. *Draquila – Italia Che Trema*. BIM Distribuzione.

Herzfeld, M. 1991. *A Place in History – Social and Monumental Time in a Cretan Town*. Princeton: Princeton University Press.

Humphrey, C. 2008. Reassembling Individual Subjects: Events and Decisions in Troubled Times. *Anthropological Theory* 8, no. 4: 357–380.

Jiménez, A.C. 2003. On Space as a Capacity. *Journal of the Royal Anthropological Institute* 9, no. 1: 137–153.

Jones, T. 2003. *The Dark Heart of Italy*. London: Faber and Faber.

Klein, N. 2007. *The Shock Doctrine*. London: Penguin.

La Repubblica. 2013. Terremoto L'Aquila, Le Verità Nascoste. Bertolaso: 'Ricostruzione tra 28 Anni'. <http://video.repubblica.it/dossier/terremoto-in-abruzzo/terremoto-l-aquila-le-verita-nascoste-bertolaso-ricostruzione-tra-28-anni/116798/115244> (accessed 10 July 2015).

Low, S.M. 1999. Spatializing Culture: The Social Production and Social Construction of Public Space in Costa Rica. In *Theorizing the City: The New Urban Anthropology Reader* (ed.) S.M. Low, 111–137. Piscataway: Rutgers University Press.

Malkki, L. 1995. *Purity and Exile: Violence, Memory, and National Cosmology among Hutu Refugees in Tanzania*. Chicago: University of Chicago Press.

Mammarella, L. 1990. *L'Abruzzo Ballerino. Cronologia dei Terremoti in Abruzzo dall'Epoca Romana al 1915*. L'Aquila: Adelmo Polla Editore.

Muehlebach, A. 2012. *The Moral Neoliberal: Welfare and Citizenship in Italy*. Chicago: University of Chicago Press.

Parboni, A. 2010. Bertolaso Indagato per Corruzione. *Il Tempo*, 11 February.

Popham, P. 2009. Berlusconi Turns Adversity to Political Advantage after Quake: The Italian Leader's Energetic Reaction to the Disaster Has Been a PR Triumph. *The Independent*, 10 April.

Putnam, R., R. Leonardi and R. Nanetti. 1993. *Making Democracy Work: Civic Traditions in Modern Italy*. Princeton: Princeton University Press.

Runciman, D. 2013. *The Confidence Trap: A History of Democracy in Crisis from World War I to the Present*. Princeton: Princeton University Press.

Saunders, G.R. 1998. The Magic of the South: Popular Religions and Elite Catholicism in Italian Ethnology. In *Italy's 'Southern Question': Orientalism in One Country* (ed.) J. Schneider. Oxford: Berg.

Schneider, J. (ed.). 1998. *Italy's 'Southern Question' – Orientalism in One Country*. Oxford: Berg.

Silverman, S. 1968. Agricultural Organization and Social Structure, and Values in Italy: Amoral Familism Reconsidered. *American Anthropologist* 70, no. 1: 1–20.

——. 1975. *Three Bells of Civilization – The Life of an Italian Hill Town*. New York: Columbia University Press.

Trapasso, P. 2010. Bertolaso Sentenzia e Irrita Anche Chiodi. <http://www.6aprile.it/featured/2010/09/10/bertolaso-sentenzia-e-irrita-anche-chiodi.html> (accessed 10 July 2015).

Yanagisako, S.J. 2002. *Producing Culture and Capital: Family Firms in Italy*. Princeton: Princeton University Press.

Yoneyama, L. 1999. *Hiroshima Traces: Time, Space, and the Dialectics of Memory*. Berkeley: University of California Press.

Jan-Jonathan Bock is a research fellow at the Woolf Institute, and an honorary research associate at Peterhouse, University of Cambridge.

6

'The People' and Political Opposition in Post-democracy
Reflections on the Hollowing of Democracy in Greece and Europe

Giorgos Katsambekis

[I]t is now quite clear that the democratic states of the capitalist world have not one sovereign, but two: their people, below, and the international 'markets' above. (Wolfgang Streeck, 'Markets and Peoples')

Wolfgang Streeck's words reflect a shared worry among contemporary democratic intellectuals, political theorists and economists, concerning a power shift evident in most developed countries of the Western world. This shift can be described as a quasi-transfer of authority from 'the people' to 'the markets' – and from popular sovereignty to technocratic virtue and administrative rationalism. In Peter Mair's (2013: 2) words, it feels today that even the 'semi-sovereignty' of the people, which Elmer Schattschneider (1960) was talking about in the 1960s, 'is slipping away, and that the people ... are becoming effectively *non-sovereign*. What we now see emerging is a notion of democracy that is being steadily stripped of its popular component – easing away from the demos.' Sociology and political theory have coined the term 'post-democracy' to designate – among other things – this hollowing of democratic institutions, that seems to have started somewhere in the early 1980s and has most probably peaked during the last two decades.

Hence, while the concept of 'post-democracy' was until recently only marginally used by radical political theorists and sociologists, today, amid an unprecedented crisis, it acquires a renewed interest and importance. Post-democracy signifies a transition that can be seen and investigated on many levels of political life and society. But what it basically designates is a *tendency* towards a depoliticised polity where decision making is increasingly slipping away from popular control and accountability, and where the people are becoming spectators rather than active citizens (Crouch 2004). In this context, my focus in what follows will be set on post-democracy's eventual dismissal of 'the people' as the legitimising authority and central symbolic reference upon which the democratic polity is based (see Canovan 2005; Laclau 2005; Lefort 1988; Rancière 2006). A discursive dismissal that constitutes both the justification of a specific neoliberal govern-mentality, already in place, and the prefiguration of a 'democracy without the demos', that seems to be the vision for certain political and intellectual elites across the Western world (see Rancière 1999; Mair 2013; Feinberg 2008).

Indeed, post-democracy's dismissal of 'the people' seems to dovetail per-fectly with the late (neo)liberal paradigm of consensual or 'post-adversarial' politics (Mouffe 2005a: 75–76). This discourse is premised on the posi-tion that the right/left distinction has run its course, that confrontation and antagonism(s) in politics are obsolete, if not harmful, and thus, that there needs to be a broad consensus on some core issues of policy making (usually concern-ing fiscal issues that are presented as 'non-political'), which are supposed to be placed beyond contestation and popular accountability (Mouffe 2013; Mair 2013). This is the gist of what is termed 'post-adversarial politics': a situation where there is no meaningful contestation or debate around the terms along which a polity is organised and functions, and where politics is reduced to the technical administration of a specific model, which in itself is never seriously challenged.

It is within this context that the people – or the 'ordinary citizens' – are losing their political priority and relevance. Popular participation (from elec-tions to trade unions and collective movements) has generally declined over the last decades. Peter Mair, in his posthumous masterpiece (2013), describes this withdrawal of the masses with great analytical clarity. This disengagement of the people can be traced in the electoral arena mainly through the increasingly low turnout levels in elections throughout Europe, but also through the increasing levels of electoral volatility (Mair 2013: 22–34). For Mair, 'withdrawal and dis-engagement are symptomatic of a growing indifference to conventional politics' (Mair 2013: 19). In his analysis, this is just one side of the same coin, the other side being the political elites who are also withdrawing from the political arena and partisan politics, becoming more closely attached to government institu-tions and the state itself. This 'twin disengagement' ultimately marks a growing gap in the heart of contemporary democracies, a gap between 'the people' and democratic power, 'the people' and the legitimation of governments, which needs to be seriously taken into account.

If this is true and yesterday's 'dark continent' is now becoming a 'grey post-democratic continent', with peoples and political elites disengaged from each other, then there is probably no better place to investigate post-democracy's excesses than crisis-ridden Greece. After tracing the signs of Greece's post-democratic transition over the last two decades, I propose that post-democratic theory is a significant tool in understanding not just the Greek political system and society today, but also the dynamics within the European Union. In its turn, the study of the Greek case might provide significant insight as to where post-democracy is heading. Admittedly, the ongoing crisis has sharpened discourses and polarisations, has pushed political subjects to take rigid positions against the administration of the crisis and eventually led the once barely convergent mainstream political forces of centre-left and centre-right (PASOK[1] and ND[2]) under the same political roof between November 2011 and late 2014. This, in its turn, created the grounds for the rise of a challenger party at the left of the political spectrum, skyrocketing the (until recently marginal) populist radical left SYRIZA[3] to power in January 2015 (see Katsambekis 2015). So, in a way, politics seems to be dynamically back on the agenda and post-democratic tendencies are being challenged through the re-emergence of new polarisations and the decline of consensus. On the other hand, due to this re-emergence, European and Greek elites have aggressively tried to suppress any popular contestation or opposition, to silence or surpass the people, revealing post-democracy's more authoritarian face. Most striking in this regard has been the chain of events that led the newly elected SYRIZA government to succumb to the pressures of its European partners for the continuation of austerity in July 2015.

In this context, my main focus will be on the discursive administration of the first phase of the crisis (i.e. before SYRIZA came to power in January 2015) and the operation of various signifiers in the elites' discourse, understood here as a set of 'systems of meaningful practices that form the identities of subjects and objects' (Howarth and Stavrakakis 2000: 3–4) through the construction of social antagonisms and collective identities and the drawing of political frontiers. Discourse, in this sense, does not only build hegemonic narratives and construct what is eventually perceived as 'normal'. It also reflects and justifies a set of already existing institutions as well as social relations and practices, while at the same time it can prefigure possible future alternatives.

My aim is to show that the popular-democratic subject of modernity, as historically incarnated by 'the people', is systematically ignored, marginalised, even stigmatised and suppressed, as contemporary European elites develop a new 'fear of the masses' – or 'demophobia' (see Marlière 2013) – and attempt their own 'revolution from above' (Balibar 2011). The general hypothesis is that the (discursive) marginalisation of 'the people' (or 'anti-populism') reflects a broader shift from the *political* (as antagonism, rupture, etc.) to the *post-political* (as management, administration, consensus, etc.) and from *democracy* to *post-democracy*; from antagonism and political debate on alternatives to 'neutral' management and 'enlightened' administration. Indeed, what the pressures of the current crisis produced wasn't a renewed open and democratic space where people could participate more, get further involved, deliberate, disagree and co-decide on issues that are affecting them equally, if not radically changing their ways of life. On the contrary, the crisis, to date, has given ground to European and Greek elites, along with various transnational or supranational institutions, like the IMF and the ECB, or internal organs of the EU (like the Eurogroup) to further consolidate their power over the national parliaments and impose an *emergency consensus*, particularly hostile to popular dissent.

Post-democracy (and the Spectre of Populism)

'Post-democracy' is a term initially coined by Jacques Rancière (1995) and consolidated in mainstream academic research through the elaborations of Colin Crouch (2004) and Chantal Mouffe (2005a) – among others. It designates a series of *tendencies* that mark a passage of modern developed democracies to norms and practices that are reminiscent of pre-democratic rule (Crouch 2004: 6). So while all the formal institutions of democracy remain in place, the centres of political decision and the very energy of political antagonism have gradually moved to somewhere else. The temple of democratic decision making is no longer the parliament, nor is the 'sovereign people' the cornerstone of the polity's legitimisation. The parliament is still there, it typically functions, but there are myriads of non-democratically controlled institutions, formal or informal, that effectively take part or seriously influence decision making, while the media and the various 'experts' have acquired a very powerful role. As for the moment that the electorate is called upon to choose its representatives, 'while elections certainly exist and can change governments, public electoral debate is a tightly controlled spectacle, managed by rival teams of professionals expert in the techniques of persuasion, and considering a small range of issues selected by those teams' (Crouch 2004: 4). And it gets even more complex if we turn our gaze from the national to the various international or supranational institutions. From the notorious rating agencies and the International Monetary Fund (IMF) to the European Union, this 'gentle monster' in Brussels (Enzensberger 2011), and large multinational corporations and financial capital, political decision is repeatedly filtered, influenced and altered over and again, leading – in several cases – democratically elected governments to impose the very opposite policies to the ones they promised, fuelling in this way frustration and political cynicism.

In Rancière's words:

> Postdemocracy is the government practice and conceptual legitimation of a democracy after the demos, a democracy that has eliminated the appearance, miscount, and dispute of the people and is thereby reducible to the sole interplay of state mechanisms and combinations of social energies and interests. (Rancière 1999: 102)

Maybe it is hard to find a better example of post-democratic rule in today's Western world, than in the EU itself, where:

> decisions can be taken by political elites with more or less a free hand. What we see, therefore, is the absence of effective representation in the European Union political system, in that … the citizens lack ultimate control … Despite the seeming availability of channels of access, the scope of meaningful input and hence for effective electoral accountability is exceptionally limited. It is in this sense that Europe appears to have been constructed as a protected sphere, safe from the demands of voters and their representatives. (Mair 2013: 108–109)

It is in this context that 'populism' becomes part of the (post-democratic) story. Since populism's main operation is the discursive construction and interpellation of 'the people' in opposition to a 'power bloc' (Laclau 2005), while post-democracy's aim is to make 'the people' disappear (Rancière 2006: 80; Feinberg 2008: 61–66), the confrontation between post-democracy and populism comes rather naturally. As Serge Halimi has recently pointed out, '[a]nyone who criticizes the privileges of the oligarchy, the growing speculation of the leading classes, the gifts to the banks, market liberalization, cuts on wages with the pretext of competitiveness, is denounced as "populist" who "plays the game of extreme right"' (Halimi 2011). Again, Rancière (2006: 80) had already highlighted that populism can be seen today as the 'convenient name' under which the denunciation and discrediting of alternatives legitimises the claim of economic and political elites to 'govern without the people', 'to govern without politics'. Halimi and Rancière's concerns are reflected in a growing literature on Europe's post-democratic trajectory, the absence of solidarity among EU members and a growing 'democratic deficit' that can bid popular sovereignty farewell (Habermas 2011; Beck 2011; Balibar 2010, 2011). In such accounts the roles of popular representation and popular participation acquire a central position in the envisaging of a break with the post-democratic regime and a radical-democratic way out of the crisis.

But instead of more popular involvement, the European elites have chosen less and less popular involvement and deliberation. The emphatic dismissal of 'populism' by the European elites (see e.g. Stabenow 2010; Cendrowicz 2012) seems to confirm Laclau's (2005: x) suspicion, that such a trend entails 'the dismissal of politics *tout court*', and 'the assertion that the management of community is a concern of an administrative power whose source of legitimacy is a proper knowledge of what a "good" community is'. 'Proper knowledge' or 'expertise' can be seen here as metonymies of the pre-democratic logic of the *arkhè*, that entails a '"normal" distribution of positions that defines who exercises power and who is subject to it' (see Rancière 2010: 30–31). Today, the logic of the *arkhè* can be better described as post-political technocracy or, following Karl Bracher (1964), 'expertocracy'.

But what does that mean for the popular component of democracy? The picture might become clearer if we now focus on the notion of 'the people' and its place within the landscape of democracy.

'The People': Clarifications on a Contested Notion

Talking about 'the people' is far from unambiguous. Democratic political theory has long struggled with the term, sometimes advocating rival conceptions of democratic agency, such as the 'multitude', 'civil society', or the 'proletariat'. References to 'the people' became a constant in political life after the passage to political modernity and the so-called 'disenchantment of the world' (Gauchet 1997). 'Popular sovereignty' and 'representation' replaced the 'Divine Right of Kings' as the legitimising cornerstone of any democratic political order. And with the kings gone, the people became the occupant of the 'empty place' of power (Lefort 1988: 225).

Today, as Margaret Canovan (2005: 2) maintains, '[t]he English term ['the people'] shares three basic senses with its equivalents in other European languages: the people as sovereign; peoples as nations, and the people as opposed to the ruling elite (what used to be called "the common people")'. And while this phenomenological distinction is adequate, we should supplement the notion of 'the people' with the element of radical *potentiality*, to adequately grasp it as the subject that emerges after the democratic rupture of political modernity (Rancière 2010), the subject that is at once the bearer of *constituent* and *constituted* power (see Kalyvas 2005). Understanding 'the people' as constituent power, means acknowledging that they 'can play an active role in terms of (re) founding and updating the higher legal norms and procedural rules that regulate the exercise of power' (Rovira Kaltwasser 2012: 189).

So the people could be better grasped as an ever-present subject/possibility, elusive and paradoxical in the sense that the very thing that 'grounds' it, might also be 'the thing that renders it impossible' (as per Rancière 2010: 86–87). In that sense, Rancière suggests that the people signifies the inscription of the 'part of those who have no part' – the inscription of the excluded, the 'uncounted', who break with the existing order and claim their inclusion, the particularity that speaks and acts in the name of 'the people', identifying itself with the whole of the community (ibid.: 33–34, 85). The people are thus seen as the specific subject of politics, where *politics* as opposed to *police* is understood as a disruptive force/process which, through the constitution of egalitarian discourses, brings into question established identities and norms, disturbs fixity and re-opens the field of contestation (ibid.: 36–37). Understood in this sense, the people becomes 'a political category' *par excellence*: 'not ... a datum of the social structure ... not a given group, but an act of institution that creates a new agency out of a plurality of heterogeneous elements' (Laclau 2005: 224).

In such an understanding of the people also lies what Rancière (2006) calls the 'scandal of democracy', which is exactly what disturbs today's anti-populist technocratic elites, who seem to call upon the Saint-Simonian dream of an apolitical 'administration of things': the fact 'that [in Democracy] the power belongs to those who have no qualification to rule' (Rancière 2011: 3). If Rancière's remarks point more towards the normative and more abstract ideal of democracy, Mair puts forth a similar argument in more concrete terms. He observes that a significant part of contemporary policy-making theory and political theory literature openly advocates that what we need today is less popular involvement in common affairs, indeed 'less democracy' (Mair 2013: 5–9). For some commentators it is clear that 'democracy is too important to be left to the politicians, or even to the people voting in referendums' (Pettit 2001). Thus, '[w]hat we need in politics today is not more democracy but less' (Zakaria 2003: 248). Such views are not confined to academia or policy-making experts, but have found their way into mainstream politics. If modern democracy could be conceptualised as an uneasy marriage between a 'constitutional component' (checks and balances, etc. – government *for* the people) and a 'popular component' (active popular participation – government *by* the people), what Mair (2013: 10) sees is that those two elements of a '"unified" sense of democracy ... are now becoming dis-aggregated, and then ... contrasted to one another both in theory and practice'. And '[o]nce democracy is divided into its popular and constitutional elements, ... it is the popular that loses ground.'

This suppression of democracy's 'popular component' – of 'the people' as constituent power – is clearly revealed in the Greek (but also European) context. But in order to highlight how 'the people' have lost ground during Greece's late post-democratic turn, we first need to take a step back and briefly describe how certain post-democratic tendencies have emerged and intensified within the last two decades.

Greece in the 1990s and 2000s: Enter Post-democracy

Greece probably shows its first clear post-democratic tendencies somewhere in the early or mid-nineties. The two major political parties, which had the support of more than 80 per cent of the electorate, had by then converged to such a point that the centre-right ND was often accusing the centre-left PASOK of having 'stolen' its programme (Bratakos 2002: 681). Both political forces claimed to be 'modernisers' and rallied for consensual politics beyond right and left, beyond 'extremes', and towards a society fully reconciled and devoid of divisions and internal antagonisms. In this consensual paradigm the 'excesses' of political passions and popular identifications around specific centres (be it a leader, a common idea or a common cause) are abandoned – if not discredited – to give place to economic pragmatism, the daily administration of everyday lives and an almost sacralised notion of (economic) growth. References to 'the people' are considered outdated and 'populist' and are soon replaced by more neutral terms, like 'civil society', the 'middle ground', the 'citizen', the 'individual' and so on.

In sharp contrast, political life in Greece during the first two decades after the fall of the military junta in 1974 was characterised by the clear distinction between left-wing and right-wing political forces that defended different programmes and built discernible and antagonistic collective identities that were held together by bonds of affective investment (see Lyrintzis 2005). By the late 1970s and throughout the 1980s, the political stage was dominated by PASOK's archetypal populism and the figure of its charismatic leader, Andreas Papandreou, that put forward the demands of the so-called 'non-privileged' for social justice, popular sovereignty and national independence against an establishment accused of monopolising political access and economic privilege in various ways since the end of the Greek Civil War (1946–1949). As a result of the highly polarised political struggle, political participation on every level was intense (party membership, trade unions, student movement, etc.) and PASOK's rhetoric, which portrayed 'the people' as being 'above institutions', as *the* ulti-mate authority, triggered a massive grassroots movement that gave it a remark-able 48.07 per cent of the vote in the 1981 elections and kept it in power until

1989 (Lyrintzis 1987; Spourdalakis 1988).[4] This was the year that PASOK faced defeat, following a massive scandal involving its leader, Papandreou. During the early 1990s, following an internal crisis, it gradually started turning 'anti-populist' and indeed more moderate; a shift that was fully realised under the leadership of the 'moderniser' Costas Simitis, in 1996, marking a remarkable passage 'from populism to modernisation' (Lyrintzis 2005: 249–252). By then, it had already come back to power, winning the 1993 elections. But we were now dealing with a new PASOK: 'By the mid-1990s ... it was clear that the new moderate pragmatic approach advanced by the PASOK government, particularly in the economy, was incongruous with the polarisation associated with the stress on the Left-Right cleavage' (Lyrintzis 2005: 246).

Polarisation and left-right dilemmas thus gave way to a discourse of consensus and a severe critique of populism, which was a way for the 'new PASOK' of Costas Simitis to denounce the party's radical past. For Simitis (leader of PASOK and prime minister of Greece 1996–2004) anti-populism had become a *sine qua non* for his project of 'modernisation' by the late 1980s. This soon became the case for his main rival, Costas Karamanlis (leader of ND from 1997, and prime minister of Greece 2004–2009), who also chose 'populism' as the 'constitutive outside' of his political project based on the so-called 'middle ground', launched in the late 1990s; a project that was described by the official communications expert/consultant of ND as a strategy of 'triangulation' (inspired by Clinton's campaign for the 1996 U.S. presidential election), a strategy that permitted ND to leave aside its right-wing identity and move to the left, occupying a strategic position at the 'centre' by appropriating many of its opponent's basic ideas (Loulis 1999).

A discourse of 'third-way' national optimism flooded the public space after the mid-1990s and is most evident in the very titles of the books by the then Prime Minister, Costas Simitis: terms like 'powerful Greece', 'powerful society', 'creative Greece', along with 'good governance' and so on, acquire here the role of key signifiers. This peculiar upward spiral of (verbal) modernising optimism peaked when Greece entered the Eurozone in 2000 and then hosted the Olympic Games in 2004. The country was at last seen as a fully integrated member of the group of the most developed and powerful states of Europe, worthy of its place in the euro area and ready to declare its own liberal 'end of history'.

All the other features described by theorists of post-democracy are here, too. In the absence of effective alternatives and political choice(s), expert management (Ladi 2005) and economic administration constituted the dominant paradigm of governance. And since political/programmatic differences were on a sharp decline, communication experts were brought to the fore, so that political antagonism could migrate and be expressed on the terrain of the electoral spectacle. Moreover, experts from the field of finance and economics acquired a prominent place; central bankers and professional academics were present to guarantee that political parties drew on the expertise of the best technocrats in pursuing the most effective administration of things. The field of the economy already reigned supreme over that of politics.

But as Chantal Mouffe has shown, political antagonism can be suppressed but never fully eliminated. It can always manifest itself elsewhere (Mouffe 2005b). So, as in other European countries, suppressed antagonism initially translated into an 'increasing moralization of political discourse' (Mouffe 2005b: 57). Since there is only one politics that is possible, and since there is no alternative, it is a matter of having a better, more virtuous political subject/manager to implement the measures that are considered objectively necessary. Unsurprisingly, then, one of the main slogans of the ND opposition against the Prime Minister Costas Simitis in the late 1990s and early 2000s was that he was the 'archbishop of corruption'. At the same time, ND claimed that it purported to *continue* on the same track of reforms, but would do so with 'humbleness', 'modesty' and through the establishment of a broad 'consensus'. Hence, the main motto of Costas Karamanlis' government as soon as he became prime minister in 2004 was 'with humbleness and modesty'.

Interestingly, the larger part of the Greek society consented to this model and for almost four decades stayed bound to the two major parties. To understand their long-lasting attachment to those parties during their post-democratic turn, one should count in the widespread culture of an individualist and hedonistic cynicism that characterised Greek political culture from the 1990s onwards (see Demertzis 1994; Diamandouros 1994). Citizens remained attached to PASOK and ND since they were more or less reconciled with the current condition, subject to a hegemonic post-political cynicism, and had given up on any possible radical change, or they simply didn't care. Of course, clientelistic networks also played a major part in securing the loyalty of broad social strata to the two major parties (see Sotiropoulos 2001).

Still, it wasn't a smooth ride all the way. The prevailing post-political consensus triggered a variety of populist reactions in the early 2000s (varying from the extreme and religious right to the radical left) which attempted to present themselves as true alternatives to a dead-end path, claiming to represent the 'voice of the people'. Although at times nationalist and xenophobic, these movements were still posing a legitimate claim: they asked for 'more democracy' and for power to be returned to the disempowered 'people'.[5] Mainstream parties and a large part of the Greek intellectual community didn't bother to engage in a meaningful political debate around the causes of the populist emergences and the occasional uncontrolled explosions of collective *pathos*.[6] Their stubborn anti-populist moral condemnation of almost any social mobilisation or reaction and any political opposition as irrational 'populism' and 'nationalism' seemed to prove anti-populism to be a self-fulfilling prophecy, *condemning the product of its suppression.*

Crisis-ridden Greece: Post-democracy at the Extremes?

The unexpected breakdown of 2010 shook previously existing alliances, subjective identities, loyalties and social compromises and initiated a radical dislocation of the Greek political system. The biopolitical paradigm soon shifted violently from individualist and hedonistic cynicism to 'punitive asceticism' (see Stavrakakis, this volume). 'We lived beyond our means', 'we consumed more than we produced', 'we wanted more than we could afford', 'the party is over', and 'we all ate the money together'[7] were characteristic mottos of a dominant discourse that spread a feeling of collective blame and guilt. The 'irresponsible populism' of the past decades that 'flattered the people' with false promises was simultaneously identified as the root of this collective pathology. Similar formulations had also flooded the public spheres in Ireland, Cyprus, Portugal, Spain and Italy.

Enter the Crisis

But let's step back a few months, in order to re-articulate the choreography of events around the Greek crisis from the beginning. In October 2009 Greece held what would prove its most critical national election after the fall of the colonel's junta in 1974. In a society stressed by the various crisis narratives and dismal predictions that followed the global financial breakdown of 2008, PASOK won the election, gaining a rather impressive share of the vote, building its campaign around key signifiers such as a 'better tomorrow', 'a just society', 'a new reborn and optimist Greece', and so on. One of its main promises was a brave redistribution of wealth and a new fairer taxation system in favour of the lower and middle social strata. In this sense, it articulated neo-Keynesian elements in its economic programme. The then government of ND under Costas Karamanlis claimed that PASOK's programme was 'deeply populist', demagogic and thus unattainable, since structural adjustments and fiscal austerity were needed to avert a looming recession. George Papandreou's infamous answer was that 'We have the money'. It was the same George Papandreou some months later who, as the Greek prime minister announced to the Greek people that, not only 'we did not have the money', but also that the country was standing on the verge of a complete economic collapse. The EU and the IMF were called to the rescue and the rest is more or less already history. The bail-out agreement offered to Greece some days later would be publicly presented as *the only viable* solution to the country's tragic situation. It was the turn of ND now – as the opposition – to react fiercely against the draconian austerity measures, but the government's response was that this was the only way to avoid national destruction, rendering, in its turn, ND's disagreement *populist* and ultimately *anti-patriotic*.

In the PASOK government's discourse a rather simplistic schema soon appeared, employing a re-signification of patriotism: Greece was under attack by the 'speculative markets', and thus all Greeks should stand together and endure the assault by implementing a serious of harsh though *necessary* measures in order for the country to survive. This schema appears at first to be populist, or even nationalist-populist since it pitted the Greek people as nation against an exterior Other (the 'markets', the 'speculators'). Nevertheless, on closer inspection, this discourse operated according to what Laclau and Mouffe (1985) call the 'logic of difference' and what Rancière (2010: 36–37) calls the logic of 'police'. It sought to absorb any division or conflict within Greek society in a greater antagonism with what was exterior to the Greek people/nation. It thus performed a contradictory double gesture: first, it overlooked any division within the Greek people/society, since it supposed that despite the particular differences the Greek people could and should be united against what appeared to be an attack from outside the nation (from the 'speculators'); and second, it treated differentially the particular categories of the population, not by institutionally absorbing their demands, but by isolating, targeting and disarming each category through a top-down diffusion of stigmatisation and blame. At first, public sector employees were targeted for not being productive enough, then the so-called 'closed professions' for distorting market competition, then the public education system for not being competitive enough and connected to the market's needs, and so on. Such a discourse would (and initially did) avert the formation of broader alliances and fronts consisting of heterogeneous social subjects – that is on the axis of equivalence – by turning the one category/class against the other.

The administration of the crisis was thus elevated to the status of the *ultimate national issue*, and the then government of PASOK under George Papandreou frequently stressed that what was needed was a new 'genuine patriotism' (see Papandreou 2011). Anyone who opposed the austerity agenda and the so-called 'troika'[8] was simultaneously branded not only *populist*, but also an *anti-patriot*. Discussion around possible alternatives was systematically suppressed, and when it was initiated, it would immediately deteriorate into a monologue about economic necessity. Political opposition was effectively suppressed. An undeclared 'state of emergency' (see Agamben 2005) would henceforth cast its shadow over any possible alternative management of the crisis, paving the way for all kinds of deviations from democratic 'normality', including the continuous violation of the constitution, the effective suspension of social welfare and civil rights, assaults on freedom of speech and an unprecedented rise in police brutality.

Social Reactions and Pressures from the EU

Already by the spring of 2011, Greek society was like a cauldron ready to explode (Kouvelakis 2011). An unprecedented GDP contraction, massive salary and pension cuts, along with soaring unemployment suggested a society on the verge of humanitarian crisis and a political system before major realignment. Indeed, the months that followed the first austerity package in 2010 witnessed various forms of massive collective action and mobilisations against the politics of austerity. From numerous national strikes and mass demonstrations, to solidarity movements, public building occupations and encampments, one could easily see that the measures taken by the government did not enjoy popular consent. After all they were clearly ineffective. Probably the most salient movement of that period – and certainly the most massive – a movement that embraced a vast multiplicity of individuals and collectivities, was that of the so-called *aganaktismenoi* that followed the demonstrations against austerity of the namesake *indignados* in Spain (May 2011). The *aganaktismenoi* can be seen here as a democratic grassroots populist movement. It articulated a multiplicity of demands and subjects that were demonstrating against the status quo in the name of 'the people'. In Rancièrian terms, the *aganaktismenoi* were a partial incarnation of 'the people': the outcasts of the crisis who were claiming an equal part, the ones without a voice who wanted to be heard, indeed the 'popular component' of democracy in action (see Katsambekis 2014; Prentoulis and Thomassen 2012).

With society boiling and the then opposition (ND) seeming unwilling to explicitly back up the austerity programme, the EU was more than worried. A few days after the first impressive gathering of the *aganaktismenoi* outside the Greek parliament the Greek party leaders met to discuss a possible agreement on a new set of harsh austerity measures to be passed by the government. After their failure to reach an agreement the following statement appeared and was widely reproduced in the Greek and international media:

> [The Commission] regrets the failure of Greek party leaders to reach consensus on economic adjustment to overcome the current debt crisis ... We expect that the efforts towards a cross-party agreement to support the EU-IMF programme will continue. An agreement has to be found soon. Time is running out. ... It is essential for the recovery of the Greek economy that all Greek parties, including the opposition parties, adopt a constructive attitude and support the EU-IMF programme and its implementation. ... The magnitude of the challenge is a test to the Greek society as a whole and therefore requires a contribution by all parties and all citizens.[9]

These are the words of then EU economic affairs commissioner, Olli Rehn. What Rehn stresses here is that dispute and disagreement on the policies which should be followed on the occasion of Greece's crisis are *not desirable* and might even be *dangerous* for the country's future. The Greek party leaders should thus urgently reach a consensus setting aside their varying views and political ideologies, because, when dealing with such a critical crisis, the choices – if any – are very limited. Indeed, what is striking in this announcement is its insistence on eliminating any political opposition in the country's political landscape (which, of course, means the elimination of politics *tout court*). It calls for consensus and cross-party agreement and emphatically repeats that '*all* Greek parties, including the opposition parties' should consent to what is described as a 'constructive attitude'. It is clear that the moment of 'consensus', that usually appeared in the Commission's discourse as advice or wishful thinking, started appearing as *raw blackmail*: 'either you all consent, or you do not see another instalment and you go bankrupt'. That is the rationale behind these words, clearly reflected in the alarming '*time is running out*'. Support for the EU-IMF programme, which by then had already malfunctioned, appears as *necessary*, and 'consensus' as the only 'constructive attitude', while disagreement between political parties is effectively suppressed.

What is immediately marginalised in such a logic is not only political disagreement as such, but also the very possibility of 'the people' as electorate to express their disagreement through their democratically elected representatives. If every political party in the parliament perforce agrees on the same plan and the same policies that are presented as an objective 'necessity' – and not as a political choice among other possible ones – then, along with disagreement, 'the people' vanishes, too, as its choices are effectively cancelled. It doesn't matter if one votes for left-wing or right-wing parties, since – when properly disciplined by the EU and the IMF – they will probably both implement the same programme.

The European Commission's demand that all Greek political parties consent on the bail-out terms and pledge to continue on the same track came a few days after the Eurogroup required that the Greek opposition should provide written commitment to the country's bail-out plan for the flow of emergency borrowing to continue. Even the German Chancellor, Angela Merkel herself, personally put pressure on the then Greek opposition leader, Antonis Samaras, to back up the austerity package and thus 'fulfil [his] historic responsibilities'[10] – *a responsibility to consent.* Concurrently, in Greece, voices were heard in the mainstream media and among pro-austerity MPs calling the politicians to step aside, to leave the stage and give their place to the 'technocrats'. The managing editor of one of Greece's leading newspapers directly asked the politicians:

> to step aside for a while, and give place to *those who know practical solutions* to do the job … Besides, today's politicians can become the best advisors on how a serious technocrat can manage the great obstacles before the recovery of the country: the partisan mechanisms, the trade unionists, the media and the interests. (Papachelas 2011; my emphasis)

According to this widespread view, the 'technocrats' appear as 'those who know better', those who are 'serious', while anything that entails elements of collective democratic practice, like political parties or trade unions, is considered an 'obstacle' that stands in the way of salvation and recovery. Democratic collective practices are considered slow and messy.

Expressions of this post-political (if not anti-political) cynicism were revealed with a new intensity when the then Greek Prime Minister, George Papandreou, expressed his intention to give 'voice to the people' and call for a referendum on the second EU-IMF bail-out deal in October 2011. The reaction of the 'markets' was immediate as stock markets plunged, causing waves of anxiety among European leaders. The Swedish Foreign Minister Carl Bildt, in true Thatcherite style, wondered on Twitter: 'I truly fail to understand what Greece intends to have a referendum about. Are there any real options?' Bildt's tweet reflected what almost every European leader was thinking at the time: 'How can a prime minister want the opinion of the people in such troubled times of crisis?', 'How could he risk a "negative" outcome?' The 'people' were seen again as ignorant masses, echoing what Balibar (1997) has described as the 'fear of the masses', characteristic of past centuries. A few days after Papandreou's announcement, he was publicly humiliated by German Chancellor Angela Merkel and French President Nicolas Sarkozy at the G20 summit in Cannes and forced to cancel the referendum. Heavy pressure was again put on the then Greek opposition and ND to accept and support the new loan agreement. So, despite ND's initial, rather superficial disagreements with the bail-out plan, the two major political parties (PASOK and ND) reached a consensus around what was described as a 'responsible attitude for the nation'.

The Commission's pleas for consensus were thus fully realised as PASOK and ND, along with the smaller extreme-right party LAOS, formed a coalition government under the ex-central banker, unelected Prime Minister Lucas Papademos. ND's leader, Antonis Samaras, sent an official letter to the European leaders expressing his commitment to the austerity agenda dictated by the 'troika' and backed by the EU. Hence, the already blurred divide between the mainstream centre-left and centre-right completely disappeared. Worse still, their alliance gave a place in government to the extreme-right for the first time in Greece's post-authoritarian history, although the two parties did not need it in order to form a parliamentary majority.

It is rather striking in this case that the EU strongly encouraged such a political alliance with a xenophobic extreme right-wing party – very often also described as populist – having previously imposed diplomatic sanctions on Austria in response to the participation of Jörg Haider's extreme right-wing populist FPÖ (Freedom Party) in the Austrian government. Evidently the EU's emphasis on economic 'necessity' and certain 'structural reforms' is very likely to translate into a cynical political 'pragmatism' that is particularly dangerous for democracy and even leads to coalitions with the 'populist' or extreme-right 'devil'.

Indeed, LAOS is a political party that belongs to the broader family of far-right xenophobic neopopulist parties in Europe, a party that since its establishment in September 2000 had been dismissed as either extremist or populist, even neo-fascist by mainstream political parties. And yet overnight it became a 'reliable political partner' and a 'responsible ally', provided it supported the austerity agenda. It seems that 'populism' appears to be dangerous (for the 'anti-populist'/post-democratic elites) only under certain conditions: *only as long as it poses a substantial threat to the established power bloc*. If it is no longer considered to be an opposing political force, a 'threat' that challenges a given constellation of power, it can become an equal and responsible ally. So, in this sense, it is not its 'populist', anti-democratic or extremist character that actually poses a threat, but rather its stance as *opposition* (see Borneman, this volume).

It was around the same time that the EU encouraged the formation of a similar government in Italy under the unelected technocrat Mario Monti.[11] As the European and international press described it, the EU saw these governments as the best way to 'calm the markets' (Wearden 2011) that appeared as quasi-living entities: they worried, they issued warnings, they expressed their dissatisfaction with current policies, and so on (Žižek 2012: 14). The elevation of the markets' logic to an ultimate criterion that supplants popular sovereignty – especially in times of crisis – was described by Colin Crouch ten years ago on the occasion of the U.S. presidential elections in 2000:

> where there was almost irrefutable evidence of serious ballot-rigging in Florida, a result which was decisive to the victory of George W. Bush, the brother of the state's governor. Apart from some demonstrations among Black Americans, there were very few expressions of outrage at tampering with the democratic process. The prevailing mood seemed to be that achieving an outcome – any outcome – was important to restore confidence to the stock markets, and that was more important than ensuring that the verdict of the majority was truly discovered. (Crouch 2004: 2)

The difference between the U.S. elections of 2000 and the imposition of the Papademos government in Greece is that, while in the first case popular reaction was only marginal and half-hearted, in the second case popular reaction was already at a historic high with hundreds of thousands rallying and camping in the streets and squares all over Greece for months. The cynical reaction of the Greek political elite to the mobilisations was graphically illustrated in the words of the then Vice President of the government, Theodoros Pagalos, who described the protesters as 'either fascists, either communists, or just assholes'.[12]

Some months later Jürgen Habermas (2011) expressed his concern that the European project would transform 'into its opposite. The first transnational democracy would become an especially effective, because disguised, arrangement for exercising a kind of post-democratic rule'. Crouch himself recognised Greece as the 'clearest case' of post-democratic rule: 'The most explicit expression of the post-democratic aspects of crisis management was the framing of the Greek austerity package, designed by international authorities in close collaboration with an association of leading bankers' (Carrigan and Crouch 2013).

The formation of the coalition government under Papademos further sharpened post-democratic tendencies within the Greek political system, leading it to new (anti-democratic) extremes. The then Minister of Education Anna Diamantopoulou (2012) proposed that this government of technocrats 'should … become one of national salvation; without time limits, with the possibility to reshuffle, *consisting of few politicians and the best [*aristoi*] of the Greeks*'. And even if that could not be achieved, Diamantopoulou still insisted that '[t]he next government, whatever the elections result might be, should be one of programmatic consensus and with a prime minister like Papademos. … Conducting national elections soon … would be a temporary victory of populism, of the anti-reformist block which is gathering forces'.

What is evident in such public interventions – coming from highly influential individuals and strongly supported by MPs and ministers at the time – is, first, a distrust of the democratic electoral process; second, what we have referred to as the '*logic of the arkhè*'; and third, an urge to eliminate opposition and establish a lasting consensus beyond popular accountability. In this case we do not just slip beyond democracy, but we are drawn back to raw pre-democratic logics.

Significantly, Diamantopoulou called upon one of the most prominent anti-democratic historical figures, Plato, to justify her call for this new aristocracy that she described as the most suitable solution for Greece. In her view, popular sovereignty and democratic elections must be suspended and the '*aristoi*' should take charge in order to solve the country's problems. It seems that both 'post-democracy' and 'elitism' would just be euphemisms for what we are truly facing in *aristocratic* claims to power like this one.

The Elections of 2012–2015 and the Rise of the (Populist) Radical Left

Despite the attempts of the Papademos government to declare itself a govern-ment of 'national salvation' and to continue functioning without time limits and without opposition, national elections were held in May 2012. Against the 'anti-populist' hysteria (or maybe partly because of it) and a prevailing xeno-phobic agenda put forth by both PASOK and ND, a Greek radical left coali-tion, SYRIZA, previously just struggling to enter the parliament, managed to persuade and effectively mobilise a noteworthy proportion of the electorate. By addressing 'the people' through a discourse that articulated a plurality of demands against the local and European elites and their policies of extreme austerity, a discourse that was indeed a populist one (see Stavrakakis and Katsambekis 2014; Katsambekis 2015), SYRIZA received an impressive 16.78 per cent of the vote and more than tripled its power. These numbers rose even more in the elections of June 2012, where SYRIZA got 26.89 per cent of the vote.

This upward dynamic did not come out of the blue. SYRIZA was probably the only party that had engaged with the demands of the *aganaktismenoi* and met them out in the streets. Its programme, embracing most of the demands of the popular movements, was based on an alternative mixture of policies involv-ing a radical break with the politics of austerity. SYRIZA, in 2012, called for a broad coalition (a 'left front') that would lead to a 'government of the Left' bold enough to annul the 'Memoranda', while supporting the country's place within the Eurozone (but 'not at all social cost'), raise taxation on big business, put the banking sector under public control, call a moratorium on debt repayment until Greek society gets back on its feet, scrap salary cuts and emergency taxes. Such claims were again stigmatised by the parties supporting austerity, European officials and media as outrageously populist and unattainable, even unthinkable – as a policy that would certainly lead the country out of the Eurozone, if not out of the EU altogether, and from there to a real economic and social hell.

Thus, as a reaction to SYRIZA's proposals, a quasi-apocalyptic discourse, marked by a strong anti-populist emphasis, was articulated by mainstream and pro-austerity parties and a large part of the media in Greece, a discourse that intensified even further after 2012, as SYRIZA maintained its upward dynamic. If SYRIZA came to power and tried to implement its programme, it was often argued, Greece would face total economic and social destruction. It would default on its debt and the army would have to intervene to protect the banks;

the supermarkets would be emptied by panicked citizens. Ostracised by the international community, Greece would face geopolitical insecurity, and even the danger of a military coup and a new civil war. A similar narrative regarding the 'populist threat' that SYRIZA posed to Europe was developed across the European public sphere. Both the party's impressive electoral results and the need to radically oppose it were very often explained with recourse to its populist message, a message that was supposed to be as dangerous as it was mesmerising (Stavrakakis and Katsambekis 2014).

In their effort to demonise SYRIZA's alternative project, Greece's mainstream parties and their organic intellectuals also used what can be called the 'theory of extremes', equating the radical left with the extremism of the Golden Dawn, an openly neo-Nazi party that made it into the parliament for the first time with an impressive 6.92 per cent. It seems then that '[t]he categorisation of the extreme right as "populist"' aimed 'above all [to] ... discredit both the left and the popular classes themselves' (Marlière 2013; see also Katsambekis and Stavrakakis 2013). In this sense, the mainstream's stance against SYRIZA at that point – both within Greece and in Europe – seems to exemplify the post-democratic tendency to suppress or even demonise political opposition and alternatives; in other words, demonisation takes the place of political confrontation.

SYRIZA eventually came to power in January 2015, ushering in a new, very turbulent period, as Alexis Tsipras' coalition government attempted, through intense negotiations with Greece's European partners, to loosen austerity's grip on the country in order to pursue an alternative path out of the crisis. When negotiations reached a deadlock, the Tsipras government (contrary to that of Papandreou some years before) succeeded in holding a referendum regarding Greece's new proposed agreement with its EU partners, in which the people overwhelmingly voted against it (the 'no' vote was more than 61 per cent). New ultimatums were nevertheless presented to Greece by its European partners, backed up with the threat that Greece could be forced to exit the euro zone (or even the EU) and thus face economic collapse, leading the Greek government to sign a new financing agreement (the third 'memorandum') that followed the same logic as the previous ones. This latest development yet again reveals the marginalisation of the people, the violation of the popular will and mandate at its most extreme. Not only was SYRIZA forced to back down on most of its programmatic promises, the overwhelming result of the Greek referendum was utterly ignored. After all, one of the most important politicians in Europe, the German Finance Minister Wolfgang Schaeuble, had quite clearly stated, regarding Greece and SYRIZA, that 'Elections change nothing. There are rules'.[13] While it remains to be seen how SYRIZA's policies and public discourse are going to be shaped within the constraints of the new 'memorandum' and whether a new major re-alignment of the Greek political system is underway, the enforcement of the new agreement – which was voted in by a broad majority in the Greek parliament, including the parties of the old two-partyism, ND and PASOK – may mark the passage from what I earlier termed 'emergency consensus' to what could now be called a *'forced* consensus'; the latest development in the evisceration of representative democracy.

Conclusion

To sum up, the permanent 'state of exception' that the Greek and European political elites have imposed on Greek society during recent years in their effort to implement a series of harsh and unpopular austerity measures has led to the articulation of a political discourse that rejects disagreement and democratic dissent and attempts to eliminate political opposition and thus the prospect of any radical change. As a result, popular will was persistently and effectively trampled in the name of 'economic necessity', and almost any opposition was branded 'populist', sometimes 'anti-patriotic' or even 'dangerous' and thus unwanted. Even national elections were dismissed by top MPs of the mainstream parties as dangerous 'populism' and the unelected *'aristoi'* were called to the rescue of the country. The view behind this stance was that the government of technocrats should extend its life for as long as it was necessary for the country to exit the crisis. In their effort to police and discipline the public sphere the media were consequently flooded with versions of the Thatcherite *'there is no alternative'* doctrine, which sought to impose an 'emergency consensus'.

But the discourse of 'consensus' (Rancière 1999: 95–121) is not worth the name, since it inevitably creates new frontiers and exclusions (Mouffe 2005a). In its paradoxical denial of cleavages and divisions it establishes new ones that often manifest in post-political, if not anti-political terrains. When 'consensus' on the austerity agenda becomes the equivalent of common sense – a synonym for rationality – thus rendering any critical voice ultimately irrational and nonsensical, today's battle, as often represented by European politicians and the hegemonic media, 'is one between those "responsible" forces advocating and enforcing austerity and those "irresponsible" ones risking debt increases and public spending' (Stavrakakis 2012: 2289). Hence anyone who speaks in the name of, or calls upon 'the people' and their dissent can be easily dismissed as an 'irresponsible populist' or a mere 'demagogue', and certainly irrational. This restrictive dualism, which in Greece often takes the form of a battle of 'enlightened rationalism versus destructive populism', leaves no place for meaningful political debate and disagreement and could ultimately fuel reactions against both democracy and the European project.

The Greek case, in all its complexity and peculiarity, is particularly important for the study of post-democracy in its ongoing phase, since it manifests most (if not all) of the symptoms described in the relevant literature, and at the same time exemplifies tendencies that are now discernible all across Europe. What is more, it probably prefigures what is to come in other countries, too. If a minimal conception of post-democracy would be a society 'that continues to have and to use all the institutions of democracy, but in which they increasingly become a formal shell' (Carrigan and Crouch 2013), something that implies a hollowing of democracy (Mair 2013), what I have highlighted here is how this 'hollowing' takes place through the marginalisation of 'the people', along with the suppression of opposition. The two processes take place simultaneously, since 'the people' – as a potential subject – always bears the possibility of discord and the mark of 'constituent power'.

The suppression of this possibility is an alarming setback, since the role of political opposition, the institutionalisation of disagreement, within democratic societies constitutes an essential feature of democratic modernity. It is actively linked to the possibility of 'the people' to make their voices heard. And this is because '[p]olitical opposition gives voice. By losing opposition, we lose voice, and by losing voice we lose control of our political systems' (ibid.: 142). What we have seen in Greece is a constant attempt to marginalise and silence any kind of popular and/or political opposition to the policies imposed by the EU and the 'troika'. When a political party (SYRIZA) expressing such an opposition rose to power, it faced extreme pressure to succumb to a new bail-out memorandum. Now, this suppression of opposition does not go without its 'side-effects' on the European level. Thus, it is perhaps no coincidence that the emblematic figure of Europe's extreme and Eurosceptic right, Marine Le Pen, had already urged denouncement of a Greek agreement with the European institutions as a shameful retreat, accusing SYRIZA that it had succumbed to the 'Euro-dictatorship', betraying its people and effectively confirming that the Front National and its likes were the only viable alternatives to this 'undemocratic' Europe, linking popular sovereignty to robust national sovereignty and democracy to a renewed nationalism.[14]

The mid-2010s have seen Europe reel in apparent shock at the significant electoral gains made by extreme, xenophobic and hard-Eurosceptic parties of the Right, in countries ranging from France and Britain to Austria and Finland. But could it be that their supporters, asphyxiating in systems of consensus, in systems that lack meaningful political opposition and alternatives, were just searching for the voices that they had lost? Could it be that the 'surplus of consensus' across Europe – that seems to suppress any kind of progressive alternative – ultimately produced the object of its denunciation: isolationist, radical nationalist or even outright anti-European opposition? Europe's efforts to tackle this question, which will necessarily also be an effort to deal with the impasses of its post-democratic transition, hold the key for the future developments that could be more or less democratic. If Europe, in its future efforts, does not find a way to creatively include popular dissent and incorporate significant elements of popular accountability, that is to effectively restore balance between the 'popular component' and the 'constitutional component' of its system in a way that aspires a new collective passion among citizens for the common European democratic project, then what we see today as occasional and local 'shocks' might just be the first cracks of tomorrow's collapse of the EU as we know it.

Acknowledgements

Some aspects of this material have been published in a previous form in *POSTData* 19, no. 2 (October 2014): 555–582. I would like to thank the publishers of that journal for their permission to reproduce them here.

Notes

1 PASOK (Panhellenic Socialist Movement) was founded by Andreas Papandreou in 1974. Emerging as a radical left political force in the 1970s, it adopted a more pragmatic and moderate profile when in office in the 1980s, before gradually joining the trajectory of third-way European social-democracy.
2 Founded in 1974 by Konstantinos Karamanlis, ND (New Democracy) is a centre-right party, one of the main pillars – together with PASOK – of the Greek two-party system (1974–2012). In 1974, it won the election with an overwhelming 54.37 per cent and formed the first government of the Third Hellenic Republic.
3 SYRIZA (Coalition of the Radical Left) was initially founded as an electoral coalition of radical left political parties and extra-parliamentarian organisations in 2004. Its main constituent, Synaspismos (founded in 1992), originates in the Greek Eurocommunist tradition. SYRIZA dissolved its participating constituents and became a unified party in July 2013, following its electoral breakthrough in May-June 2012.
4 This is not to offer a romanticised picture of Greece's 'thriving democracy' before its post-democratic turn. The so-called 'hyper-politicisation' of the 1970s and 1980s came with its own perils (clientelism, cronyism, nationalism, emphasis on the leader's charisma, etc.) However, a major achievement of the PASOK government during the 1980s was 'the empowerment of social groups that had never enjoyed any significant share of power' (Lyrintzis, 2005: 149), a sharp contrast to post-democracy's de-emphasising of popular accountability and sovereignty.
5 We should remember that while '[p]opulist movements are widely regarded, especially in Europe and Latin America, as threats to democracy, [they] explicitly claim to be true democrats, setting out to reclaim power for the people' (Canovan 2004: 244).
6 At least five significant moments/incidents disturbed 'politics as usual' in that period: 1) 1999's large and heterogeneous rallies against the capture of Abdullah Otsalan, the outlawed leader of Turkey's Kurdistan Workers' Party, who had been hiding in the Greek Embassy in Nairobi; 2) the so-called 'people's rallies' [*laosynakseis*] organised by the Greek Orthodox Church as a reaction to the exclusion of religion from identity cards in 2000; 3) the emergence in 2000 of Giorgos Karatzaferis and his party LAOS (which means 'the people' in Greek), which introduced to the Greek political scene a nationalist-populist mobilisation with bold xenophobic characteristics; 4) the massive and at times violent (against immigrants, especially Albanians) gatherings and celebrations in the centres of big cities after Greece won the European Football Championship in 2004; 5) the anti-authoritarian protests by Greek youth in December 2008 after the assassination of a fifteen-year-old in central Athens by a police officer.
7 This last one coming from the then Vice President of the government, Theodoros Pangalos.
8 'Troika' refers to the tripartite committee responsible for supervising the policies implemented in Greece after the first bail-out agreement in 2010. It is comprised

of the European Commission (EC), the European Central Bank (ECB) and the International Monetary Fund (IMF).
9   <http://www.dailytelegraph.com.au/time-is-running-out-for-greece/story-fn6e1m7z-1226064509769> (accessed 27 July 2015).
10 <http://www.bbc.co.uk/news/world-europe-13901936> (accessed 18 March 2013).
11 In the case of Italy, the populist bogeyman for Europe is Beppe Grillo and the Five Star Movement (see Bock, this volume). It will be interesting to see what happens if in the future Grillo changes his mind and compromises with the austerity agenda. Wouldn't he then be branded a 'responsible' leader and a reliable European ally?
12 Interview for Canal 5, 30 November 2011.
13 <http://www.bbc.com/news/world-europe-31082656> (accessed 20 July 2015).
14 <http://www.lepoint.fr/politique/grece-marine-le-pen-denonce-l-eurodictature-europeenne-25-02-2015-1907828_20.php> (accessed 27 August 2015).

References

Agamben, G. 2005. *State of Exception.* Chicago: University of Chicago Press.
Balibar, E. 1997. *La crainte de masses.* Paris: Galilee.
———. 2010. Europe: Final Crisis? Some Theses. *Theory & Event* 13, no. 2: <http://goo.gl/xC5Cw> (accessed 11 June 2011).
———. 2011. Europe's Revolution From Above. *The Guardian,* 23 November.
Beck, U. 2011. Créons une Europe des citoyens! *Le Monde,* 26 December.
Bracher, K.D. 1964. Problems of Parliamentary Democracy in Europe, *Daedalus* 93, no. 1: 179–198.
Bratakos, A. 2002. *The History of Nea Democratia.* Livanis: Athens.
Canovan, M. 2004. Populism for Political Theorists? *Journal of Political Ideologies* 9, no. 3: 241–252.
———. 2005. *The People.* Cambridge: Polity Press.
Carrigan, M., and C. Crouch. 2013. Five Minutes with Colin Crouch. <http://blogs.lse.ac.uk/politicsandpolicy/archives/30297> (accessed 18 May 2014).
Cendrowicz, L. 2012. 10 Questions with European Commission President José Manuel Barroso. *Time,* 21 May.
Crouch, C. 2004. *Post-democracy.* Cambridge: Polity Press.
Demertzis, N. (ed.). 1994. *The Greek Political Culture Today.* Athens: Odysseas.
Diamandouros, N. 1994. *Cultural Dualism and Political Change in Post-Authoritarian Greece.* Madrid: Instituto Juan March de Estudios e Investigaciones.
Diamantopoulou, A. 2012. Speech at the Open Discussion 'For Greece, Now!' <http://goo.gl/PZoiV> (accessed 15 March 2013).
Enzensberger, H.M. 2011. *Brussels, the Gentle Monster: Or the Disenfranchisement of Europe.* London: Seagull Books.
Feinberg, J.G. 2008. The Unfinished Story of Central European Dissidence. *Telos* 145: 47–66.
Gauchet, M. 1997. *The Disenchantment of the World: A Political History of Religion.* Princeton: Princeton University Press.
Habermas, J. 2011. Europe's Post-Democratic Era. *The Guardian,* 10 November.
Halimi, S. 2011. Un raisonnement de fou. < https://www.monde-diplomatique.fr/2011/06/HALIMI/20653> (accessed 25 July 2015).
Howarth, D., and Y. Stavrakakis. 2000. Introducing Discourse Theory and Political Analysis. In *Discourse Theory and Political Analysis: Identities, Hegemonies and*

Social Change (eds) D. Howarth, A. Norval and Y. Stavrakakis, 1–23. Manchester: Manchester University Press.

Kalyvas, A. 2005. Popular Sovereignty, Democracy, and the Constituent Power. *Constellations* 12, no. 2: 224–244.

Katsambekis, G. 2014. The Multitudinous Moment(s) of the People: Democratic Agency Disrupting Established Binarisms. In *Radical Democracy and Collective Movements Today: The Biopolitics of the Multitude Versus the Hegemony of the People* (eds) A. Kioupkiolis and G. Katsambekis, 169–190. Farnham: Ashgate.

———. 2015. The Rise of the Greek Radical Left to Power: Notes on SYRIZA's Discourse and Strategy. *Línea Sur* 3, no. 9: 152–161.

Katsambekis, G., and Y. Stavrakakis. 2013. Populism, Anti-populism and European Democracy: A View from the South. <http://www.opendemocracy.net/can-europe-make-it/giorgos-katsambekis-yannis-stavrakakis/populism-anti-populism-and-european-democr> (accessed 27 July 2015).

Kouvelakis, S. 2011. The Greek Cauldron. *New Left Review* 72: 17–32.

Laclau, E. 2005. *On Populist Reason.* London: Verso.

Laclau, E., and C. Mouffe. 1985. *Hegemony and Socialist Strategy.* London: Verso.

Ladi, S. 2005. The Role of Experts in the Reform Process in Greece. *West European Politics* 28, no. 2: 279–296.

Lefort, C. 1988. *Democracy and Political Theory.* Cambridge: Polity Press.

Loulis, Y. 1999. *Triangulation*, Athens: I. Sideris.

Lyrintzis, C. 1987. The Power of Populism: The Greek Case. *European Journal of Political Research* 15, no. 6: 667–686.

———. 2005. The Changing Party System: Stable Democracy, Contested 'Modernisation'. *West European Politics* 28, no. 2: 242–259.

Mair, P. 2013. *Ruling the Void: The Hollowing of Western Democracy.* Verso: London.

Marlière, P. 2013. The Demophobes and the Great Fear of Populism. <http://www.opendemocracy.net/philippe-marli%C3%A8re/demophobes-and-great-fear-of-populism> (accessed 4 July 2013).

Mavris, Y. 2013. An X-ray of the Golden Dawn. *Efimerida ton Syntakton*, 1 July.

Mouffe, C. 2005a. *On the Political.* London: Routledge.

———. 2005b. The 'End of Politics' and the Challenge of Right-Wing Populism. In *Populism and the Mirror of Democracy* (ed.) F. Panizza, 50–71. London: Verso.

———. 2013. *Agonistics.* London: Verso.

Papachelas, A. 2011. Let Them Step Aside. *Kathimerini*, 25 September.

Papandreou, G. 2011. Speech at the Greek Parliament on National Issues. <http://archive.papandreou.gr/papandreou/content/Document.aspx?m=13224&rm=11084662&l=2> (accessed 4 July 2013).

Pettit, P. 2001. Deliberative Democracy and the Case for Depoliticising Government. *University of New South Wales Law Journal* 24, no.3: <http://www.austlii.edu.au/au/journals/UNSWLJ/2001/58.html> (accessed 4 July 2013).

Prentoulis, M., and L. Thomassen. 2012. Political Theory in the Square: Protest, Representation and Subjectification. *Contemporary Political Theory* 12, no. 3: 166–184.

Rancière, J. 1995. *On the Shores of Politics.* London: Verso.

———. 1999. *Disagreement: Politics and Philosophy.* Minneapolis: University of Minnesota Press.

———. 2006. *Hatred of Democracy.* London: Verso.

———. 2010. *Dissensus: On Politics and Aesthetics.* London: Continuum.

———. 2011. The Thinking of Dissensus: Politics and Aesthetics. In *Reading Rancière: Critical Dissensus* (eds) P. Bowman and R. Stamp, 1–17. London: Continuum.

Rovira Kaltwasser, C. 2012. The Ambivalence of Populism: Threat and Corrective for Democracy. *Democratization* 19, no. 2: 184–208.

Schattschneider, E.E. 1960. *The Semisovereign People: A Realist's View of Democracy in America.* Chicago: Wadsworth.

Sotiropoulos, D. 2001. *The Peak of the Clientelist State.* Athens: Potamos.

Spourdalakis, M. 1988. *The Rise of the Greek Socialist Party.* London: Routledge.

Stabenow, M. 2010. EU-Ratspräsident Van Rompuy: Anlaufstelle für Merkel und Sarkozy. *Frankfurter Allgemeine Zeitung,* 9 April.

Stavrakakis, Y. 2012. Beyond the Spirits of Capitalism? Prohibition, Enjoyment and Social Change, *Cardozo Law Review* 33, no. 6: 2289–2306.

Stavrakakis, Y., and G. Katsambekis. 2014. Left-wing Populism in the European Periphery: The Case of SYRIZA. *Journal of Political Ideologies* 19, no. 2: 119–142.

Streeck, W. 2012. Markets and Peoples: Democratic Capitalism and European Integration. *New Left Review,* 73: 63–71.

Wearden, G. 2011. European Debt Crisis: Papademos Named as Greece's New PM. <http://www.guardian.co.uk/business/blog/2011/nov/10/eurozone-crisis-italy-greece> (accessed 4 July 2013).

Zakaria, F. 2003. *The Future of Freedom: Illiberal Democracy at Home and Abroad.* New York: Norton.

Žižek, S. 2012. *The Year of Dreaming Dangerously.* London: Verso.

Giorgos Katsambekis holds a PhD in political science from the Aristotle University of Thessaloniki.

7

Debt Society Consolidated?
Post-democratic Subjectivity and its Discontents

Yannis Stavrakakis

... we who lay bare the aggressiveness that underlies the activities of the philanthropist, the idealist, the pedagogue, and even the reformer. (Jacques Lacan)

I never lost as much but twice,
And that was in the sod.
Twice have I stood a beggar
Before the door of God!

Angels – twice descending
Reimbursed my store –
Burglar! Banker – Father!
I am poor once more! (Emily Dickinson)

The ongoing economic crisis in Europe and beyond is usually discussed in more or less technocratic ways. Attention is paid to the stress tests applied to the banking sector to safeguard its supposed resilience, to the technicalities of deficit reduction and supposedly neutral structural readjustments and reforms. Instead of illuminating what is at stake, such a narrow approach rather obscures understanding and limits the scope of meaningful theoretico-political intervention. It has also allowed and even panegyrically legitimised the reproduction and circulation of a so-called 'success story', a narrative declaring the end of the crisis and a return to 'normality' – even in the hard-hit European South.[1] And yet this 'normality' may be a euphemistic reference to the consolidation of a new model of human sociality, of a new articulation of the social bond, marking a significant advance in the neoliberal restructuring of economic, political and psychosocial relations, a perpetual continuation of crisis with other means.

From Michel Foucault to David Harvey (occupying the antipodes), critical theorists of neoliberalism have managed to illuminate many aspects of these developments (Foucault 2008; Harvey 2005). More recently, Saskia Sassen has added to Harvey's 'accumulation by dispossession' (Harvey 2005: 159) the concept of 'expulsion' to talk about the recent aggressive, even *brutal* turn marking pathologies of late capitalism such as growing inequality (ibid.: 1). Expulsions involve a process of hierarchical distribution of populations and forms of life that amounts to a 'savage sorting'; although it emanates from institutions and processes marked by increasing complexity it is governed by both 'brutal simplicity' and 'simple brutality' (ibid.: 4). The attempted transformation of Southern Europe illustrates well this *brutality* through the massive expulsion of the middle classes from jobs, welfare services and even their homes (ibid.: 214).[2] What is thus clearly revealed is the radical shift in the driving principles of the social order away from those dominant during the Keynesian era: the systemic edge passes from a logic of *incorporation* to a logic of *expulsion* (ibid.: 221). From this point of view, Greece, Spain and Portugal are not unique cases; deeper structural conditions and trends are revealed here. Furthermore, this expulsion dynamic is now 'hardwired into the normal functioning' of the system (Sassen 2014: 37, 76). The emerging 'normality' is everywhere a normality 'marked by extremes in unemployment, poverty, suicide, displacement from home and land, incarceration' (Sassen 2014: 76). In Lauren Berlant's words, the 'new normal' denotes thus an enforced adjustment 'to the process of living with the political depression produced by *brutal* relations of ownership, control, security, and their fantasmatic justifications in liberal political economies' (Berlant 2011: 261, emphasis added); in a thoroughly perverse mode, what is supposed to mark the end of the crisis signals the *normalisation* of its effects.

Political theory has also been busy in accounting for the political aspect of these developments, that is to say for *political dispossession*, for the *expulsion of popular strata from decision-making processes* and the *dislocation of incorporation dynamics*. Take for example the introduction of the category of 'post-democracy', outlined in greater detail by Katsambekis (this volume) and the editors' introduction. The multiple 'hollowings' of democracy that this term refers to are also presented in dominant discourses as a new 'normality', as the new normal functioning of democracy in which democratic form is reduced to the 'necessities' of globalised capital, *popular sovereignty* is replaced by *market sovereignty* and mechanisms of political representation by the functioning of rating agencies:

> From an allegedly defunct Marxism, the supposedly reigning liberalism borrows the theme of objective necessity, identified with the constraints and caprices of the world market. Marx's once scandalous thesis that governments are simple business agents for international capital is today an obvious fact on which 'liberals' and 'socialists' agree. The absolute identification of politics with the management of capital is no longer the shameful secret hidden behind the 'forms' of democracy; it is the openly declared truth by which our governments acquire legitimacy. (Rancière 1999: 113)

Obviously the welfare state was not perfect (poverty, inequality and racism, among others, obviously existed), but it allowed considerable upward mobility for its citizens, which is no longer the case in the age of expulsion. The

Keynesian era, though far from ideal, nevertheless exhibited constitutive systematicities that were about mass production as well as mass consumption. This is no longer the case (Sassen 2014: 14, 221). Nor were the democratic political forms associated with the liberal democracies of the welfare state period perfect, but they did indicate some sort of articulation between the egalitarian (democratic) and the liberal traditions enabling a slow radicalisation of democracy (Crouch 2004: 3; Mouffe 2009). What we seem to be witnessing currently is the end of this era and the *consolidation* of a new 'normality'. And yet it is impossible to account for the ways in which this consolidation is attempted within the context of the current administration of the crisis without taking into account the psychosocial dimension, without examining how *subjectivity* and collective identification are reshaped and manipulated in the emerging 'debt society', without capturing the technologies of domination used in the management of the crisis. Obviously, economy and politics never exist in isolation from one another. Hence, for Crouch, the post-war type of democracy offering 'major opportunities to the mass of ordinary people actively to participate, through discussion and autonomous organizations, in shaping the agenda of public life' (Crouch 2004: 2) would be inconceivable without the social compromise reached 'between capitalist business interests and working people' (ibid.: 7) and vice versa; similarly, today, as Sassen highlights, what seems to be at stake in processes of (predominantly economic) expulsion is not only financial survival, but 'the question of membership and constitutive participation' (Sassen 2014: 222).

Hence, to view neoliberalism and its administration of the crisis as an economic phenomenon – especially in the technical sense – would mean to insist on a conception which is both thin and incomplete, not to mention that it remains 'too closely bound up with the sermonizing discourse of the advocates of neoliberalism'; a thicker notion needs to identify the frames and the machinery through which neoliberalism is currently actualised, revealing it as 'a transnational political project aiming to remake the nexus of market, state, and citizenship from above' (Wacquant 2010: 212–213). Indeed neoliberalism – especially in its German ordo-liberal version – should not be identified with *laissez-faire*, with the result of a spontaneous natural order, but rather 'with permanent vigilance, activity, and intervention' (Foucault 2008: 132, 161). It denotes a state in which 'there may be as many interventions as in a policy of planning, but their nature is different' (Milksch in Foucault 2008: 133) as they aim at conditioning the 'framework' for a possible market economy intervening on the 'population' and a variety of other social factors thus constituting a veritable 'policy of society' (Foucault 2008: 140–141, 146). If this is a side of neoliberalism that has often and remarkably been overlooked by both apologists and detractors (Wacquant 2010: 214), the attempted consolidation of debt society provides an opportunity to arrive at a more complete picture. At the same time, and most crucially, it also reveals how both economic and political processes in their mutual engagement cannot significantly influence behaviour without engaging with the (discursive and affective) mechanisms of subjection, interpellation and identification through which subjectivity and identity are continuously constructed, dislocated and reconstructed.

Deepening Post-democracy and the Multiple Faces of Debt

The passage from early to late modernity is generally associated with a process of gradual (relative) *democratisation*, in both the political and economic realms. Politically, representative democracy has enjoyed an unprecedented global spread; in the West especially, political and social rights seemed to have flourished up until quite recently. Economically, we have witnessed a 'democratisation of consumption' with the gradual spread of a consumerist culture of 'luxury'. Having emerged with the 'conspicuous consumption' typical of court society, this ethos gradually colonised the *bourgeoisie* and then the lower classes, creating a predominantly consumerist society. Up to a certain point both processes progressed together, and this is how the system managed to co-opt popular pressure and social movements and create relative stability: by largely replacing *prohibition* with *commanded enjoyment*, and disciplinary power with the productive regulation of desire. As we have already seen, both pillars of this process are currently in crisis and a new post-democratic normality replacing economic and political incorporation with exclusion is being consolidated. The crucial question is how.

To the extent that it marginalises broad sections of the population and overturns major economic and political advances of the last two centuries, *how is the passage to this new regime achieved without the development of significant discontent and overwhelming resistance?*[3] It is important to note that, at first, the post-democratic dynamic did not affect the 'democratisation of consumption', although it signalled a significant increase in inequality. This delicate balancing act was accomplished through the *accumulation of debt*. The loss of political and social rights went largely 'unobserved' to the extent that the lower and middle strata could still function as consumers by getting more and more loans. Indeed, up until the crisis, 'the build-up of debt, first public and then private, helped preserve liberal democracy by compensating citizens for low growth, structural unemployment, deregulation of labour markets, stagnant or declining wages, and rising inequality' (Schäfer and Streeck 2013: 17). This way, the hegemony of finance managed to exchange rights for credit and debt. Thus, if the welfare state was instrumental in sustaining 'mass consumption' through income redistribution, in *consumerist post-democracy*, 'consumer credit has taken the role that belonged to the welfare state in the Fordist regime' (Marazzi 2011: 126–128).

It is here, however, that things acquire an extra psychosocial *gravitas* with immense economic, social and political implications. Although Maurizio Lazzarato fails to inscribe his analysis within the long sociological and/or psychoanalytic tradition on ethics, morality and the spirits of capitalism, his impressive *The Making of the Indebted Man* offers a revealing account of how the hegemonisation of economic behaviour by debt/credit has had enduring effects well beyond the economic field. Starting with the role of Christianity that 'interiorizes' debt as 'feeling of guilt' (Lazzarato 2012: 77–78) and then drawing primarily on Nietzsche and Deleuze, Lazzarato cogently shows how debt involves a special type of power relation 'that entails specific forms of production and control of subjectivity – a particular form of *homo economicus*, the "indebted man"' (ibid.: 30). The creditor-debtor relationship involves thus a complex ethico-political process constructing a *type of subjectivity* that is both accountable and guilty: 'Economic production and the production of subjectivity, labor and ethics, are indissoluble' (ibid.: 49). Thus debt seems to operate at the psychosocial intersection of power, morality and the economy.

It was this system that facilitated the whole banking crisis of 2008. Once interest rates rise, once the housing market stalls, once banking risk assessment models fail, 'the whole mechanism of income "distribution" through debt and finance collapses' (ibid.: 111). Surprisingly, however, although the crisis initially seemed to provide the condition of possibility for a progressive re-politicisation of the economy – highlighting the need to reverse the trend of 'deregulation' – it is currently being used in a bid to reinforce further the neoliberal post-democratic orthodoxy, at least within the European context. Having first encouraged the spirit of loan-dependent consumerism, having allowed a prolonged bankers' party, the same neoliberal power-bloc uses debt – now passed onto state budgets – in order to reverse democratisation. Now the process of de-democratisation, which first affected the political field, is also affecting consumption; the consumerist society of 'commanded enjoyment' is violently turning back into a society of prohibition, of dispossession and expulsion. By turning private into sovereign debt, by individualising and spreading the blame for both of them (public and private debt), 'the blow to neoliberal governmentality from the subprime crisis will, in the short run, be transformed into a victory for the universal debt economy' (Lazzarato 2012: 122). Indeed, without taking into account this multi-modal function of debt, its ability to operate in a plurality of levels, its historical/subjective association with shame and guilt, it is impossible to make sense of the way the crisis has been managed up to now, producing and consolidating 'debt society'.

Not only has neoliberalism, since its emergence, been founded on a logic of debt (Lazzarato 2012: 25); most crucially, using the threat of sovereign debt default, the neoliberal power bloc 'seeks to follow through on a program it has been fantasising about since the 1970s: reduce wages to the minimum, cut social services so that the Welfare State is made to serve its new "beneficiaries" – business and the rich – and privatize everything' (Lazzarato 2012: 10). Ironically, we here encounter the bizarre reversal marking the end of the 'democratisation of consumption' process. If debt/credit was initially used to safeguard our access to consumption in an increasingly unequal society, if it functioned to sustain our aristocratic fantasies of 'conspicuous consumption', now it violently 'brings us back to a [very different] situation [equally] characteristic of feudalism, in which a portion of labour is owed in advance, as serf labour, to the feudal lord'

(Baudrillard in Lazzarato 2012: 13). This feeling of historical regression, of an 'uneven and combined development' moving backwards to meet its supposed culmination, is something to which we will return again and again in this text. And debt must occupy a privileged place in a much-needed *rhythmanalysis* of capitalist (post-)democracy to the extent that it seems to function as the psychosocial *hinge* not only between economy and politics but also between antithetical articulations of the two (promoting an ethics of prohibition and sacrifice or one of commanded enjoyment).[4] It is only now, perhaps, on account of this paradoxical inverted causality, that Walter Benjamin's 'Capitalism as Religion' fragment, written in 1921, acquires its true meaning. Capitalism, in Benjamin's view, is a 'debt-producing' and 'guilt-producing' cult (Benjamin 2005: 259). And if, in 1921, Benjamin had to register the impossibility of fully developing this insight, postponing this exercise for 'later', what if this 'later' is now (Weber 2008: 252)? By describing capitalism as the 'first case of a blaming, rather than a repenting cult', aiming not at relieving debt/guilt through repentance, but at its universalisation, Benjamin (2005: 259) may have prefigured processes that visibly mark our current predicament.

What then if debt is not only a problem but also a mechanism of domination, in other words a solution of sorts? What if the sense of guilt it creates is so pervasive precisely because it precedes its current deployment and builds on *subjective infrastructures* sedimented in the *longue durée* leading them to new heights? Being, for the last few years, the experimental laboratory of cutting-edge neoliberal and other strategies, Greece provides the perfect ground to test the validity of these hypotheses.

Crises usually disturb dominant representations, shake up our sense of continuity and generate new narratives attempting to regulate the social bond, often in favour of pre-existing social hierarchies. After many years of being subjected to such narratives, we can certainly map them with great accuracy. I am referring mainly to the dominant discourse of European institutions, which is also accepted and largely reproduced by mainstream intellectuals and the media in Greece. Examined in its genealogical unfolding (before and after the crisis) this discourse is itself marked by a certain irregularity or discontinuity. Where is this located? Almost overnight the country that entered the euro and hosted the Olympics winning unconditional international acclaim, the EU's agent and preferential business partner in the Balkans, a valued market for European commodities (from lucrative arms deals and overpriced medical supplies to luxury cars and hi-tech products), became the *sick man* of Europe, a *bête noire* to be ridiculed, condemned and disciplined in the most severe and exemplary way. *How did this become accepted? Together with the punishment that followed it?*

In mapping the discourses that expressed this gigantic disciplining operation, driving a huge experiment in violent downward social mobility and neoliberal restructuring, we encounter a process of creating and sustaining shame and guilt – and thus legitimising punishment (in the form of radical impoverishment, sky-rocketing unemployment, liquidation of labour and other social rights). A series of metaphors are enlisted here to substantiate blame: medical and pedagogical, anthropomorphic and zoomorphic, they all seem to prepare the ground (social as well as subjective) for the legitimisation of a harsh punishment (Stavrakakis 2013b, 2014). It is important to note that, especially during its early stages, this disciplining operation relied a lot on the pastoral cultivation of a particular 'ideal ego' with which every Greek citizen had to identify in order to satisfy the European gaze, the big Other, and be properly 'readmitted' into the Eurozone family of 'normal' member states. Failure to do so in the eyes of European institutions is then bound to produce feelings of guilt and shame and eventually to attract the sadism of the superego:

> the 'ideal ego' stands for the idealized self-image of the subject (the way I would like to be, I would like others to see me); the Ego-Ideal is the agency whose gaze I try to impress with my ego image, the big Other who watches over me and propels me to give my best, the ideal I try to follow and actualize; and the superego is this same agency in its revengeful, sadistic, punishing, aspect. (Žižek 2006: 79)

All three modalities have been instrumental in the administration of the Greek crisis. Initially, the emphasis was placed on the asymmetric dialectic between ideal ego, the model of a new truly European Greece to come, and Ego-Ideal, the European gaze overseeing the country's transformation, rewarding the advances and punishing the setbacks. This was not entirely unexpected given the long pedigree of such a positioning throughout modern Greek history. Indeed, one of the aspirations of the revolution for independence from Ottoman rule (1821) was to create a 'European state' (Skopetea 1988: 27). And yet the realisation of this aspiration was, from the beginning, subject to significant asymmetries: it was 'symptomatic of the dependent nature of the new state that the Greeks were not a party to the treaty of May 1832 between Britain, France, Russia and Bavaria which settled the terms under which King Otto was to accept the throne and which placed Greece under the "guarantee" of the "Protecting" powers' (Clogg 1992: 47). The resulting association between independence and dependency affected both politics and culture marking the paradoxical choreography between the emerging modern Greek identity and its big Other, its symbolic guarantor: Europe.

Each of these poles operated diachronically on a plurality of registers; thus Europe would comprise, among others, a 'Europe as model', the blueprint Greece had to follow, as well as a 'Europe as observer' (Skopetea 1988: 163). Being under constant observation, feeling at all times the ambivalent European gaze, both fascinated and disappointed by Greece, increasingly shaped a type of identity oriented towards the continuous need to prove to Europe the worth of modern Greek achievement (ibid.: 164–165). What was continuously judged here was the required 'progress' of the new state – not only in terms of numerical indices of economic, administrative and educational performance, but also and primarily in terms of institutional function and 'popular' mentalities – following its 'entry exams' (the war of independence) and its generous acceptance into the civilised European world, the EEC, the EU and, finally, the Eurozone (ibid.:

225–227). Consequently, to the extent that the European gaze diachronically oscillates between admiration and contempt, in Greece, likewise, guilt alternates with indignation in an unmistakably superegoic tit-for-tat.

Even in the nineteenth century, a dialectic of indebtedness marked the imaginary regulation of the identifications at stake: if modern Greece owed its political independence and survival to Europe, could Europe ignore the role of (ancient) Greece as the cradle of European civilisation (ibid.: 167)? As becomes evident from the way this question is posed, Europe is the privileged pole here and modern Greece emerges as the dependent variable, the one demanding recognition, support and even affection from the European Other. This is clearly when the relationship of Greeks to Europe acquired the symptomatic form of an enduring and troubling 'complex' (ibid.: 169). Throughout modern Greek history this choreography often escalated into a superegoic climax, sometimes even involving debt and bankruptcy. Today it is again the superego in 'its revengeful, sadistic, punishing, aspect' that seems to run the show. And debt is once again of paramount importance.

Debt as Psychosocial Hinge

What was the *proof* of Greece's failure, the *symptom* of its illness, the justification for a further post-democratic turn in its governance? What was the indisputable evidence that constituted the basis of blame, the source of shame and guilt? The answer is simple, the *accumulation of debt*. Here, however, some puzzling paradoxes start to emerge. How is it possible that the policies imposed to remedy this problem (the economic and moral failure of excessive debt), while gradually bringing the deficit under control, only promise to 'stabilise' debt in 2020, when it will be almost at the same level it was at in 2008–2009, at the start of the crisis? Isn't that revealing of the fact that, at least during this delicate phase (these lines are written in January 2015), debt functions both as a failure and a pathology to be remedied but also – and most crucially – as a controlling mechanism to be sustained and used in the 'proper' ways? On the one hand, debt is declared unethical *après coup*, blame for it is retroactively individualised – ownership is ascribed to particular states, groups and individuals, largely ignoring broader systemic inequalities – and a pound of flesh is demanded from all – with the normal exclusion of the power bloc. On the other, debt is accepted as here to stay, as something that needs to be stabilised and protected – even 'cultivated' – in order to be used as a tool to *threaten, subject and control*. How else could one interpret Mario Draghi's admission that a restructuring of Greek debt – currently standing at an astonishing 174.9 per cent of GDP – is 'neither necessary nor useful' (Draghi 2014)? Indeed, no one today can escape the web of indebtedness. This applies not only to Greece, but to a wide range of institutional entities and subjects, from states that are obliged to bail out their collapsing banks to students, who, instead of scholarships now receive loans, so that their lives start overdetermined by a huge burden.

How is it possible, however, for so many people to accept this course of events given that debt accumulation constituted a thoroughly ethical behaviour within late capitalist consumerist societies? In other words, how is it possible for debt to turn overnight from good to bad object, to use Melanie Klein's (1984) terminology? From an accomplishment to a failure for which each and every one (from states to individuals) is fully accountable and for which eternal suffering can be the only reward? How can debt function so effectively as a *hinge* between antithetical formulations of the social bond? There is, indeed, plenty of evidence to suggest that the assumption of shame and guilt is always already presupposed as a long-term subjective infrastructure well before its every (contingent) historical instantiation. Clearly some sort of pre-existing propensity needs to be posited in order to explain the fact that today many are forced to feel ashamed and guilty because of their (national, family and personal) indebtedness, while a few years ago the same people were actively encouraged to accumulate credit and debt in order to spend, consume and enjoy. Back then guilt plagued only those who could not keep up with the generalised/democratised spirit of 'conspicuous consumption'. In that sense, this propensity has nothing to do with the particular (very different if not contradictory) injunctions involved.

Evidently, what is at stake with credit and debt is something that goes far beyond economics and involves subject formation at the most profound level. To quote Lazzarato (2012: 29), 'debt acts as a "capture", "predation", and "extraction" machine on the whole of society, as an instrument for macroeconomic prescription and management, and as a mechanism for income redistribution. It also functions as a mechanism for the production and "government" of collective and individual subjectivities'. It is the realm of *subjectivity* that stands at the epicentre of this functioning: 'debt breeds, subdues, manufactures, adapts, and shapes subjectivity' (ibid.: 38–39). This problematic of the emergence of a new type of subjectivity is by no means unique to Lazzarato; for example, Dardot and Laval have also recently focused on the emergence of what they call an 'entrepreneurial' or 'neoliberal subject', illuminating how neoliberalism 'direct[s] from within' governments, peoples and individuals, and is not only destructive but also 'productive of certain kinds of social relations, certain ways of living, certain subjectivities' (Dardot and Laval 2014a: 3). It has to be studied as a rationality structuring the actions of the rulers as well as the conduct of the ruled (ibid.: 4). But by highlighting the role of debt, Lazzarato allows a better understanding of the multiple and even antithetical ways in which this new subject can be constituted and manipulated.

In my view, however, it would prove extremely productive to add a further psychosocial twist to Lazzarato's take on this production of neoliberal forms of subjectivity. If such subjective construction works through the (impossible) assumption of *duty, shame and guilt* and their political regulation, it makes sense to register what psychoanalysis adds to this picture when it acknowledges the same operations as founding gestures of modern subjectivity. Referring to Klein and especially to the good/bad object distinction, Lacan (2006: 111) observes that 'the superego appears at so early a stage that it seems to form contemporaneously with the ego, if not before it'. Positing the 'fatal inevitability of the sense of guilt', Freud (1982 [1929]: 69) had also described guilt as something concomitant with human sociality, as an unavoidable result of ambivalence related to the struggle between Death and Eros, a conflict set 'going as soon as men are faced with the task of living together'. In fact, within psychoanalytic literature, both the development of a sense of guilt and the function of the superego acquire a strong socio-political relevance; by overdetermining subjectivity they emerge as shaping the social bond and stabilising the economic and political order.

Let me highlight some of Freud's observations that may be relevant for our analysis. Firstly, guilt has to be dissociated from a linear causal framework relating it to some prior action of the subject, whether individual or collective. Although initially our understanding of guilt relates to someone having 'done something which he knows to be "bad"' (ibid.: 61), in actual fact, it does not make a lot of difference whether something bad has indeed been committed or has remained at the level of mere *intention*. Second, the judgement of recognising something – whether act or intention – as 'bad' does not originate from within the ego but indicates a significant 'extraneous influence' (ibid.: 61). What is, however, the motive behind our *submission* to such an extraneous influence which may arbitrarily disregard the desires and satisfactions of the ego? Cognisant of her/his ontological helplessness, of her/his reliance on others, one is always fearful of losing the love of her/his community. At the same time, Freud adds, 'loss of love' is coupled with fear of 'punishment' (ibid.: 61). This is where the superego emerges to strengthen this process of subjection: 'Thus we know two origins of the sense of guilt: one arising from the fear of an authority, and the other later on, arising from the fear of the super-ego' (ibid.: 64). The superego thus constitutes a continuation of 'the severity of external authority' which it, in part, replaces (ibid.: 64). As Norbert Elias has magnificently supported with his sociological evidence, the success of an external authority in influencing behaviour relies on its ability to enlist the complicity of the subject itself in its subjection through the establishment of 'internal' mechanisms of control reproduced as habits: 'The prohibitions supported by social sanctions are reproduced in individuals as self-controls ... This ... is clearly the state of affairs which Freud tried to express by concepts such as the "superego"' (Elias 2000: 160).

Dardot and Laval (2014b) argue that '[t]he main innovation of neoliberal technology precisely consists in directly connecting the way a person "is governed from without" to the way that "he governs himself from within"'. Such a connection, however, has always been there to the extent that no socio-political stability, not even a relative one, can be achieved without it; without, that is, what Lacan describes as the 'pacifying' dimension of the Ego-Ideal: the function of superegoic guilt – associated with subjective indebtedness towards the Other – as the *hinge* between subjectivity and the social order through the connection it establishes between 'libidinal normativeness' and 'cultural normativeness' (Lacan 2006: 95). It is important, however, to register the different modalities through which this connection operates, which relate to a multiplicity of alternating faces consisting of at least two major variants: prohibitive and brutal (Freud) as well as permissive and generative (Lacan). In fact, Lacan was perhaps the first to highlight the plasticity of this structure when he linked the (consumerist) command 'Enjoy!' with the superego: 'The superego is the imperative of jouissance – Enjoy!' (Lacan 1998: 3). We can thus infer that both enforced *accumulation of debt* – a central moral imperative of what Todd McGowan (2004) has called a 'society of commanded enjoyment' – as well as *stigmatisation* and *punishment* of indebtedness – the violent return to a 'society of prohibition' – constitute internal if antithetical moments of the same mechanism, using subject construction in the service of a (neoliberal) overdetermination of the social bond.

And this works both ways. One should not forget that the gesture of renouncing enjoyment, within any society of prohibition, can also 'generate a surplus enjoyment of its own' and thus 'the superego injunction to enjoy is immanently intertwined with the logic of sacrifice: the two form a vicious cycle, each extreme supporting the other' (Žižek 2006: 81). And vice versa: the consumerist injunction to enjoy never delivers on its liberating promises, revealing the command to enjoy merely as 'a more nuanced form of prohibition' (McGowan 2004: 39). It is, above all else, the common superegoic infrastructure that facilitates the shifts from one modality to the other, revealing the psychosocial continuity behind major economic, political and behavioural shifts.

What is the nature of this continuity? From a psychoanalytic point of view, the continuity has to do with the self's *radical ex-centricity*, as Lacan would put it; on the realisation that, instead of being 'something autonomous and unitary', instead of being a source of certainty, ego identity is something 'deceptive', which only serves as 'façade' for our complex 'unconscious mental activity' (Freud 1982 [1929]: 3). In a consistent Freudian way, the Lacanian subject is devoid of the autonomy that 'the discourse of freedom' assigns to it. Such a picture can only be of a 'fundamentally biased and incomplete, inexpressible, fragmentary, differentiated, and profoundly delusional character' (Lacan 1993: 145), to the extent that it disavows our constitutive reliance on the Other – through identification processes – which enables the construction of all sense of identity conferring, at the same time, upon it an ultimately alienating character: *desire is always the desire of the Other*. The continuity in question involves, thus, the reliance of our desire on processes of subjection to the socio-symbolic order, on the *extimate* influence of the cultural and political superego, simultaneous extraneous and intrinsic, hated and loved.

If Lacan's deconstruction of autonomy and his theory regarding the cultural and political overdetermination of subjectivity draws on Freud and Kojeve's Hegel, in Frederic Lordon's opinion, '[n]o one strove to establish the absolute generality of the heteronomy of desire more than Spinoza' (Lordon 2014: 15). It may not be a coincidence after all that, as the story goes, Lacan used to keep a chart of Spinoza's *Ethics* in his room while at school. What is at stake here is what Lordon terms our 'passionate servitude' in which 'the real chains are those of our affects and desires' (ibid.: 16–17). This is a schema of radical *exodetermination* similar to the one psychoanalysis puts forward; and the similarities extend to highlighting its different modalities as well as to demonstrating that exodetermination can take at least two distinct forms analogous to the two types of superegoic overdetermination we have highlighted: prohibition and commanded enjoyment. In Lordon's words, '[c]oercion and consent are forms of the lived experience (respectively sad and joyful) of determination. To be coerced is to have been determined to do something but in a state of sadness. And to consent … is to live one's obedience, but with its intrinsic burden relieved by a joyful affect' (ibid.: 40). Lordon's Spinozist understanding of continuity in change offers thus an additional grounding to our psychoanalytic argument and is worth citing at length:

> For one is determined to assent just as one is determined to suffer: whichever state of mind one is in, it is always the product of exodetermination, and from this standpoint all states of mind are strictly alike. But only from this standpoint; in other respects they are very different, and it is not for nothing that they make those who experience them say sharply contrasting things, such as 'I consent' versus 'I yield'. Their true difference however always comes back to the fundamental polar opposition between the joyful and the sad. One can see a sign of the displacement of this difference in the double meaning of words such as 'enthralled' and 'captivated', which refer both to tyrannical enslavement and to enchanted acquiescence. In both cases one is indeed chained – to the order of causal determination – but with opposite affects in each. The difference is surely not minor, but nor is it what it is commonly believed to be – in any case it is not the difference between the free will that says yes wholeheartedly and the one that was temporarily made to yield by a superior force. Those who consent are no freer than anyone else, and are no less 'yielding' than the enslaved; only, they have been made to yield differently and thus experience their determination joyfully. (ibid.: 52–53)

It is, at the macro-level, the constitutive character of exodetermination and debt's privileged position within the underlying dual superegoic infrastructure overdetermining subjectivity which has thus allowed, at the micro-level, the power bloc of the debt economy to use 'the latest financial crisis as the perfect occasion to extend and deepen the logic of neoliberal politics' (Lazzarato 2012: 29). In Greece, this programme has initiated a spiral of unimaginable social destruction; in the words of the current (January 2015) Prime Minister, Antonis Samaras (who was rapidly transformed from a harsh critic to its foremost supporter), 'Greece lost about 25% of its pre-crisis GDP, the Greeks lost about 40% of their standard of living in just 4 years, while unemployment skyrocketed: 27% for the general population and more indeed than 60% for the youth!'[5] Obviously Greece is not alone in being forced to follow this path; from the United Kingdom's zero-hour contracts to Germany's systemic exploitation of migrant East European workers, this is a pan-European trend; nevertheless, Greece remains one of the current hotspots of this aggressively imposed neoliberalism. As Sassen notes, what has been happening in Southern Europe (and elsewhere) is no less than a violent redefinition of 'the economy'. It is still very unclear what this can produce in terms of presentable economic indices and growth; regardless, the cost is extremely high and involves, at the ground level, a 'brutal restructuring' (Sassen 2014: 43). What thus ensues can be described as an 'economic version of ethnic cleansing in which elements considered troublesome are dealt with by simply eliminating them ... The unemployed who lose everything – jobs, homes, medical insurance – easily fall off the edge of what is defined as "the economy" and counted as such. So do small shop and factory owners who lose everything and commit suicide. And so do the growing numbers of well-educated students and professionals who emigrate and leave Europe all together' (ibid.: 36).

Universal Cruelty: Post-democracy Radicalised?

One of the tentative conclusions to be drawn from our analysis is that the management of the crisis involved a continuous dialectic between subjectivity and the social bond using well-tested technologies of domination that purport to sublimate what appears as ambivalence and contradiction (encouraged accumulation of debt and punishment) into a mutual engagement sustaining the dominant power bloc and, in fact, deepening the grip of neoliberal capitalism, of 'debt society'. In order, however, to fully account for the subjective/collective imposition of this dialectic, for its political effectiveness, one would also need to take into account its recent mutations. We have discussed a process of creating and sustaining shame and guilt and thus legitimising punishment – but what if it also works the other way round? Maybe what permits debt to turn overnight from positive to negative, from good to bad object, is *also* the brutality and meaninglessness of the punishment itself – as well as its universal application. Paradoxically, the harsher and the more uncalled for the punishment, the easier it is for this shift to be accepted.

What if, in other words, the performativity of the punishment itself retroactively ascribes to past behaviour the stigma of an excessive, immoral, irrational pathology? Here, punishment seems to retroactively produce guilt, almost bypassing blame. Only thus can it continue to function even when its semblance of reasoning has started to evaporate, as happened in Greece.[6] What is at stake here is a mechanism that, from a certain point onwards, works predominantly through pain, through a 'mnemotechnics of cruelty' (Lazzarato 2012: 40–41), which inscribes the promise of debt repayment on the body itself. In Shakespearean terms, a pound of flesh, a limb has to be extracted (ibid.: 43) in order for this power structure to produce the surplus of meaningless despair that will allow it to be accepted fatalistically – or so the logic goes.

In the first stages of the crisis the imposition of the austerity avalanche involved and relied on its meaningful packaging, its embellishment with an ideological meaning able to secure a minimum of hegemonic consent – even one based on fear, blame, moralism and demonisation. During the last period, however (up until the time of writing, January 2015), a variety of indications signal the passage into a new phase – albeit one that is all too familiar to students of the long history of power relations. Decision making has gradually stopped claiming any concretely meaningful foundation; it lost any interest in winning consent – even through fear and extortion, through the manipulation of ideal ego and Ego-Ideal. What remains is, thus, its brutal imposition, superego in its most revengeful, sadistic form, 'reduced to something, which cannot even be expressed, like the *You must*, which is speech deprived of all its meaning' (Lacan 1991: 102).

Brutal aspects of neoliberalism have been sought up to now in evidence pertaining to incarceration trends in the United States and globally (Wacquant 2010). This is obviously important because it substantiates the relationship between the neoliberal economics of austerity and the collapse of the welfare state with a turn towards the *aggressive* enforcement of state policies and the repression of dissent: 'The misery of American welfare and the grandeur of American prisonfare at century's turn are the two sides of the same political coin' (ibid.: 203). In Greece, this despotic turn has been felt both in the treatment (incarceration) of illegal immigrants as well as in the implementation of a 'zero tolerance' strategy, which attempts to aggressively regulate the public space and insulate it from protest; following the violent eviction of the *indignants* from the squares and similar shifts in the tactics involved in monitoring public demonstrations, universities have recently emerged as a major site of contestation. It is also astonishing that at a time of major economic collapse and indignation, mayors of big Greek cities have proposed to insulate the urban centre from political rallies, now supposed to take place in the periphery so as to stop disrupting the shopping centre and the smooth functioning of the market (as if it was protest that disrupted the market and not the shrinking of spending power). It seems that even in an ailing economy, or maybe especially in an ailing economy where a new social order is being consolidated, consumption practices – now open to a shrinking minority – are bound to become inexorably linked to security logics: 'Places of consumption must seem like safe places to shop: places where "our type of people" venture' (Papanicolaou and Rigakos 2014: 18) and from which the losers as well as the detractors of progress have to be violently excluded.

It would be a mistake to judge these developments one by one, or to try to evaluate them separately in their own right; no doubt, some of them capitalise on pre-existing pathologies in order to use them in legitimising the deepening of the post-democratic mutation of capitalist democracy. What is, however, striking here is the asymmetry between the alleged democratic pathology to be remedied and the despotic solution imposed: instead of restoring democratic functioning, the solutions implemented often bracket democracy altogether. It is therefore crucial to assess the timing of their cumulative implementation and their positioning within the shift of domination techniques away from the (relative) permissiveness of the post-authoritarian period and into a radicalised post-democracy verging on brutal decisionism. This is evident in the discourse of mainstream politicians but also in a series of direct actions escaping the field of policing and security. Most emblematic among numerous examples was the decision in June 2013 to shut down ERT, the Greek public radio and television. The thoroughly unexpected and violent blackening of the screens, which shocked the international community and provoked an instant popular reaction and a major political crisis, has only highlighted the nihilist characteristics of the dominant policies implemented under the auspices of European and international institutions (Stavrakakis 2013a). In a similar vein and in ways disproportionate to any conceivable pre-existing pathology affecting these institutions, it was decided to liquidate whole branches of state functioning, like municipal police, without any previous consultation or debate. Even more recently, the eight most important public universities in Greece – already savagely hit by huge budget reductions and salary cuts – have been ordered by the government to move a substantial number of their administrative staff overnight – in some cases exceeding forty per cent – into a so-called 'availability' status – effectively bringing them to their knees. No wonder that the rectors of the biggest Greek universities, whom nobody in Greece would accuse of oppositional bias, have protested budget cuts that have reached – compared to 2009 – the astonishing level of 74 per cent for the University of Athens and 81.4 per cent for the University of Thessaloniki (Papamatthaiou 2014). The continuation of the functioning of these historic institutions in the future is consequently in serious doubt.

It is also important to note that this despotic shift is thoroughly consistent with what international financial institutions dictate. Consider the widely reported 'mistake' made by the IMF in calculating the effect of the measures implemented on GDP contraction (Blanchard and Leigh 2013). In the face of such an astonishing admission of undercalculation with disastrous consequences for the Greek economy and following calls from all political sides to relax the current policies, the troika insisted on Christine Lagarde's motto: 'implementation, implementation, implementation!' (Reuters 2012).

Most important in all these examples is to focus not on the 'what', on the concrete content of the policy shifts, but on the 'how', on the mechanics of their imposition. Distanced from any real argumentative support, the measures implemented openly reveal their functioning in favour of establishing a nihilistic system of domination through cruelty. This seems to be their only meaning and purpose. Aren't all of these signs of a gradual reversal of the transformations in penal and domination styles Foucault had observed? We seem to return to an era when punishment could 'exceed in savagery the crime itself' (Foucault 1995: 9). Obviously 'the punishment-body relationship is not the same as it was during the torture in public executions' (ibid.: 11); and yet the *collapse of meaning* characteristic of brutal nihilism seems to be directly targeting bodies, bodies that are increasingly suffering beyond any reasonable and proportionate expectation and without any remotely persuasive ascription of blame; bodies that more and more appear not as an intermediary level but as a 'constituent element' (ibid.: 11) of the exercise of power.

What we encounter here is, perhaps, superego at its purest, the sadistic superego in 'its senseless, blind character, of pure imperativeness and simple tyranny' (Lacan 1991: 102):

> the cruel and insatiable agency which bombards me with impossible demands and which mocks my failed attempts to meet them, the agency in the eyes of which I am all the more guilty, the more I try to suppress my 'sinful' strivings and meet its demands. The old cynical Stalinist motto about the accused at the show trials who professed their innocence ('the more they are innocent, the more they deserve to be shot') is superego at its purest. (Žižek 2006: 80)

Whether this openly sadistic turn will herald the triumph or trigger the collapse of the policies implemented is impossible to predict. At any rate, if cruelty could be interpreted as a sign of weakness, this is not because it contradicts a humanist perspective. From a psychoanalytic perspective consistent with the duality of the drives both aggressiveness and cruelty are constitutive of human communities. 'Men are not gentle creatures who want to be loved' (Freud 1982 [1929]: 48), at least, this is not the whole picture:

> they are, on the contrary, creatures among whose instinctual endowments is to be reckoned a powerful share of aggressiveness ['cruel aggressiveness' as Freud later termed it]. As a result, their neighbor is for them not only a potential helper or sexual object, but also someone who tempts them to satisfy their aggressiveness on him, to exploit his capacity for work without compensation, to use him sexually without his consent, to seize his possessions, to humiliate him, to cause him pain, to torture and to kill him. (ibid.: 48)

As Lacan has observed, one only has to leaf through a book of works by Hieronymus Bosch to encounter an atlas of all the aggressive fantasies tormenting mankind (Lacan 2006: 85). Furthermore, although civilisation attempts to limit this aggressiveness (Freud 1982 [1929]: 49) its effects remain ambivalent and partial: it is difficult to banish it, easier to channel it in ways benefiting the formation and cohesion of communities – in order to get bound by libido they need to channel aggressiveness outwards (ibid.: 51), to a suitable outgroup (the Jews, the immigrants, etc.). Thus cultural and political ways to limit aggressiveness may sometimes increase unhappiness, ushering in a destructive dialectic: 'What a potent obstacle to civilisation aggressiveness must be, if the defense against it can cause as much unhappiness as aggressiveness itself' (ibid.: 80).

Moving beyond humanist sentimentalism, a *critique of cruelty* can only emanate from an assessment of its inherent ambivalence and its ethico-political implications. On the one hand it should be clear that, although operating at a zero degree of meaning where, as we have seen, suffering seems to be the only meaning left, such an openly aggressive turn into universal cruelty does not signify a turn into a post-hegemonic era where power becomes purely biopolitical, operating beyond meaning and representation (cf. Lash 2007; Beasley-Murray 2010). On the contrary, it functions as a signal of strength, of hegemony: 'The preeminence of aggressiveness in our civilisation would already be sufficiently demonstrated by the fact that it is usually confused in everyday morality with the virtue of strength' (Lacan 2006: 98). To put it in slightly twisted Althusserian terms, by revealing the poverty of contemporary ideological state apparatuses, the crisis forces repression itself to acquire an ideological meaning. Indeed, although aspects of the Althusserian distinction between repressive and ideological state apparatuses may partially resemble the post-hegemonic one between real and representation, to the extent that the first functions through violence exerted on bodies while the second functions through ideology (Althusser 2014: 244), the introduction of the distinction calls for further clarification, which calls into question its purity and highlights the representational value of violent and brutal domination itself:

> I can clarify matters by correcting this distinction. I shall say rather that every state apparatus, whether repressive or ideological, 'functions' both by violence and by ideology, but with one very important distinction …
>
> This is the fact that the (Repressive) State Apparatus functions massively and predominantly by repression (including physical repression), while functioning secondarily by ideology. (There is no such thing as a purely repressive apparatus.) (Althusser 2014: 244)

And yet, beyond its *façade* of strength, this meaning reveals the vulnerability of the power structure. As Lacan has put it, the turn to cruelty constitutes an unmistakable indication that power feels the presence and the pressure of an adversary that needs to be recognised even if only in order to be crushed: 'But this very cruelty implies humanity. It targets a semblable, … it is in the fight to the death for pure prestige that man wins recognition from man' (Lacan 2006: 120). This applies even to torture: 'For the contempt for conscience that is manifest in the widespread reappearance of this practice as a means of oppression hides from us what faith in man it presupposes as a means of enforcing justice' (ibid.: 113). In fact, although, at first, this turn can be interpreted as taking the logic of the superego to its sadistic extremes, at the same time it foreshadows its *implosion*. This is simply because, by increasingly relying on the cruel aggression of an external authority, it undermines the superego as internal authority; and vice versa, the turn to universal cruelty only becomes necessary by the inability of the cultural superego to guarantee the reproduction of the socio-political order. It is here that regression acquires its proper psychoanalytic connotation to the extent that the sequence leading to the erection of the superego, as described by Freud, is arguably reversed:

> First comes renunciation of instinct owing to the fear of aggression by the *external* authority (this is, of course, what fear of the loss of love amounts to, for love is a protection against this punitive aggression). After that comes the erection of an *internal* authority, and renunciation of instinct owing to the fear of it – owing to fear of conscience. In this second situation bad intentions are equated with bad actions, and hence come a sense of guilt and a need for punishment. The aggressiveness of conscience keeps up the aggressiveness of the authority. (Freud 1982 [1929]: 65)

In that sense, although superficially functioning as shibboleths of strength, brutal nihilism and universal cruelty may signal a withdrawal of the superego revealing the heteronomy implicit in the construction of neoliberal subjectivity and thus increasing its vulnerability, lessening its hegemonic grip, since, in the words of Althusser (2014: 245), 'no class can hold state power over a long period without at the same time exercising its hegemony over and in the Ideological State Apparatuses'.

Conclusion

As we have seen, at a psychosocial level, the management of the (Greek) crisis involved a continuous dialectic between subjectivity and the social bond, using well-tested technologies of domination sustaining the dominant power bloc; the multiple mechanisms which allow debt to function as a potent psychosocial hinge are crucial here. Within this framework, what initially appears as antithesis and contrast conceals an *extimate* superegoic continuity. We have thus seen how, while in the first stages of the crisis the imposition of the austerity avalanche involved and relied on its meaningful packaging – sustaining shame and guilt and thus ideologically legitimising punishment and 'reform' – during the last period a variety of indications signal the passage into a new phase in which the suffering of bodies and its resignification in terms of an ideology of strength acquires priority bypassing blame. At any rate, political theory is thus faced with a new challenge: how is one to assess the establishment and consolidation through cruelty of 'neoliberal' debt society? Does it constitute a sign of further post-democratisation? Or does it signify a passage beyond post-democracy? If so, into what exactly? Even if no conclusive answer is currently forthcoming, it may be the time to start posing the question.

Colin Crouch seems to be in favour of the first course:

> The entire way in which the crisis has been managed has been evidence of a further drift towards post-democracy. First, the Anglo-American financial model that produced the crisis in the first place was designed by a politico-economic elite that corresponds to my concept, as bankers moved in and out of the revolving doors in Washington, designing policies to suit their firms. Then the management of the crisis itself was primarily a rescue operation for banks at the expense of the rest of the population. The most explicit expression of the post-democratic aspects of crisis management was the framing of the Greek austerity package, designed by international authorities in close collaboration with an association of leading bankers. (Carrigan and Crouch 2013)

What if, however, the management of the crisis itself increasingly functions in ways one would find very difficult to make compatible with even the most formal definition of (post-)democracy? What if the consolidation of debt society driven by what Sassen (2014: 13) calls 'predatory formations' and transforming institutions like the European Union into 'political monsters' (Beck 2011), is drawing us into a terrain of what, currently, can only be signified as a contradiction in terms, as authoritarian or 'totalitarian democracy'? (Harvey 2014: 292; Marazzi

2011: 141). What if it signals a fuller actualisation of what Sheldon Wolin (2008: xvi) had highlighted as a set of tendencies pointing 'in a direction away from self-government, the rule of law, egalitarianism, and thoughtful public discussion, and toward … "managed democracy," the smiley face of inverted totalitarianism'? In that case, to speak about democratic recession, *malaise* or dysfunction, even about post-democracy, would probably be insufficient.

When commentators like Wolfgang Streeck diagnose that democracy as we knew it is already 'effectively suspended' in countries such as Greece, Ireland and Portugal (Streeck 2011: 26) then we may need to consider the possibility that the turn to universal cruelty we have attempted to capture in this text could indicate a 'master-desire [that] no longer tolerates restrictions on its strategic moves and embraces the idea of no longer having to take the other into consideration' thus evolving into some sort of 'tyranny' (Lordon 2014: 30–31). Apart from revealing neoliberalism as 'constitutively corrosive of democracy' (Wacquant 2010: 218), this recent turn of limitless and nihilistic imposition could very well be seen as following, once more, a 'totalitarian' orientation (Lordon 2014: 47). Not necessarily in the classic meaning of the term but in the sense that it elicits *total* subordination and submission. And yet, such a 'total' enforcement of superegoic brutality could also indicate an *implosion*, a 'liquidation of the super-ego', to use Bernard Stiegler's expression (Stiegler 2014: 7) and may be further undermining its *pacifying* function. Arguably such a radical undermining will be untenable in the long run. From Machiavelli to Gramsci and from Spinoza to Althusser we know that '[c]ontradictory as it may sound, tyrants would rather be loved!' it is more efficient to rule with love rather than with fear (Lordon 2014: 34, 40). Somehow the sad affects resulting from cruel exodetermination will have to be transubstantiated into a 'regime of joyful affects' (Lordon 2014: 47). Sustainable superegoic guilt presupposes both.

The new normality has been unable to win and sustain the active endorsement, even the complicity, of large sections of the population in the South and beyond. Its rapid and brutal imposition has, of course, triggered powerful psychosocial mechanisms of revalorisation turning debt from 'good' to 'bad' and camouflaging brutal nihilism as hegemonic strength. A critical mass of subjects have adopted, as a result, a position of 'cruel optimism', to use Lauren Berlant's terminology. This is how Berlant defines it:

> A relation of cruel optimism exists when something you desire is actually an obstacle to your flourishing. It might involve food, or a kind of love; it might be a fantasy of the good life, or a political project. … These kinds of optimistic relation are not inherently cruel. They become cruel only when the object that draws your attachment actively impedes the aim that brought you to it initially. (Berlant 2011: 1)

Thus, the so-called 'success story' about the end of the crisis could be seen as 'a bad life that wears out the subjects who nonetheless, and at the same time, [still] find their conditions of possibility within it' (ibid.: 27). What we seem to encounter here is, at first, an attitude of disavowal of the menacing reality. In a collapsing world – where fantasies like 'upward mobility, job security, political and social equality, and lively, durable intimacy' are fraying – it refers to the 'sustaining inclination to return to the scene of fantasy that enables you to expect that this time, nearness to this thing will help you or a world to become different in just the right way' (ibid.: 2). Such cruel optimism, characteristic of an in-between period, in which old attachments die a violent death but new ones cannot be generated yet, cannot last forever. The more the superego function is liquidated, the more alternative fantasies and administrations of desire will emerge, the less it will be able to sustain its grip.

In order to avoid the eventual collapse of cruel optimism, the fermenting of discontent and the ensuing political radicalisation of the lower and middle classes, the systemic edge may have to re-energise once more the movement of the pendulum between the two spirits of capitalism, between cruel prohibition and enforced enjoyment, arriving at a new distribution or combination. Will this prove feasible? What if, by reducing politics to a zero degree of meaning, by liquidating the superego, by impoverishing sociality and ethical imagination, its recent movements and especially its nihilistic turn have ushered in an era of profound 'spiritual misery' (Stiegler 2014: 6–7)? If, in the 1990s, it was still appropriate to refer 'to a new "spirit" of capitalism, it may now be more urgent to be thinking about a new "stahlhartes Gehause" – a new steel-hard casing, better known as the "iron-cage"' (Otsch et al. 2014: 248). What then if a new distribution or combination between the two spirits has been denied by a long process in which neoliberalism seems to be deepening a pre-existing process of 'destruction of spirit by capitalism' (Stiegler 2014: 2)? This will be a real challenge for our ethical imagination, meaning the ways in which 'technologies of the self, forms of subjectification and imagined relations with others lead to novel ways of approaching social transformation' (Moore 2011: 15). In particular, will we manage to push forward a democratic renegotiation of our constitutive heteronomy? Will we prove worthy of the task?

Notes

1   This is, for example, the case in Greece where this return to normality, orchestrated by the then governing parties and celebrated by mainstream media, had been regrettably antagonised by the proverbial pessimists, including recent reports that, in 2013, 35.7 per cent of the Greek population were found to be at risk of poverty and social exclusion (Eurostat 2014).
2   This brutal turn has also marked political developments in the South during the last few years; see, in this respect, Stavrakakis (2013b).
3   The link between worsening economic/political conditions, discontent and democratic resistance is never automatic. In fact, resistance may not be the more predictable outcome in such conjunctures. Yet it would be wrong to imply that no resistance at all has been observed in the global landscape: developments in Latin America during the last fifteen years should be taken into account in this respect. Slowly but steadily the European South has also been witnessing the emergence of a series of democratic movements with hegemonic pretensions.

4   This may indicate some analogies with Derrida's logic of *différance*.
5   <http://www.primeminister.gov.gr/2013/10/04/12384></u> (accessed 10 October 2013).
6   This has not happened only in Greece; the trend is widespread. In the United
     Kingdom, for example, David Cameron's 2013 initiative to take away key benefits
     from the under-25s was quickly criticised as a display of 'downright venality, wicked-
     ness and *cruelty*' (Fog 2013, emphasis added). See also, in this context, the debate
     around the 'inhumanity' of the decision of the U.K. government to stop supporting
     European search and rescue operations in the Mediterranean Sea (Birrell 2014) as
     well as the 'brutality' characteristic of the profit-driven reorientation of the university
     system (Warner 2014).

References

Althusser, L. 2014. *On the Reproduction of Capitalism: Ideology and Ideological State Apparatuses*. London: Verso.

Berlant, L. 2011. *Cruel Optimism*. Durham: Duke University Press.

Beasley-Murray, J. 2010. *Posthegemony*. Minneapolis: University of Minnesota Press.

Beck, U. 2011. Créons une Europe des citoyens! *Le Monde*, 26 December.

Benjamin, W. 2005. Capitalism as Religion. In *The Frankfurt School on Religion* (ed.) E. Mendieta, 259–262. New York: Routledge.

Birrell, I. 2014. Britain's Refusal to Save Migrants is an Act of Inhumanity. <http://www.theguardian.com/commentisfree/2014/oct/28/britain-refusal-help-migrants-inhumanity> (accessed 22 July 2015).

Blanchard, O., and D. Leigh. 2013. *Growth Forecast Errors and Fiscal Multipliers*. Cambridge, MA: NBER Working Paper No. 18779.

Carrigan, M., and C. Crouch. 2013. Five Minutes with Colin Crouch. <http://blogs.lse.ac.uk/politicsandpolicy/archives/30297> (accessed 22 July 2015).

Clogg, R. 1992. *A Concise History of Greece*. Cambridge: Cambridge University Press.

Crouch, C. 2004. *Post-Democracy*. Cambridge: Polity Press.

Dardot, P., and C. Laval. 2014a. *The New Way of the World: On Neo-liberal Society*. London: Verso.

———. 2014b. The New Way of the World, Part I: Manufacturing the Neoliberal Subject. *e-flux* 51: 1–8.

Draghi, M. 2014. Mario Draghi: 'Neither Necessary, Nor Useful a Restructuring of Greek Debt'. < http://www.tanea.gr/PrintArticle/?article=5180918> (accessed 22 July 2015).

Elias, N. 2000. *The Civilizing Process: Sociogenetic and Psychogenetic Investigations (Second Edition)*. Oxford: Blackwell.

Eurostat. 2014. More Than 120 Million Persons at Risk of Poverty or Social Exclusion in 2013. News release 168, 4 November.

Fog, A. 2013. David Cameron's Assault on the Young isn't Callous – It's Much Worse Than That. <http://www.theguardian.com/commentisfree/2013/oct/03/david-cameron-under-25s-assault/print></u> (accessed 22 July 2015).

Foucault, M. 1995. *Discipline and Punish: The Birth of the Prison*. London: Vintage.

———. 2008. *The Birth of Biopolitics: Lectures at the Collège de France, 1978–1979*. Basingstoke: Palgrave.

Freud, S. [1929] 1982. *Civilization and its Discontents*. London: The Hogarth Press and The Institute of Psychoanalysis.

Harvey, D. 2005. *A Brief History of Neoliberalism*. Oxford: Oxford University Press.

————. 2014. *Seventeen Contradictions and the End of Capitalism.* London: Profile Books.

Klein, M. 1984. *Envy and Gratitude and Other Works, 1946–1963.* London: Vintage.

Lacan, J. 1991. *The Seminar of Jacques Lacan. Book I: Freud's Papers on Technique, 1953–4.* New York: Norton.

————. 1993. *The Seminar of Jacques Lacan. Book III: The Psychoses, 1955–56.* London: Routledge.

————. 1998. *The Seminar of Jacques Lacan. Book XX: Encore, On Feminine Sexuality, The Limits of Love and Knowledge, 1972–3.* New York: Norton.

————. 2006. *Écrits.* New York: Norton.

Lash, S. 2007. Power after Hegemony: Cultural Studies in Mutation? *Theory, Culture and Society,* 24, no. 3: 55–78.

Lazzarato, M. 2012. *The Making of the Indebted Man.* New York: The MIT Press/ Semiotexte.

Lordon, F. 2014. *Wiling Slaves of Capital: Spinoza & Marx on Desire.* London: Verso.

Marazzi, C. 2011. *Capital and Affects.* New York: The MIT Press/Semiotexte.

McGowan, T. 2004. *The End of Dissatisfaction? Jacques Lacan and the Emerging Society of Enjoyment.* Albany: SUNY Press.

Moore, H. 2011. *Still Life: Hopes, Desires and Satisfactions.* Cambridge: Polity Press.

Mouffe, C. 2009. *The Democratic Paradox.* London: Verso.

Otsch, S., P.P. Pasqualoni and A. Scott. 2014. From 'New Spirit' to New Steel-Hard Casing? Civil Society Actors, Capitalism, and Crisis: The Case of Attac in Europe. In *New Spirits of Capitalism?* (eds) P. du Gay and G. Morgan, 231–250. Oxford: Oxford University Press.

Papamatthaiou, M. 2014. Dramatic Call for Financial Support from the Universities of Athens and Thessaloniki. <http://www.tovima.gr/PrintArticle/?aid=655768> (accessed 22 July 2015).

Papanicolaou, G., and G. Rigakos. 2014. *Democratizing the Police in Europe: With a Special Emphasis on Greece.* Vienna: transform!

Rancière, J. 1999. *Disagreement: Politics and Philosophy.* Minneapolis: University of Minnesota Press.

Reuters. 2012. IMF's Lagarde Repeats Implementation Mantra. *Kathimerini (English Language Edition),* 11 May.

Sassen, S. 2014. *Expulsions: Brutality and Complexity in the Global Economy.* Cambridge, MA: The Belknap Press.

Schäfer, A., and W. Streeck. 2013. Introduction: Politics in the Age of Austerity. In *Politics in the Age of Austerity* (eds) W. Streeck and A. Schäfer, 1–25. Cambridge: Polity Press.

Skopetea, E. 1988. *The 'Model Kingdom' and the Great Idea.* Athens: Polytypo.

Stavrakakis, Y. 2013a. Dispatches from the Greek Lab: Metaphors, Strategies and Debt in the European Crisis. *Psychoanalysis, Culture and Society* 18, no. 3: 313–324.

————. 2013b. Brutal Nihilism. *Chronos,* no. 2: <http://www.chronosmag.eu/index. php/y-stavrakakis-brutal-nihilism.html> (accessed 22 July 2015).

————. 2014. Debt Society: Psychosocial Aspects of the Greek Crisis. In *The Psychosocial & Organization Studies: Affect at Work* (eds) M. Fotaki and K. Kenny, 33–59. Houndmills: Palgrave.

Stiegler, B. 2014. *The Lost Spirit of Capitalism.* Cambridge: Polity Press.

Streeck, W. 2011. The Crises of Democratic Capitalism. *New Left Review* 71: 5–29.

Wacquant, L. 2010. Crafting the Neoliberal State: Workfare, Prisonfare, and Social Insecurity. *Sociological Forum,* 25, no. 2: 197–220.

Warner, J. 2014. An Open Letter to the Education System: Please Stop Destroying Students. <https://www.insidehighered.com/blogs/just-visiting/open-letter-education-system-please-stop-destroying-students> (accessed 22 July 2015).

Weber, S. 2008. *Benjamin's Abilities.* Cambridge, MA: Harvard University Press.

Wolin, S.S. 2008. *Democracy Incorporated: Managed Democracy and the Specter of Inverted Totalitarianism.* Princeton: Princeton University Press.

Žižek, S. 2006. *How to Read Lacan.* New York: Norton.

Yannis Stavrakakis is Professor of political science at the Aristotle University of Thessaloniki.

8

Politics after Democracy
Experiments in Horizontality

Marianne Maeckelbergh

This chapter traces a shift from the early 2000s when transnational social movements framed their grievances in terms of a 'democratic deficit' and the production of a 'democratic alternative' to what today might better be described as the emergence of a post-democratic political subjectivity which seeks to develop a viable political system for *after* democracy – one that will be better than democracy. While this post-democratic subjectivity has a different historical trajectory in each of the many localities where this 'horizontal' politics is emerging, it is nevertheless striking that it is emerging simultaneously across localities. This chapter explores some of the notable commonalities across several key sites of political unrest since the early 2010s and places these practices in relation to the transnational social movement history they share.[1]

Recent decades of protest have embodied a continuous experimentation with 'open' anti-hierarchical forms of politics (Graeber 2008, 2013; Juris 2008; Maeckelbergh 2009; Razsa and Kurnik 2012; Sitrin 2006; Sitrin and Azzellini 2014). The twenty-first century has so far been a time of experimentation with new forms of political subjectivity that are not based in predetermined ideologies or clearly defined sets of demands. Instead, social movement practices of 'participatory' and 'horizontal' politics that have been on the rise for over fifty years (and have existed, of course, for much longer) finally took centre stage in the public sphere, and for a moment, this 'horizontal politics' could not go unnoticed. That these movements were connected to a crisis of democracy was quite clear from the start. The year 2011 started with a wave of revolutions in the Middle East and North Africa, instigated against authoritarianism and, according to popular accounts, in the name of 'democracy'. In Spain, the 15 May (15M) movement, named for the day people first started taking over public squares across Spain and occupying them on 15 May 2011, began with the slogan of 'Real Democracy Now'. In the United States, the Occupy movement that occupied Zuccotti Park near Wall Street on 17 September 2011 and then many other parks and squares across the country and the world, were heard chanting 'this is what democracy looks like', a chant that was also commonly heard in the early 2000s in the alterglobalisation movement.

The prevalence of critiques of contemporary democracy stemming from these movements and their repeated demands to make the economy, the country, the city, politics in general 'more democratic' has led many to interpret these movements as being fundamentally about restoring democracy in the era of financial capitalism. Others, who have been participating in and studying the alterglobalisation movement, the 15M movement and Occupy have argued that these movements are not about restoring democracy, but about *reinventing* democracy to ensure that democracy will mean something very different in the twenty-first century than it has meant in the past (Graeber 2002, 2013; Juris 2008, 2012; Maeckelbergh 2009, 2012; Razsa and Kurnik 2012). This chapter builds on this literature in order to suggest that the political practices and subjectivities being produced through contemporary social movement praxis are so different from dominant forms of democracy (representative, liberal, electoral, etc.) that it might not make analytic sense to bring both forms of politics under the same label of 'democracy'.

When I first started researching social movement responses to the 'democratic deficit' at the turn of the twenty-first century, it seemed to me that the best way to understand these movements and what they were fighting for was to see them as movements that were developing their own qualitatively different forms of democracy. The way I understood what movement actors were trying to achieve was by making a distinction between democratic structures and democratic values. I argued that part of the movement actors' political aims was to create new democratic structures that could better fulfil democratic values such as equality, liberty, participation, diversity (see Maeckelbergh 2009, 2011, 2012, 2013a). Although I wrote short caveats and footnotes to explain that there was also a more critical perspective within the movement that rejected democracy entirely and that this perspective should not be ignored when discussing the role of democratic ideals within social movement praxis, I had largely ignored this perspective because it represented such a small subset of actors and it seemed so at odds with the dominant narratives and practices of most movement actors.

Over the years, however, I have discussed this analytical perspective with many activists across the world and especially in the past few years, I have encountered more and more critiques of democracy not only as a set of political structures, but also as a moral ideal. These critiques have usually come down to activists explaining to me that what I hadn't understood is that even though a lot of people use the word 'democracy' in discussions and everyday movement practices, democracy remains the system of oppression under which we are currently living. Democracy, as presented in this specific narrative, is the political system that has systematically maintained inequality and is what they are struggling against. Democracy should be recognised and presented not as a solution, they say, but as a set of political structures that serve to disempower people. The argument continues that as long as we keep using the term democracy to refer to the movement's own political practices, we will never be able to make clear that oppression is inherent to democracy as a form of governance. So, while the term most frequently used by most activists to describe what they desire is 'democracy', perhaps it is not the best analytical term given that it does not allow for a consideration of the tension that emerges between the existing democratic system and experiments with new political systems.

In this chapter I first explore some of the values implicit in the elaborate deci-sion-making procedures that social movements have slowly designed over the last half-century (at least) to promote a form of radical equality, today dubbed 'horizontality', which is viewed by participants as a potential replacement for political systems based on representation and electoral politics. I discuss these emerging political practices elsewhere at length as an example of 'democracy' in order to argue that these movement structures are better suited to fulfill-ing democratic values than the structures of representation, elections and the nation state. Activists might add new adjectives to the term democracy, ranging from participatory, to direct, to real, to horizontal, but all these adjectives stand in a conflictual relationship to what most of us have known democracy to be in the past. In the description of horizontal politics that follows, I hope to present, but not resolve, this tension for the reader by engaging the arguments of move-ment actors who more explicitly reject democracy, to see what this tension might say about democracy itself.

The discussion of democracy, post-democracy and horizontal politics as non-democracy presented here takes as its starting point the argument of a minority of movement actors (that democracy is a systematic way of disempowering the public with a stamp of global legitimacy) in order to delve into the many ways in which horizontality is different from democracy. I present some of the more critical attitudes and perspectives on democracy that I have encountered within transnational social movement networks, with special emphasis on the critical voices emerging in recent years. By introducing ethnography from a diversity of interconnected contexts (Egypt, Greece, Spain, the United States and the United Kingdom) I hope to show that the emerging post-democratic political subjectivities, while in no way unambiguously post-democratic, are intertwined in a globally interconnected trend of growing antagonism towards representa-tive and electoral democracy and a growing scepticism towards the idea that democracy could ever be coupled with values such as equality and liberty.

This line of argumentation draws on over ten years of ethnographic field-work within transnational social movement networks and countless conversa-tions with movement actors about the meaning of their political practices. In these deep discussions about political ideals and political practices, the differ-ences between democracy when spoken about by our leaders and democracy when spoken about by activists becomes clear. I hope to show that the meaning and perhaps long-term significance of horizontal politics is transforming in the 2010s because it is being practised within a political context that is growing more sceptical of democracy as a political ideal. In contrast to Crouch (2004) and Rancière (1995), this chapter, therefore, not only characterises the contem-porary political moment and contemporary nation states as post-democratic in a negative sense, but it also presents the political alternatives being developed by people around the world as a potential positive alternative to replace these post-democratic nation states. In other words, I present horizontality as the political form that is intended to come *after* democracy. This transition from democracy to horizontality is the counterfactual ideal guiding movement politics.

The Field of Horizontality

My choice to construct the field as a multi-sited, global field is the result of my analytical focus not on a specific location, site or group of people, but on the political process of horizontal decision making. This horizontality is taken as the subject of study, and it transcends multiple sites of occupation. There are important internal differences in each location, but all the multiple localities are part of a common process of experimentation with horizontal forms of politics. The models being developed are not exactly the same everywhere, and not all movement actors perceive themselves to be a part of a global and histori-cal process (though surprisingly many do). The differences between the many localities also generate important analyses, but to understand the implications of these different political uprisings all happening in one historical time period, it is essential to consider these movements as part of one internally diverse, multi-sited field.

I have been researching these horizontal practices since the early 2000s, starting with the alterglobalisation movement, and have watched these prac-tices re-emerge in slightly altered forms in the 15 May movement in Spain, the movements of the squares across Europe, the Occupy movements, the Gezi resistance in Turkey, and in the aftermath of the February 2014 upris-ings in Bosnia-Herzegovina. Throughout my research into horizontal politics, I have been actively involved in social movement decision-making practices locally and transnationally, including in the organisation of the World Social Forum in 2004, the European Social Forum in 2003 and 2004, the anti-G8 mobilisations in 2003, 2004, 2005, 2007 and 2008, and the anti-NATO and anti-UNFCCC protests in 2009. Most recently I have been doing fieldwork during repeated short visits to Athens, Barcelona, Cairo, Istanbul, London, Madrid, New York, Oakland, Thessaloniki and Tuzla between 2011 and 2014. Most of the research since 2011 was part of my work as co-producer on the globaluprisings.org film series. Working on the film series meant that I not only had access to video interviews that I conducted myself, but also to many more unedited video interviews (carried out in most cases by my co-producer Brandon Jourdan) and to hours and hours of raw footage, including of impor-tant events at which I had not always been present. Throughout all of these moments and research locations, I have followed horizontal decision making, people and practices to explore the way these practices are given meaning both locally and internationally, participating in many hundreds of meetings in twenty different countries.

The choice to frame the field transnationally is also a political choice. Over the past years the movements around the world have been treated by mainstream media, politicians and commentators as disparate and isolated incidents. This is quite a different picture from the one that emerges when you go from one place to another. In each location people speak of and analyse events happening far away and claim to be inspired by and connected to those events. Some people travel frequently between the different sites of uprising, transferring skills and knowledge. Others come together in large international gatherings at specific moments to exchange and learn from each other. The moments of convergence as well as the exchange of information across these contexts makes it difficult to regard such events as disconnected from one another.

If we accept that these struggles are connected, then one of the questions that emerges is which historical frame ought to be applied for understanding these movements? Rather than place these movements within their national or local histories, it is important to explore the transnational history of movement organising that has shaped so many of the everyday movement practices emerging around the world. This allows us to see the experiments with horizontality and the rejection of democracy not as a new practice or idea, but as the continuation of an ongoing process that goes back into history, not only in Spain, the United States, Egypt or Greece, but rather, and especially, in the moments of convergence between movements internationally over the past few decades. It also helps us to see that this experiment is unlikely to end any time soon and will most likely continue until the fundamental tension at the heart of the movements is resolved: the question of how to create meaningful political participation in the governing of our everyday lives.

Possibilities: Creating New Political Systems Here and Now

I have no interest in protesting, I have an interest in demonstrating an alternative. (December 2011, New York City)

We see that the institutions we have do not serve the people and evidently are being delegitimised by the actions we're seeing here and we think we need to build a political, economic, social and environmental alternative. (September 2012, Madrid)

From the start, movements such as Occupy and 15M have baffled spectators and commentators due to their refusal to shape clear demands aimed at politicians. The lack of demands, however, should come as no surprise when we consider the nature of the grievances being expressed and the scale of the political project being embarked upon. There are no politicians or representatives that can deliver the type of social change these movements desire. An ethnographic look that goes beyond simple movement slogans to examine the daily practices of movement actors makes it very clear that their aims surpass a politics of making demands on leaders, to become instead a politics that aims to make the existing system redundant:

For people that think that economic, political and social justice is reducible to a set of demands, they're just wrong. This is a structural issue that is happening globally and it is a crisis of capitalism. We want to ask better questions and be in dialogue about what the answers are going to be but we're in no rush. (September 2012, New York City)

Over the past decades, social movements internationally have created thousands of sites of horizontally organised democracy, envisioned as a prefiguration of an alternative to representative democracy, in order to create space for solutions to emerge for the many crises we face today – economic, environmental, political. The rise of prefiguration as a strategy of social change within movement networks has deep roots, especially in anarchist and autonomous organising (see Franks 2003). The specific historical trajectory for prefiguration in contemporary movements in Europe and the United States is connected to the movements of the 1960s, where prefiguration came to the fore as part of what is often dubbed a 'cultural revolution', which involved not only transforming political structures but also transforming oneself and each other directly. Prefigurative politics was given new inspiration by the Zapatista uprising in Chiapas, Mexico from 1994 onwards, which inspired several generations of activists worldwide. Experiments with a politics of *Horizontalidad* in Argentina after the 2001 crisis helped to introduce the notion of horizontality to movements around the world. With the rise of the alterglobalisation movement, many scholars pointed out the central importance of prefiguration, arguing for the need to understand movement practices as a reflection of its goals (Graeber 2002; Juris 2008; Maeckelbergh 2011; Polletta 2002; Smith 2008; Teivainen 2008). As Juris (2008: 295) argues, 'radical anti-corporate globalisation activists are not only seeking to intervene within dominant public spheres; they are also challenging representative democracy, in part by developing their own directly democratic forms of organizing and decision making'. Movement actors today continue this strategy of actively pursuing more horizontal, direct, participatory forms of democratic decision making as an embodiment of a more inclusive and egalitarian model of governance.

Since the 1960s, social movement praxis has grown increasingly oriented towards the creation of elaborate egalitarian decision-making structures. These decision-making practices are part of a prefigurative turn within social movement praxis and have most often been interpreted and written about as 'experiments with democracy' (Breines 1989; Epstein 1991; Graeber 2002, 2008, 2013; Juris 2008; Polletta 2002; Maeckelbergh 2009; Razsa and Kurnik 2012). These experiments have been labelled with many different adjectives, most commonly as 'participatory' or 'direct' democracy and most recently as 'horizontal' democracy. These horizontal forms of politics are intricately tied to an ideological rejection of representation as a democratic structure. As Michael Hardt recently put it:

Starting in Egypt and then very consciously in Spain [there was a] refusal of representation, both the electoral system and party structures and even representatives of the movement itself. That questioning of representation goes with a reinvention of democracy itself. Trying to reclaim democracy is both a continuation and an extension of the horizontal organization and experimentation with democracy that has gone on for at least the last ten years. (September 2012, unpublished interview)

Horizontal decision making, usually referred to simply as 'horizontality' or 'horizontalism' not only rejects representation, but it also rejects the structure of the nation state. Horizontality replaces the nation state with the network as the basic structure of governance. These network structures take many forms, but at least two can be identified. First, the use of decentralised working groups networked through a general assembly or a 'spokescouncil' (that is, a meeting of members from each working group). And second, the creation of inter-neighbourhood assemblies to coordinate between neighbourhoods. While most decisions can be taken within the working groups or neighbourhoods, the larger meetings are essential to bring together people from the various, at times geographically dispersed, working groups or neighbourhoods to discuss proposals and coordinate actions.

Since 2011, horizontality has been increasingly critiqued by movement actors. The forms of horizontal decision making enacted in the many squares around the world were never the perfect embodiment of the ideal. Many of these critiques were connected to the general assembly structure, which became a centralised authority and created the impression, or in some cases the rule, that people needed permission from the general assembly before taking action. In Barcelona during the occupation of Plaça de Catalunya, many people complained that this de facto centralised authority was disempowering and had the effect of delegitimising any actions not explicitly approved by the assembly. The same dynamic was present in the Occupy groups I witnessed where the decision-making procedures were quite rigid. As a result, the process was viewed as simultaneously too bureaucratic and too chaotic, and most importantly, as out of their hands. Both people who were actively engaged in the assemblies and people who had abandoned the process expressed the same sense of powerlessness *vis-à-vis* the movement's own decision-making structures. Those whose more anti-democratic perspectives I will address in the next section often argued that the process of horizontal decision making within Occupy and related movements was focused entirely on form and not content – meaning that the procedures of decision making were applied in a rigid way, ignoring the non-hierarchical, autonomy-oriented political principles.

These critiques are important not only because they highlight the very real limitations that were encountered in the moment that horizontal decision making spread across the world, but also because these are the critiques that will inform future experiments in non-hierarchical political decision making. Viewed historically, the internal critiques of movement decision making have been essential to the improvement of these practices. When the movements of the 2010s are viewed from an international perspective, we see a learning process. In Spain especially, the movement acted quickly to decentralise the assemblies to the neighbourhood level and over time the notion of autonomy came to the fore as the key concept that had been missing in people's understandings of effective non-hierarchical decision making. This lesson learned in Spain was actively referenced in Turkey when neighbourhood assemblies, dubbed forums, spread rapidly in the aftermath of the Gezi uprising in late May and early June 2013. The forums in Turkey intentionally took a different form (more of a decentralised space for the expression of grievances and less of a decision-oriented process) from those of the 15 May or Occupy movements to avoid reproducing some of the same mistakes.

In each embodiment of horizontal decision making the specific problems encountered are different and the lessons learned manifest themselves in various forms (in some cases being taken up and incorporated into the process directly), but often they lead to a degeneration of the process at that specific time and place. Despite the limitations of these processes in specific times and places, over time and across contexts, we can see some important ways in which these horizontal networked forms of decision making are transforming the way many people think about key values underlying democracy. First, horizontality is based on a different belief about how equality functions. It starts from the assumption that there can never be perfect equality. Consequently, equality is not something that can be created by an authority. Second, horizontality emphasises and embraces the diversity of the public and, ideally, allows for people to collectively coordinate divergent courses of action and to produce multiple solutions to a problem. Finally, horizontality creates structures for incorporating conflict into the decision-making process, ideally by offering autonomy to those who disagree. All three of these dimensions of horizontality are difficult in practice, and the importance of these values becomes most apparent not when they are perfectly embodied, but rather when they are *not* perfectly embodied. These values are so essential to the process that a lack of equality, diversity or autonomy within the process is perceived as a violation of the process.

Understanding what is specifically meant by these values is, therefore, important to understanding the politics – i.e. the content – of horizontality. Horizontal politics rests upon a notion of equality that is very different from the type of equality enshrined in representative democracy. Within representative democracies, equality is created through the negation of difference, by giving each citizen one vote regardless of their status in society. This 'one man, one vote' policy creates the illusion of equality, but it has never been sufficient to overcome the myriad inequalities that permeate society, and has never resulted in the interests of all sections of society being represented equally in government. Horizontality builds on the feminist principle that argues that declaring all people equal does not make all people equal. Horizontal decision making is based on the assumption that a political system in which equality is declared to officially exist, but in which inequality is not confronted, merely serves to reproduce inequality. In Occupy Wall Street this desire (never fully achieved) to actively create equality through the decision-making process was described as follows:

The NYC General Assembly uses a form of 'pure' democracy. Unlike a representative democracy in which an individual or group is elected to speak for you and may
actually not do so, direct democracy ensures that all voices are heard, none above
another. Instead of utilising a voting system, which ensures a minority group is
ignored or oppressed, the NYC General Assembly utilises a consensus process to
come to decisions on important issues. Consensus, based on the consent of individuals within a larger group, is a participatory dialog used to reach a general sense
of agreement by all members of the assembly. (Occupy Wall Street 2011)

Here, equality is assumed to be impossible under a system of voting since it auto-
matically silences minority opinions. Since giving everyone an equal vote does
not lead to equality, new structures for generating equality over time become
necessary. Embodying this form of equality requires that everyone involved in
the process be prepared to confront their own privilege and prejudice and this
confrontation is not always a welcome realisation.

Horizontality, therefore, is a political system in which everyone who participates has to take responsibility for continuously limiting power inequalities
as they arise between participants. The specific structures developed to help
people take on this responsibility are slightly different everywhere, but some
are common across localities. First, the use of hand signals was common across
most contexts. These are used to express agreement, disagreement, to organise
the discussion and to keep the flow of conversation on topic. Second, in most
places guidelines such as the 'step up, step back' principle and complex systems
for taking turns were developed, in an attempt to ensure that everyone could
be heard and that some would not dominate. Facilitators encourage people to
notice how much they speak and there are strict anti-oppression guidelines
against saying or doing anything racist, sexist or oppressive. These guidelines
are slightly different everywhere and across time, and were more clearly articulated in some places than in others. One very clear set of guidelines were those
developed in Oakland, California:

Ground rules:
1. **Step up, Step back** (monitor your own involvement: not too passive, not too
dominant; make sure that the time and space not monopolized by white men, for
example)
2. **Active listening**
   - Actively engaging with speaker: nodding, affirmative gestures
   - Don't multi-task while someone else is speaking
   - Possible: not raising hand until someone else is finished speaking
3. **Allow Space for disagreement**
4. **Don't blame/ shame/ attack**
5. **Speak for yourself, Use I statements**
6. **Progressive Stack & Diversity of facilitation techniques**
   - Have people who self-identify with marginalized groups put higher on the
   stack
   - EX: people of color, woman, trans, queer, ...
   - ALSO, can put people who have talked a lot lower on stack ... Facilitators
   - Discuss this ahead of time so it is not on facilitator to decide how to manage

7. **Practice 'both/ and' thinking not just 'either/ or'**
   - more than 1 reality exists
   - EX: should we go to gov. and beg/ ask for stuff or create our own world ... actually both are possible
   - be mindful of 'neither/ nor' possibility
   - EX: glass half -full, half- empty? One could also say: glass is partly full of water and partly full of air
8. **Oops, Ouch, What's up with that?** (& positive hand gestures)
   - What's up with that?: if something may be an ouch, this is an option that asks for clarification and can open up discussion

(Occupy Oakland facilitation training, original emphasis and formatting)

In the 'General Assembly Script' of Occupy Wall Street in New York it was explicitly stated that the aim of these rules, here called 'tools', is not to control people but to make the decision-making process as accessible as possible for everyone:

> This process is a set of tools to make the most directly democratic, horizontal, participatory space possible; each tool (hand signals, etc.) is about opening space – not rule making. ('General Assembly Script' as of 10/17/11)

The aim of all the meeting guidelines is to ensure not only that people can have equal input into a political process, as in one man, one vote, but that the outcomes of political decision making also reflects the diversity of the input. In majoritarian systems the minority opinion is voted out. In horizontality these opinions matter and the decision-making process, when it works well, should leave room for these opinions to be expressed. Achieving this last form of equality – equality in outcomes – however, is much harder than an imagined equality of inputs, and despite the creation of several structures to support these multiple and equal outcomes, it often proves difficult. In addition to the many critiques outlined above, many people voiced concerns that not all voices were being heard – quite the contrary. In critiques of Occupy especially, participants pointed out the many ways in which the occupations were reproducing the racism, sexism and heteronormativity of society at large and there were continuous conflicts about transforming the political process in order to challenge these hierarchies.

In the above set of rules we see very clearly the intention to avoid thinking about political options in either/or and neither/nor terms, but instead participants are encouraged to think about ways in which the things they want *and* the many things others might want can *all* be possible. While the common democratic tendency, even in 'alternative' models of democracy such as deliberative democracy, is to strive for agreement and uniformity within a geographical region, horizontal decision making is based on network structures that, in principle, require no such uniformity. The advantage of a network structure over that of the nation state as a political formation is that a network can split into multiple hubs without compromising the unity of the network as a whole. People with divergent interests can pursue different projects without resulting in political instability of the whole network. Networks are made of links between hubs and clusters and so there is no need for centralised authority (which does not mean that this authority cannot arise as movements have learned over the years).

Networks also have no fixed constituency. The lack of an identifiable constituency has the advantage of erasing strict lines of inclusion and exclusion (though this does not resolve processes of exclusion), but it also has the disadvantage that universal suffrage is impossible. Consequently, to ensure that everyone can fully participate in the decisions that most affect their lives, new notions of political participation are required. The guidelines mentioned above are part of these new structures for political participation, but they are only the starting point. These practices are the main site for the political innovation necessary to reinvent and create an increasingly horizontal form of politics.

The main aspect of horizontality that is coming to the fore in recent movements is the awareness that the main aim is not to enact a series of decision-making procedures, but to ensure empowerment and autonomy for people in collectively determining their own lives through decentralised networks rather than powerful centralised nation states. Movement actors are intentionally, and at times unintentionally, creating a system of rights that does not rely on a centralised authority to ensure these rights. As a Slovenian activist cited in Razsa and Kurnik (2012: 250) puts it, here using the term direct instead of horizontal, but expressing the same principles:

> Direct democracy for us means that we reject the transfer of rights and powers to any sovereign. So we have to find new ways to produce rights – by defining them such that we simultaneously build our power to realize them ... the process of producing together new claims, new rights ... is as important as the content of the rights.

Here again we see the prefigurative notion that the political process is as important as (crucially: not more important than) the political content because the political process is linked to the political content. This is similar to the Zapatista model of rights – demand your rights, fight for your rights, but do so as part of a larger political process of self-determination in which people decide collectively what they need and how they can help each other fulfil these needs (Speed and Reyes 2002). When rights claims become part of a struggle for self-determination they are taken out of the realm of democratic politics. The pursuit of self-determination as a primary goal transforms how people view themselves and their roles as political actors:

> People that tell us what a social movement should look like haven't really factored in that we are living in the twenty-first century and that the issues are very different. What we are discovering together is new ways of organizing that are horizontal that are empowering to communities that actually teach people to take their lives into their own hands. (September 2012, New York City)

The idea of a political subject as someone who takes their life into their own hands as part of a community that is aimed at teaching others to do the same is a profoundly different political subject from the one who enters the polling station alone and leaves it alone to cut their losses when their candidate is either not victorious or disappoints once in office. Whether both can be thought of as democratic subjects is perhaps a question of terminology. Certainly both subjects have been shaped in an era of rhetoric about political participation, about social change though active engagement in public life, dominated by an imagined potential for change within and through an ideal and idealised political system called 'democracy'. They do so in what Crouch (2004) calls a post-democratic context marked by democratic structures that serve primarily elite interests. This post-democratic moment exists in a necessarily close relation to the moral power of all things democratic, but as an expression of its loss. Consequently, the movements mobilise the language and values of this morally dominant paradigm to claim that the movements are the ones who have 'real' democracy, that horizontality is 'real' democracy, not the politicians who have now become unquestionably post-democratic in their pursuit of elite interests. However, as a result this tension means that the way movement actors speak about democracy is highly contradictory – rejecting the democracy they have been given by the nation state and claiming another democracy as the solution. This inherent tension, together with the problems that movement actors encounter within their own decision-making practices, has been leading to more and more overt critiques of the very notion of democracy itself as the framework for emancipatory politics. In the next section I turn to some of these voices that are emerging around the world to interrogate further what this rejection might mean about the state of democracy at the current historical juncture.

Impossibilities: Democracy's Empty Promises

Although these newly emerging forms of horizontal governance certainly share most of the key values we've come to associate with and expect from democracy, perhaps labelling these newly emerging practices as 'democratic' obscures more than it illuminates. There are many voices within the movement that prefer to distinguish their own form of politics from democracy to make the radical differences clearer. While agreed upon terminology is still lacking, the main concepts that tend to take the place of democracy for these movement actors are horizontalism, anarchism and an anti-state version of communism. But none of these terms have the same widespread support and moral legitimacy that the notion of democracy has.

Since the term democracy retains a great deal of moral weight among populations worldwide, the question arises of how to relate to this term and how to use it both in analysis of movement practices and in day to day political organising. Not using the term 'democracy' runs the risk that leaders governing in the interest of an elite few can continue to claim that they are democratic and therefore have the moral authority of ruling on behalf of the people, but continuing to use the term 'democracy' to describe the alternative forms of governance emerging to increase people's empowerment runs the risk of depoliticising these new practices by equating them with forms of governance that many people have experienced as disempowering.

It also confuses the analysis to refer to two such different political structures with the same term. For now, or until a new term emerges, it seems nearly impossible to challenge 'democracy' without claiming to be for 'democracy'. Nevertheless, there are many movement actors who do just this. The critiques of democracy are not simplistically for or against democracy as an abstract concept – they are against specific forms of governance and specific political practices and values. Consequently, the degree to which we interpret the positions held as being against democracy rather than against a specific subset of assumptions or practices commonly associated with democracy is based more on the larger political perspective of the people speaking than on any single quote. For example, in December 2011, just as the first post-revolutionary democratic election was getting started in Egypt, some of the revolutionaries who had been active for years in various social movements under Mubarak (worker's movements, pro-Palestine, anti-war, etc.), were far from enthusiastic about the potential benefits of democracy. Many of these revolutionaries were opposed to viewing democracy as a 'solution' to the problems they faced because these problems were also economic problems created by capitalism and its institutions, always with specific mention of the International Monetary Fund (IMF). The introduction of democracy was perceived as meaningless in the face of such uniform and disastrous economic policies. Their own lives would not be improved as long as the larger political structures, including democracy, were not changed. As one Egyptian revolutionary put it:

> Elections almost have this magical sense to them. But when it comes down to it there's actually very little value in that process because it is not allowing for change. It is not actually at all empowering the people to have their voice heard. ... There is a real crisis of governance and I don't think it's just limited to Egypt, it's a global crisis. (December 2011, Cairo)

Indeed, everyone wanted to make clear to me that none of the violent oppression had ended. The Supreme Council of Armed Forces (SCAF) continued to rule, only now (meaning early December 2011) they did so with the veneer of legitimacy that democracy brought with it. Early December 2011, however, was not only the start of the elections in Egypt, it was also only weeks after the attack on revolutionaries on Mohammed Mahmood street in central Cairo, which has since become an iconic moment in the historical trajectory of the Egyptian revolution. Election booths and bloody bodies on the same street were the images that these revolutionaries wanted to bring home to me.

This combination of bloody bodies on the street and 'democratic' rule continued until the democratically elected leader, Mohamed Morsi, was overthrown/ ousted by a popular revolt and/or military coup – or a popular revolt that was hijacked by the military (the choice of how to describe the events of this day is politically loaded and varies greatly depending on who you ask – in any case there were millions of people on the street on 30 June 2013 demanding Morsi's resignation). In its short-lived term in office, democracy was experienced as a political process that easily exists in conjunction with extreme levels of violent oppression. *This* was the political point that the revolutionaries my co-producer and I spoke with were adamant to make clear to the international audience of the film we were making at the time.

Although the post-democratic regime in Egypt is proving itself to be even more repressive than the democratically elected regime before it, what is important here is not whether authoritarian dictatorship is more violently oppressive than democracy. To engage in this debate would be a distraction – we should not have to choose between various forms of violent oppression. What is important to the analysis here is that these revolutionaries did not interpret the combination of democracy and violent oppression as surprising, as unique to Egypt, or as the result of a 'transition' period. Instead, those we spoke with saw democracy as a political system that is intricately tied to forms of violent repression everywhere in the world. The problems with democracy in Egypt were contextualised in relation to a wave of worldwide rebellion. As another Egyptian revolutionary put it reflecting on democracy as a political system:

> We are seeing people in Europe, Western Europe and the U.S., living in the streets and occupying space because apparently the democratic process has not brought much to them. (December 2011, Cairo)

These internationally well-networked Egyptian revolutionaries were echoing a sentiment present across the contexts I have witnessed over the past few years: disillusionment with democracy. This disillusionment is perhaps nowhere as strong as in Greece, where for some it has gone well beyond a mere critique of democracy to a rejection of the entire political system. The aim, as one person put it, is not to remove one leader and replace him with another:

> This is not a national liberation movement and it's not about bringing down a certain government. That means nothing. Since the beginning of the crisis we've brought down two governments and we keep going. There's going to be a few more, that's no problem anymore. That's fairly easy. The question is to be able to build a movement. (October 2012, Athens)

This quote presents all democratic governments, regardless of which party or person is elected, as *inevitably* impotent. In some cases, democratically elected officials are not only viewed as incapable of representing their interests, but are, similarly to Egypt, often viewed as intentionally seeking violent conflict between leaders and the public. As another person put it:

> Well from what I can see most people no longer recognise the state and the powerful, but they have no way of resisting against an armed people. We are a peaceful people, yet there is going to come a time when it's going to be our lives against theirs. And I think that's what they want, I think they really want to turn this country into a state of civil war. (October 2012, Athens)

When democracy is viewed as not only incapable of representing the people's interests, but also as intentionally acting violently against its people so that it can continue to pursue the interests of financial elites, the post-democratic moment takes on new meaning and the crisis of legitimacy facing democracy reaches new heights. When people start to view democracy as a system of perpetual disenfranchisement and repression, it is not surprising to find that the alternatives the movements are building themselves are cast in language other than that of democracy.

In Greece, as in most places, however, this move is double. There are also extensive experiments with new political forms that are explicitly referred to as 'democratic', often invoking the direct democracy of ancient Athens. The use of this language was especially popular in the summer of 2011, when the movement of the squares was large and growing across the country, and it is still very important to many people active in the ongoing anti-austerity protests. However, Greece also has one of the strongest anti-authoritarian movements in Europe – an active 'antagonist' movement complete with social centres and an 'anarchist neighbourhood' in central Athens where one finds many people who refuse to refer to these political practices as 'democratic' for the reasons described above.

We find similar sentiments in Spain, where the movement of the squares united under the slogan 'real democracy now'. With 187 home evictions a day across the country, it is not surprising that people in Spain question the functioning of democracy. While most people in the 15M movement would frame their own political programme as one *for* democracy, but a different *kind* of democracy, critiques of democracy as a political ideal are also present. In both Greece and Spain the strongest critiques come from the more anarchistic and/or anti-state end of the political spectrum – which has a long and rich history in both countries. Some of these voices argue for the need to move away from the term 'democracy', pointing out the ways in which the movement's horizontal practices reproduce democracy's inherent faults:

> As much as the ideologues of direct democracy try to hide the conflict between the notion of rights and the ideal of freedom, there's no getting around this fact.[2] The principles of democracy were drafted by elites interested in mediating class conflict and allowing the preservation of a class society. A struggle, to challenge the foundations of this system, must be antidemocratic. (Gelderloos 2011)

Continuing to fight for 'democracy', even with the added adjective 'direct', Gelderloos argues, will inevitably lead to the preservation of inequality and hierarchy because the system was created precisely for this purpose. He is not alone in believing that the concept of democracy cannot be repurposed. Nevertheless, despite the clear disillusionment and antagonism with democracy, it remains difficult to argue that these movements as a whole are movements against democracy. What we see emerging is an ongoing argument within these movements that they *should* be against democracy. The arguments against democracy have not yet won the internal movement discussion, however, and most movement actors continue to refer to their own political ideals and practices as 'more democratic' than those of the nation state and its representatives. As one activist in Madrid put it:

> It's a battle for meaning, to define what we mean by democracy. We, the multitudes in the street, want to define it as the conflict that opens, that maximises liberties for a larger number of people, for larger swathes of the population. ... We're here to say no, that we do not want to submit to the markets. We want a democracy that is designed for life, for people, for our needs, to achieve more and more happiness. Not to work for the profits of the one per cent. (September 2012, Madrid)

Here again we see the belief that democracy is a meaningless political system as long as the economic system remains unchallenged and unchanged. Democracy cannot exist where markets decide instead of people. However, this extreme disillusionment with the way democracy functions is, for this person, not the same as a rejection of democracy as an ideal, whereas the disillusionment expressed by many others, amounts to a total rejection of democracy as a political system. This tension is inherent to the post-democratic moment and it cannot be fully resolved because the democratic values (liberty, participation, self-determination) that are lost in the process of actually enacting democracy remain tied to their history as democratic values even when they are enacted through horizontal political structures that bear little or no resemblance to elections, governments, nation states or representative politics.

The specific history of democracy in each country also plays a role in shaping how strong people's ties are to the rhetoric of democracy when faced with its limitations. In both the United States and Spain, two key sites of struggle in the 2010s so far, the use of the term democracy to describe people's own political aims and actions was widespread. Still, an activist in the United States reflecting on Occupy in the aftermath of lessons learned from the 2013 uprisings in Turkey and Brazil recently reflected:

> I think the fact that we used the word 'democracy' within Occupy to describe our aims was part of why we were unsuccessful. We really missed an incredible opportunity to politicise the public and make clear where their real oppression was coming from. We need to make it clear that it is not political structures that are legitimate, but people's needs. (August 2013, Chapel Hill)

Political discourse may shift as people everywhere grapple with the need for a new vocabulary to describe a truly emancipatory form of politics that they believe is possible and which they know is necessary in the face of increasingly repressive democratic governments that represent elite interests instead of 'the people'.

Choosing to frame the social movement practices not as democratic but as a form of politics poised to replace democracy, is, however, also politically problematic. Two important arguments need to be made about the politics of this choice. First is the historical view in which it can easily be claimed that the empirical reality of democracy so far has always been a highly unequal, hierarchical and exclusive form of governance and that it should therefore not be held up as the best possible form of governance we can imagine and pursue. This view would favour the choice to stop using the term 'democracy' to refer to emancipatory movement practices. Second is the argument that our current governments are not democratic at all, where democracy refers implicitly to a 'just' form of government presumed to have existed in the past, and which is represented as an ideal type of governance. In this framework, the movements struggling against current political and economic policy would not be doing so in and against legitimate democratic governments, but against non-democratic rulers. Viewing contemporary social movements as fighting in contexts that are anything but democratic can be useful in that this shifts the boundaries of what is considered 'acceptable' political action(s) and goal(s). As I have argued elsewhere (Maeckelbergh 2013b), during the 2011 revolution, protestors in Egypt were often hailed as 'peaceful pro-democracy' protesters (i.e., 'good' people) in media reports, while those in Madrid, who were being far less confrontational, were accused of staging a coup on democracy (i.e., 'dangerous'/'bad' people), in part because Egypt was considered to be a non-democratic country and Spain was considered to be an exemplar of democracy. To argue that 'democratic' governments today are not democratic would have considerable political value because it would open up a space for political action that is considered illegitimate in democratic contexts (see Marcuse 1965; Paris 2003).

These two uses of democracy, however, are terminologically contradictory. We have to choose. Either we accept that we are currently living under 'democracy' and look at the empirical embodiment of democracy as a system of governance that has always excluded, repressed and alienated some people while benefitting others, or we take democracy to mean, by definition, a system of morally good governance in which the people rule themselves, in which case we cannot say that we have ever lived under 'democracy'. Of course one might argue that these two processes are the same: that democracy as systematic inequality is a temporary state that will eventually lead to democracy as equality (the transition theory) which will somehow materialise over the course of history. The future will be more democratic than the present because the ideal, even though it has not yet been realised, will grow closer as time progresses. In this historical moment, however, when we see a trend towards increased repression, growing inequality and the inability of representative politics to respond to people's diverse interests – anywhere in the world – this latter narrative of inevitable progress is hard to demonstrate empirically or argue convincingly.

Conclusion: Who/What Is and Is Not Democratic Anymore?

I have tried to show that there is an inherent tension in framing any set of political practices as simply democratic or post-democratic. Democracy itself means so many different things that it becomes difficult to identify when a political system or practice is no longer democratic. The tension between two fundamentally irreconcilable uses of the term 'democracy' – between democracy as an actual governing practice of exclusion and oppression and democracy as an ideal of participation and freedom – also lies at the heart of tensions found in movement practices. Shifting the analytical focus to the question of 'post-democracy' does not resolve this terminological ambiguity. Definitions of democracy that reduce democracy to the material presence of particular governing structures such as elections or political parties are at a disconnect with arguments about post-democracy since these rely largely on a notion of democracy that invokes the possibility for civic engagement and the successful representation of the people's will (Crouch 2004; Rancière 1995).

Furthermore, a deeper issue arises when we look beyond definitions to an examination of the historical and contemporary record. To say that post-democracy is present when electoral debate becomes a 'tightly controlled spectacle, managed by rival teams of professionals ... considering a small range of issues selected by those teams' and especially, when behind this spectacle 'politics is really shaped in private by interaction between elected governments and elites that overwhelmingly represent business interests' leading to a political system that 'increasingly cedes power to business lobbies, [where] there is little hope for an agenda of strong egalitarian policies' (Crouch 2004: 4) assumes that electoral debate was at some point something other than a tightly controlled spectacle, and that democracy once functioned as the pursuit of egalitarian policies.

With the notion of post-democracy, the solution to large-scale political disenfranchisement becomes the return to the supposed original, earlier moment of democracy, the time in the past when democracy still represented the people's interests. This imagined past, is, however, a past which the historical record would bring into question. When the flaws found in the current historical period are interpreted to indicate a post-democratic moment, or interpreted as the result of a crisis of democracy rather than simply as a result of democracy itself, democracy is let off the hook. This reading obscures the fact that democracy has always been a highly unequal and exclusionary political system (Agamben 2005; Alexander 2012; Held 1996) and the definition of post-democracy, therefore, could just as well function as a definition of democracy itself.

If we view the historical record from the perspective of those who have had no meaningful political voice under democracy, we see that the improvement required to 'fix' democracy may well be so extensive that it becomes meaningless to bring both political systems, democracy and the alternative (to) democracy, under the same terminology. Horizontality is a bottom-up, open-ended political process that intentionally leaves both the future and the constituency of politics indeterminate. Within horizontality, unity is eschewed in favour of diversity, goals are left open to be determined through participation, autonomy is privileged over coherent ideologies, and the ideal organising structure is decentralisation through networks instead of centralisation through nation states. However, even the horizontal structures being developed are not developed in a vacuum; they, too, are defined by the history of democracy as the dominant political paradigm of our times. Political systems do not replace one another overnight (not even through revolution). The tension that underlies the ethnography presented in this chapter is that people are shaped by their experiences and assumptions about democracy even as they try to develop new forms of governance. Many elements of 'democracy' continue in the social movement alternatives described here, while many others are explicitly rejected or transformed. It is a process of embracing the elements that are viewed as positive, such as liberty, equality and participation (transforming the meaning of these values in the process), and rejecting the elements that are viewed as disempowering, such as elections, voting and fixed representation.[3]

While at first this process, for most participants, is about pursuing and improving democracy, political subjectivities start to change and the divide between the existing democracy they are resisting and the desired democracy they are building grows so large that the two political systems can hardly be equated. However, since democracy is not only a set of political structures, but also a globally dominant moral order, the move away from democracy as a universally acknowledged 'good' requires fundamental political transformations across many locales at once. The many different histories through which democracy has arisen, from the French and American revolutions, the post-World War Two and anti-colonial era and the fall of the Soviet Union, to the recent round of revolutions in the Middle East and North Africa, lead in each case to quite a different set of disappointments, disenchantments and disasters. And yet, in each of these places there is a shared dissatisfaction with democracy, and the precise form, nature and consequences of this dissatisfaction deserve further attention.

In this chapter I have explored some ways in which I have encountered the dissatisfaction with democracy in my own ethnography of transnational social movement praxis over the past ten years. These perspectives range from the rejection of democracy as a moral good to the rejection of democracy on the basis that it is not working. These perspectives reflect different political experiences and histories, but are in no way mutually exclusive. This chapter explores these perspectives as an insight into the transitory and ambiguous process of political transformation away from democracy and towards a post-democratic form of politics that can replace democracy with a form of horizontal politics that comes *after* democracy. While in the past I have somewhat unintentionally presented social movement practices as part of a linear process of perfecting democracy, here I engage with the view that democracy is the dominant political system which never has and never could bring with it the ideals and values that we often attribute to it. I choose to turn the tables in this way so that I can make sense of the emerging anti/non-democracy attitudes and practices found within social movement networks today – practices that are future oriented, that are meant as the building blocks of the political system to come after representative democracy or instead of democracy, but which are considered to be better than democracy, even when cloaked in the language and values of democracy. Nevertheless, the political consequences of choosing to frame movement practices as post/non-democratic and nation-state practices as democratic are important, as this approach allows today's ruling elite to retain the moral legitimacy associated with the term democracy – and this is a power that is regularly used against these movements.

Despite these important political risks, when we view the post-democratic moment in this way we see that it does not have to be a negative signifier that alludes to something we once had in the past but have now lost. Instead post-democracy can be an invitation, a break in the moral dominance of democracy as the ultimate political form to allow for an expansion of the many political imaginaries that are being developed around the world today. The struggle over what comes after democracy is important because there are many signs in the world today that what might come after democracy will be worse, not better, than what we have seen so far. Whether this opening can lead to a form of governance that is better able to meet people's needs depends very much on how repressive contemporary democratic governments are prepared to become. At the moment, I fear most democratically elected governments internationally have very little limit to the repressive mechanisms they are prepared to unleash in order to protect their increasingly post-democratic mode of rule.

Exploring these newly emerging forms of horizontal governance, therefore, is not only important as an ethnographic exercise that helps us to understand transnational social movements, but as an examination of other forms of governance that are possible beyond representative democracy. While it is useful to critique the growing influence of elites on politics within current political systems, whether they are democratic or not, it is important to look beyond improving existing democracies in search of alternative governing systems, given the many problems that have always plagued democratic government. The political practices described in this chapter indicate that perhaps we can use this historical moment, when democracy is undergoing a legitimation crisis, in which people all over the world are realising that their governments do not represent their interests, to break with the moral authority of democracy in order to pursue and invent a better form of governance for after democracy. One thing is for certain, we cannot linger in the post-democratic moment because it is by definition characterised by the liminality of no longer and not yet. At some point soon the post-democratic moment will need to move forwards towards something else. For some this desired move is a move toward the idealised history of a democracy for the people (that never was, but nevertheless is no longer), for others it is a move toward new forms of governance.

Acknowledgements

Many thanks to the participants of the Wenner-Gren sponsored Post-Democracies workshop held at the University of Cambridge in April 2013 for their thoughtful feedback on a paper that became the basis for this chapter. Thanks to the Democracy and Media Foundation for sponsoring the film series that has been the basis for this research. A particular thanks to Nick Long and

Joanna Cook for greatly improving this chapter through their crucial comments and critical engagement with the ideas expressed here.

Notes

1   This choice to contextualise these movements in relation to a shared transnational history does have the unfortunate consequence of obscuring the particularities of each place. Wherever possible I have included a few reflections on the many differences between these locations, emphasising some of the more interesting and relevant divergences. Nevertheless, given the enormity of these differences and the fact that they do not affect the argument directly, it has neither been possible nor necessary to include detailed references to all of these historical trajectories.
2   This conflict between 'rights' and 'freedom' is described very well in the previous section through the quotes from Razsa and Kurnik (2012) and Speed and Reyes (2002). Rights are granted to us by a centralised power that can just as easily take them from us and which becomes more powerful than us through the very act of granting us rights. Freedom, on the other hand, could be understood as similar to collective self-determination, which we create together for ourselves and for each other.
3   There are many moments and forms of representation that continue in this political process, but none of these are fixed (representation rotates, is fluid, switches from one person to the next in any given meeting). For more on the forms of fluid and temporary representation present in horizontal politics see Maeckelbergh (2009).

References

Agamben, G. 2005. *State of Exception.* Chicago: University of Chicago Press.
Alexander, M. 2012. *The New Jim Crow.* New York: The New Press.
Breines, W. 1989. *Community and Organization in the New Left 1962–1968: The Great Refusal.* New Brunswick: Rutgers University Press.
Crouch, C. 2004. *Post-Democracy.* Cambridge: Polity Press.
Epstein, B. 1991. *Political Protest & Cultural Revolution.* Berkeley: University of California Press.
Franks, B. 2003. The Direct Action Ethic from 59 Upwards. *Anarchist Studies* 11, no. 1: 13–41.
Gelderloos, P. 2011. Reflections for the US Occupy Movement. <http://www.counterpunch.org/2011/10/14/reflections-for-the-us-occupy-movement/> (accessed 6 April 2013).
Graeber, D. 2002. The New Anarchists. *New Left Review* 13: 61–73.
———. 2008. *Direct Action.* Oakland: AK Press.
———. 2013. *The Democracy Project.* London: Allen Lane.
Held, D. 1996. *Models of Democracy.* Stanford: Stanford University Press.
Juris, J. 2008. *Networking Futures.* Durham: Duke University Press.
———. 2012. Reflections on #Occupy Everywhere: Social Media, Public Space, and Emerging Logics of Aggregation. *American Ethnologist* 39, no.2: 259–279.
Maeckelbergh, M. 2009. *The Will of the Many.* London: Pluto.
———. 2011. Doing is Believing: Prefiguration as Strategic Practice. *Social Movement Studies* 10, no. 1: 1–20.

————. 2012. Horizontal Democracy Now: From Alterglobalization to Occupation. *Interface* 4, no. 1: 207–234.

————. 2013a. Learning from Conflict: Innovative Approaches to Democratic Decision Making in the Alterglobalization Movement. *Transforming Anthropology* 21, no. 1: 27–40.

————. 2013b. What Comes After Democracy? *Open Citizenship* 4, no. 1: 74–79.

Marcuse, H. 1965. Repressive Tolerance. In *A Critique of Pure Tolerance* (eds) R.P. Wolff, B. Moore Jr. and H. Marcuse. Boston: Beacon Press.

Occupy Oakland. 2011. Facilitation training. <http://bit.ly/faciliators> (accessed 6 April 2013).

Occupy Wall Street. 2011. Introduction to Direct Democracy <http://www.nycga.net/group-documents/intro-to-direct-democracy---facilitation-training/> (accessed 20 October 2011).

Polletta, F. 2002. *Freedom is an Endless Meeting*. Chicago: University of Chicago Press.

Paris, J. 2003. The Black Bloc's Ungovernable Protests. *Peace Review* 15, no. 3: 317–322.

Rancière, J. 1995. *On the Shores of Politics*. London: Verso.

Razsa, M., and A. Kurnik 2012. The Occupy Movement in Žižek's Hometown: Direct Democracy and a Politics of Becoming. *American Ethnologist* 39, no. 2: 238–258.

Sitrin, M. 2006. *Horizontalidad*. Oakland: AK Press.

Sitrin, M., and D. Azzellini 2014. *They Don't Represent Us*. London: Verso.

Smith, J. 2008. *Social Movements for Global Democracy*. Baltimore: Johns Hopkins University Press.

Speed, S., and A. Reyes 2002. 'In Our Own Defense': Rights and Resistance in Chiapas. *Political and Legal Anthropology Review* 25, no. 1: 69–89.

Teivainen, T. 2008. Global Civic-Driven Democratization as Political Agency. In *Civic Driven Change: Citizen's Imagination in Action* (eds) A. Fowler and K. Biekart. The Hague: Institute of Social Studies.

Marianne Maeckelbergh is Associate Professor of cultural anthropology and development sociology at Leiden University and a Marie Curie IOF Visiting Scholar at the University of California, Berkeley.

Index

www.ingramcontent.com/pod-product-compliance
Lightning Source LLC
Chambersburg PA
CBHW070924030426
42336CB00014BA/2525